Doing Without

doing without

Women and Work after Welfare Reform

Jane Henrici, editor

The University of Arizona Press   Tucson

The University of Arizona Press
© 2006 The Arizona Board of Regents

LIBRARY OF CONGRESS CATALOGING-IN-PUBLICATION DATA
Doing without : women and work after welfare reform /
Jane Henrici, editor.
     p. cm.
   Includes bibliographical references and index.
   ISBN-13: 978-0-8165-2512-6 (hardcover : alk. paper)
   ISBN-10: 0-8165-2512-9 (hardcover : alk. paper)
   1. Public welfare—United States. 2. Welfare
recipients—Employment—United States. 3. United
States—Social policy. I. Henrici, Jane.
HV95.D63 2006
362.83'840973—dc22
                              2006008572

Manufactured in the United States of America on acid-free,
archival-quality paper containing a minimum of 50% post-
consumer waste and processed chlorine free.

11   10   09   08   07   06   6   5   4   3   2   1

Contents

Part Three Working to Help

Doing Without

introduction

Jane Henrici, Laura Lein, and Ronald J. Angel

This volume provides a glimpse into how low-income women and their children live with decreasing public assistance under the neoliberal approach to government currently dominant in the United States. As chapter authors consider material collected through a long-term, multisite, and multimethod project after the implementation of welfare reform, they challenge popular and governmental assumptions about poverty that legitimate current American welfare policy and practice.

We argue that four fallacies about poverty pervade U.S. social welfare policy; this list agrees with and adds to that described by Albelda (2001a):

1. *The economy is a level playing field for all people.* A core premise of neoliberalism is that an unfettered market, while it fosters trade, allows individuals to compete equally for employment and access to goods and services. Throughout the global economy, neoliberalism remains the dominant economic and political paradigm that has affected work conditions during and since welfare reform's implementation. Analyses of the global economy that use methods such as the Gini coefficient and Human Poverty Index reveal a range of gendered and racialized inequalities in income distribution, regional development, and human rights among and within nations, including those with a predominantly neoliberal approach such as the United States. Using data from original interviews with members of households in three cities, the following chapters show that competitive opportunities are not equally available to everyone in the United States.

2. *Workers in low-wage jobs can support a household on their own.* Although such a belief may seem naïve on its face, welfare policy is

based on the unsubstantiated assumption that low-skill, entry-level jobs provide enough income and benefits for families to subsist and even thrive (Albelda 2001a). Adults often find jobs to support themselves and their dependents temporarily, but the research informing these chapters followed families for years, before and after a national economic "boom," and found their long-term situations unstable at best.

3. *Extended families, kinship, and neighborhood networks can sustain families through hardships in the absence of adequate public aid.* A basic assumption of federal "compassionate conservatism" is that families, fathers, and the commercial and nonprofit private sector are better positioned than the government to meet the needs of poor families. A related, even older belief affecting policy is that lower-income households, particularly those "of color," invariably have large extended kin networks. This view assumes the presence of individual fathers and community or kinship networks, and imagines a set of poor extended families and local private programs with resources both presently sufficient and able to grow along with demand. The families discussed in this book do not always receive help from others or find programs that can adequately provide a new safety net to replace what has been cut from government aid.

4. *Welfare is a dependency trap.* Rooted in the "culture of poverty" debates of the 1960s and 1970s, the assumption that welfare becomes a trap remains a powerful belief. The presumption is that, in comparison to others, individuals who regularly seek help lack a work ethic; that by receiving aid they are discouraged from developing one; and that, as a result, they lack self-esteem. However, U.S. families of all income and asset levels receive social welfare and use assistance such as insurance benefits, tax exemptions, subsidized medical care, educational grants, and credit extensions (Abramovitz 2001). There is no evidence that program participation, in and of itself, creates dependency. In fact, as documented in the following chapters, poor families have less access than others to many subsidized programs, even as they work long hours to support themselves.

Taken as a whole, these four fallacies imply that poverty results from the failures of individuals and families rather than from larger economic and social institutions. These beliefs also have a diferential impact on the primary targets of welfare reform policies: low-income women. They have particularly serious negative consequences for poor African American women and their children. The myths about welfare and poverty create an ongoing dilemma for poorer mothers as they struggle to reconcile their roles as parents with their roles as employees.

In the following chapters the authors call these fallacies into question by noting discrepancies with poorer women's experiences and histories. Although recent welfare policies have been successful in removing people from the cash assistance rolls, the research presented in these chapters contributes to the growing body of evidence pointing to the failure of the new welfare policy to provide families with real solutions to their economic vulnerability.

Doing Without: Women and Work after Welfare Reform presents a set of chapters that draw on material collected as part of Welfare, Children, and Families: A Three-City Study, a large-scale longitudinal, multisite, multimethod research project. Researchers surveyed, interviewed, and observed families and service providers in low-resource neighborhoods from 1999 to 2002 in Chicago, Boston, and San Antonio. Although some of the chapters draw from data from the larger study, the focus of this book is on the particular experiences of families and service providers in San Antonio, analyzed by researchers representing a range of perspectives.

In the following sections, we provide the context for the findings of the Three-City Study, including a brief discussion of welfare reform legislation and policy changes and their impact on recipients and delivery systems. We then move to a discussion of our particular approach to studying this dramatic change in federal legislation. A description of the methodology of the Three-City Study follows. We include a brief introduction to the city of San Antonio and conclude with a summary of the major themes to be addressed by the authors in subsequent chapters.

In 1996, the U.S. federal government passed legislation that radically transformed the system of public financial assistance for the poor across the nation. The Personal Responsibility and Work Opportunity Reconciliation Act (PRWORA) changed public cash assistance from an entitlement, as it had evolved under the old Aid to Families with Dependent Children (AFDC) program, into a system of temporary support with lifetime eligibility limits known as TANF, the acronym for Temporary Assistance to Needy Families.

PRWORA, known unofficially as welfare reform, also instituted a "work first" policy in collaboration with other programs and legislation implemented simultaneously in housing and child care programs. Along with time limits for cash assistance, "work first" emphasizes the goal of "self-sufficiency." Mothers are expected to work outside the home or engage in training that will lead to employment as a condition for receiving cash benefits and other forms of help. That help, whether in the form of coupons or subsidies, is only available for a limited period, again emphasizing the new focus on temporary assistance. The requirements for TANF in particular are stringent. In order to receive it a woman must engage in employment-related activities, prove income and asset eligibility, cooperate in enforcing child support by her children's father, and, if using subsidized child care, make copayments for child care (Cherlin et al. 2001b).

Certain state governments, including that of Texas, took initiatives as early as 1995 to ensure that individuals, notably unmarried mothers of dependent children, worked at paid employment rather than relying on government cash support. As a result of the "work first" policy, many women in the United States have joined the growing number of the working poor, laborers whose wages are too low to pull them out of poverty, while denying them the small additional margin that limited cash assistance can provide.

Some of the frustrations connected to public aid are not new, whereas others, rather than resulting from welfare reform, have emerged from the broader cultural and economic context that had its origins in the early 1980s (Edin and Lein 1997; Fraser and Gordon 1994; Gilens 1996; Harris 1993; Katz 2001; Kingfisher 1996; Mink 1990, 1995; K. Newman 1999; Orloff 1996; Sainsbury 1996). As is the case throughout the global economy, the current situation in the United States is one of diminishing public support combined with unreliable wages, vulnerable employment benefits, and often unsafe working conditions for low-wage women (Kingfisher 2002b; Navarro 1998; J. O'Connor, Orloff, and Shaver 1999; Sassen 1998, 2000, 2002; Shields and Evans 1998). In addition to national policy trends, local policies continue to create unique problems and barriers that low-income women as well as some advocates seek to surmount and occasionally challenge (Edin and Lein 1997, Kingfisher 1996, Mink 1995, J. O'Connor 1996, Stack 2002).

As chapters in this book show, low-income women in need of support, and the public- and private-agency workers who are charged with the task of determining client eligibility and measuring their progress, all struggle with decreasing funding for limited services while contending with the growing stigma attached to receiving welfare. In fact, the need to seek aid for even a single crisis can pit a woman against both government case workers and community service providers, who themselves may have only limited resources to allocate, within the large and confusing system (Fink et al. 2001; Mink 1998; Morgen 2001; A. O'Connor 2001; Peterson, Song, and Hershey 2002; Reisch and Bischoff 2002; Reisch and Sommerfeld 2002; Thomas 1998).

As these chapters also describe, the effort to find and keep a job can cost a low-resource family a great deal. Low-income women with children spend a great deal of time and energy, as well as valuable personal resources, in their attempts to find and keep employment. They engage in a range of training activities, often take multiple jobs, and deal with the disruptions associated with short-term employment (Moffitt and Cherlin 2002). This cost is often so high in comparison to the benefits received, particularly in a low-payment state such as Texas, that many families continue to struggle even during times of high employment.

Flexibility in Context and Identity

Among other findings, these chapters illustrate the degree to which the context in which families struggle continues to change. Alterations at national, state, and local levels interact and affect individual and household adjustments in decisions, actions, and narratives.

Neoliberalism supports the devolution of responsibility for social welfare from national to more localized entities and from the public to the private sphere. Proponents argue that regional governments, and commercial and nonprofit businesses, know more about local needs and should be given the power to allocate resources accordingly. However, this process of devolution has been often incomplete and limited in the resources allocated to it (Hays 2003).

In response to the rapidly changing policy and resource environment in which they live, the low-income women we talked to must remain alert and flexible themselves as they seek out options and resources. At the same time that they enter into irregular, low-wage work they must also rely on unstable sources of support for child care, health care, housing, and personal safety. In addition, the agency workers who are involved in implementing or mitigating the effects of system changes must be flexible as well, often falling behind in their own adaptations to the changing instructions and directives that reach them.

The recognition of a fluid and changing political, social, and economic environment is reflected in women's descriptions of themselves and their families. As we will see, personal descriptions—of who they are, what they have done, and what they should aspire to—change in response not only to actual circumstances, but also to legislative, economic, and demographic changes in cities, states, and neighborhoods. Under welfare reform, many low-income mothers along with social service providers have, on occasion, adopted the vocabulary of self-sufficiency and personal responsibility.

Many of the women with whom we spoke, seeking aid or providing it, respond to as well as occasionally reproduce stereotypes about race, ethnicity, and gender that are embedded in thinking about welfare and welfare reform (Dill et al. 1998; Edin and Harris 1999; England, Christopher, and Reid 1999; Gilens 1996; Kushnick and Jennings 1999; Mink 1990, 2002; Neubeck and Cazenave 2001, 2004; K. Newman 2001; Reisch and Sommerfeld 2002; Schneider 2000b; Thomas 1998). Important racial and ethnic dimensions of identity and experience emerge in our research and analyses, particularly in perceptions of housing policy and interactions with schools, nonprofit agencies, and welfare offices. However, most of the discussions of race and ethnicity among the low-income families we interviewed were overshadowed by more clearly articulated experiences related to poverty and social class; in contrast, conversations on race, ethnicity, and national origin were salient if problematic among neighborhood organization workers, as Henrici points out (chap. 9).

Race and ethnicity are, like all constructs of identity, such complicated and contested concepts that no single vocabulary can fully represent them. Senior researchers on the Three-City Study chose the broadly inclusive terms, *African American*, *European American*, and *Latin American* in order to consider differences in experiences among large numbers of families in Chicago, Boston, and San Antonio without claiming to depict all of their forms of self-identification.

In San Antonio in particular, with reference to the third category, women identified themselves primarily as "Mexican," or "Hispanic," while a very few identified themselves as "Puerto Rican." Although the immigrant population of San Antonio has grown rapidly over the past few years and become more diverse, the majority population of San Antonio is better characterized as Latino; this term describes American citizens of Mexican or other ancestry who might or might not have direct identification with Spanish- or Portuguese-speaking national cultures. In chapters comparing the three cities and looking at their conditions broadly, we use "Latin American," whereas in chapters that deal with more specific contexts and concerns we use "Mexican American" or "Hispanic," and less often "Latino" and "Latina." Puerto Rican women contributed to our study in different cities, but the relatively few Puerto Ricans or women of mixed Puerto Rican and either African American and/or Mexican American ancestry interviewed in San Antonio tended to choose one or the other of those latter identities as they described their experiences with race and culture growing up and dealing with work and government institutions in that city. Fortunately, an extensive and growing literature exists on contemporary definitions of identity, but for a few important contributions to this, please see Daniel D. Arreola (2004), Nancy Foner and George M. Fredrickson (2004), Louise Lamphere et al. (1993), Gilda L. Ochoa (2004), and Clara E. Rodriguez (2000). Further, a growing number of scholars focus on race and ethnicity specifically with reference to the aftermath of welfare reform. These include Bonnie Dill et al. (1998); Martin Gilens (1996); Kenneth J. Neubeck and Noel A. Cazenave (2001); Michael Reisch and David Sommerfeld (2002); Jo Anne Schneider (2000b); Sanford F. Schram, Joe Soss, and Richard Fording (2003); and Susan L. Thomas (1998).

Description of the Three-City Study Methodology

The combination of qualitative and quantitative material that appears in this book is an established but still uncommon method called for in several recent reviews of existing poverty research (Korneman 2002; A. O'Connor 2001; Russell and Edgar 1998). The Three-City Study consisted of multiple components: a survey developed by anthropologists, economists, sociologists, and developmental psychologists with an intensive examination of developmental issues of young children in the families that were surveyed; a long-term ethnographic study of a separate sample of poor families, similar in income to those in the survey; a simultaneous and parallel ethnographic study of families that included a family member with a significant disability; and an ethnographic study of the focus neighborhoods in which all of the families lived.

The goal of this design was to understand the lives of low-income families and the potential impact that welfare reform might have on their children from as many salient perspectives as possible. This triangulation of methods allowed for a number of views of the impact of welfare reform on individuals, families, neighborhoods, and services, from multiple methodological and disciplinary perspectives. The study methodology represents an innovative and powerful approach to understanding complex social phenomena. Each component of the methodology will be described in more detail below. For additional detail about the study methodology, see Winston et al. (1999).

The survey was collected in two waves, the first of which was carried out from March to December 1999 in preselected low-income neighborhoods in Boston, Chicago, and San Antonio. As part of the selection criteria, each household contained at least one child younger than four, or one child between the ages of ten and fourteen, ages that the developmental psychologists on the team deemed to be of particular developmental importance. Most households included other children as well. Forty percent of the survey families were receiving cash assistance at the time of the interview and, as we will see, very few had private (whether commercial or nonprofit) health insurance. The survey collected extensive information that included, but was not limited to, income, education, job training, earnings, employment, health, private health care coverage, Medicaid, welfare use, and social program participation. The second survey was conducted between September 2000 and May 2001 and collected information concerning changes since the first interview. A third wave is in preparation at the time of writing. In this volume, we draw on information from the first and second waves of the survey to frame and generalize discoveries from the ethnographic component.

The ethnographic component primarily focused on in-depth interviews and observations with a smaller number of families over an extended period. Families were selected from the same neighborhoods where survey participants were recruited. The ethnographic sample design called for interviewers to recruit sixty families in each city, including African American, Latin American, and European American families. A smaller group of families that included a family member with a serious disability was also selected. The ethnographic families were contacted between June 1999 and December 2000. About 40 percent of the families were Latin American, 40 percent African American, and 20 percent European American. Each city was represented by roughly the same number of families.

The study plan called for each interviewer in the ethnographic component of the study to work with six or seven families. To the extent possible, ethnographers met with each family for open-ended interviews an average of once or twice a month for between twelve and eighteen months and then again approximately six months and twelve months later. Although most meetings occurred in families' homes, ethnographers also accompanied family members to the grocery store, family celebrations, welfare offices, and a number of other family errands and activities. Topics addressed during these ethnographer visits included health and health care access, experiences with social welfare agencies, education and training, work experiences and plans, family budgets and economic strategies, parenting and child development, and support networks, among other issues.

These family interviews and observations were accompanied by extensive neighborhood ethnographies in which researchers collected information on community resources (Winston et al. 1999). Data were collected over a three-year period from 1999 to 2002 in typically one-time interviews with service providers and community activists in each city. This Neighborhood Study material is both complementary to that of the Family Studies in that it presents something of an alternative viewpoint to the changed benefits system; it also provides additional information on the context surrounding families' efforts to survive.

At each site, experienced ethnographers supervised graduate student ethnographers through regular team and individual meetings. Teams also had access to internal consultants who advised ethnographers encountering challenging family situations, such as mental illness or domestic violence. In addition, ethnographers received cross-site training about data management and analysis in order to ensure consistent and high quality data across the sites for all of the components.

The data management program NUD*IST version 4 was used to organize and maintain the massive amounts of data generated by this project. All documents were de-identified and received a family identifier code. Families were then assigned pseudonyms, which have been used in subsequent papers and publications, including this book, along with pseudonyms developed specifically for this work. Extensive field notes and interview transcriptions were converted into NUD*IST4 documents and all of those tagged into basic categories (called "buckets" or "nodes") were then encrypted and sent to the central ethnographic office at Pennsylvania State University. A team of coders there read the files and classified them even further. As is typical of most qualitative projects, data collection and analysis were simultaneous and iterative.

Project researchers used a number of strategies for analyzing the survey and ethnographic data. Some employed quantitative techniques both to examine the material across multiple locations and to analyze the data within sites. Others took an interactive synthesis approach, combining variable and case-oriented perspectives to explore patterns of interaction between policy and family response in each city. Others explored the qualitative data from a grounded theory perspective, examining the experiences of individual women and their families, and similarities and variations among families of different ethnicities in each city (Miles and Huberman 1994; Winston et al. 1999).

This book focuses on the city of San Antonio, which typifies the non-unionized and industrialized South and Southwest in contrast to the unionized, and de-industrialized Northeast and Midwest. National trends suggest that public aid at all levels will continue to retract, at the same time that labor market growth is confined largely to temporary and part-time low-wage workers in service sector, freight, and medical industry jobs. For this reason, San Antonio is useful case study since it provides a present-day example of where other U.S. cities and states may well be heading.

The data for this study were drawn from interviews with 628 women who were participants in the first and second waves of the survey component of the Three-City Study, as well as in-depth interviews with seventy-five women from the San Antonio ethnography who resided within three neighborhoods that ranged from high to low levels of community resources and population densities. The San Antonio site alone produced more than thirteen hundred documents that include field notes and transcriptions over a four-year period (1998–2002).

Because the project was focused on families with preschool-aged children, researchers initially approached community agencies that house child and day care centers, including the sole Head Start contractor. A few organizations directly expressed initial reluctance to participate due to skepticism about whether the results could be used to help their own communities. Most organizations reviewed the project's documentation and welcomed researchers as volunteer workers.

Researchers talked to staff in fifteen private nonprofit community centers with child care facilities, two of which were faith-based. The San Antonio team also looked for families through governmental and nongovernmental health and housing facilities. However, health agencies could not provide contact information for families, and staff members were unwilling to contact families on behalf of the ethnographers. Low-cost housing organizations turned out to have time and resource constraints, as did the smaller child care centers. Both sets of agencies could rarely provide contacts for interviews but were nevertheless resources for observations collected by fieldworkers about institutional responses to welfare reform.

Meanwhile, staff at the San Antonio Housing Authority (SAHA) provided enormous assistance in locating low-income families as well as participating in interviews themselves. As a result, the San Antonio participants in the ethnography include a greater proportion of public housing residents than low-income residents in San Antonio as a whole. This is important to remember because, as Salcido will discuss (chap. 4), reliable housing is critical to a family's overall stability. Therefore, these families—even when facing a considerable range of challenges and obstacles—may be relatively more stable than their counterparts, who relied on market-rate housing.

In an effort to support recruitment efforts and foster reciprocity, the San Antonio ethnographers offered participating organizations policy information, public presentations of study findings, computer training, and grant proposal assistance. A range of incentives was provided to nongovernmental agencies or their staff members when appropriate, from supplies for day care centers to public lectures for agency conferences. Furthermore, student field ethnographers spent time volunteering in after-school and weekend projects in order to meet children and their parents directly and diminish feelings of unease about talking to researchers, as well as to help out with organizational activities. With repeated visits from ethnographers, service providers responded with more trust and openness and, as time for introductions occasionally became available, help. After establishing and keeping contact with roughly forty agencies and program workers, researchers met low-income families through direct contact, staff introductions, or occasionally through lists provided by service providers.

The same pool of public and private agencies provided the core of interviews for the Neighborhood Study, although a variety of other individuals working with municipal, federal, and private concerns in the communities also spoke with project researchers. Respondents in the three study neighborhoods provided ethnographers with detailed narratives that are rich material for an exploration of trends in the city in general and those neighborhoods in particular.

Organization of this Book

The chapters that grew out of this study are organized into three sections. The first section deals with general conditions of many poorer women's lives and their efforts to find work following welfare reform. Lein, Benjamin, McManus, and Roy explore the ways that low-income single mothers manage when they are both unemployed and no longer on TANF and the implications of those strategies for their families. The authors argue that unemployment may be a choice that some women make in an effort to resolve the tension between their roles as mothers and low-wage workers. Drawing on their own earlier work and the work of other researchers, Lein et al. illustrate that low-wage jobs are marked by variable hours, lack of benefits, and low wages. Mothers' ability to retain paid work depends on their ability to identify and retain affordable, reliable child care and transportation. In very few cases were women able to use their jobs to acquire health insurance for all family members. Furthermore, mothers often quit or were fired when they or their children became ill, when child care failed, or when a job became too demanding for a woman with untreated medical conditions. Low-wage jobs neither lifted these mothers' households out of poverty nor stabilized them with the kinds of benefits necessary to sustain both work and family life.

Bruinsma concentrates on the relationship specifically between child care and employment. She suggests that even when they are able to obtain child care subsidies, some mothers are reluctant (or even refuse) to leave their children in what they perceive as inferior and even unsafe child care settings while they work. Other mothers find that child care center hours cannot be reconciled with their work schedules. Bruinsma connects these challenges, in part, to the larger neoliberalist trends that have driven welfare reform. That perspective obscures women's responsibilities of private caregiving as mothers and daughters at the same time that it views all adults as "gender-neutral-worker-citizens" who are responsible for and capable of competing in a market that prizes flexibility.

Miller and Henrici address the policies that underlie job training and job readiness for TANF recipients, but that fail to provide the larger set of necessary subsidies. The authors look at matters from the recipients' perspectives and, to an extent, from that of caseworkers in the public and private mix of the Welfare-to-Work system. Henrici and Miller conclude in particular that San Antonio's limited implementation of the legislation has resulted in fewer, rather than more, job training options. They describe a neoliberalist service delivery system focused on restricting access to governmental support while emphasizing rapid entry into the labor market. They contrast this system with a holistic set of vocational skill development and family supports, such as child care, that are recommended to help women most readily discriminated against in hiring or advancement, particularly among racial and ethnic minorities. In the authors' assessment, "work first" programs have been successfully implemented according to some measures, but many women eligible for that assistance have not found or kept jobs, and their need for education and training remains present without an adequate response.

In the second section, authors describe other obstacles for low-income women seeking security and stability, and offer their own views about these obstacles. Salcido explores expressed longings for private homes among low-income Latinas who have limited prospects of reaching that goal. Furthermore, she introduces the idea that restricted housing options directly interfere with a mother's ability to care for her children. San Antonio housing has concentrated low-income mothers in low-resource, high-crime neighborhoods where they perceive their children to be at risk. Mothers have been torn between choosing the advantages of remaining in subsidized housing, which is inexpensive and connects them with additional programs and resources, and avoiding the dangers posed to their children.

Angel and Lein discuss how the decline of access to Medicaid affects mothers and their children. Many mothers who are employed find they are not offered employer-based health insurance. If insurance is offered, they cannot afford employee contributions and copayments required to cover their families. Of the populations participating in the Three-City Study, the most likely to be uninsured were those who were employed, lived with a partner, and were Latino. However, almost all of the mothers interviewed experienced periods when health insurance lapsed for one or more members of their households. For these families, medical treatment that was needed might be delayed or foregone entirely. Alternatively, families might incur substantial debt to pay for treatment. Debt and lack of access to medical care have profound impacts on family security and stability.

Continuing to focus on health and its relationship to family economic difficulties, Skinner, Lachicotte, and Burton study the link between poverty and disability. Disability can be caused or made worse by environmental and social conditions associated with poverty, and it can create financial problems for families, thus contributing to their poverty. Using data from all three of the cities studied, the authors demonstrate that recent welfare reforms have implications for all low-income families but may affect those with members who have disabilities to a greater extent. Caregivers find it extremely difficult to locate and keep paid help, as well as adequate care for children with moderate to severe disabilities. In addition, many of the caregivers themselves have or develop chronic health problems and disabilities. The difficulties in these situations are compounded when welfare caseworkers are not properly trained to screen for disability and fail to understand the limitations that disabling conditions pose for families. Chapter 6 examines the difference that disability makes for low-income families in the context of welfare reform and how caregivers of children with disabilities are positioned within and act upon wider social welfare systems.

H. Bell, Lohman, and Votruba-Drzal's analysis responds to gaps in the literature about domestic violence as it affects low-income women and their work. The authors utilize the longitudinal nature of the survey and ethnographic data to analyze the relationships among work, receipt of welfare, and intimate-partner violence by examining those who have experienced domestic violence. With this approach, H. Bell and colleagues explore the link between women's experiences with domestic violence and their ability to maintain stable employment. Their findings help contextualize earlier research that finds no direct, consistent link among domestic violence, work, and receipt of welfare among low-income women. Recognizing the diversity of violent relationships and understanding how these relationships may change over the life cycle holds promise for focusing interventions and helping women more effectively.

The third section of the book takes data from research within public and private organizations directly involved with attempts to aid women and their households. H. Bell tackles the issue of how low-income single mothers are identified and positioned from the perspective of caseworkers charged with putting these mothers to work. Although acknowledging the parenting roles of TANF clients, these caseworkers continue to support and uphold the "work first" mandate, even when the policy creates genuine dilemmas for clients. Rather than question the system that produces these dilemmas, H. Bell finds that, for the most part, caseworkers focus on clients' personal failings and lack of motivation.

Henrici continues this exploration. She examines the personal narratives of nonprofit organization workers who reflect on their experiences and viewpoints. She considers how service providers sometimes counter their own efforts to assist others and, by inconsistent demands and assessments, can add to the difficulties poorer women face. Henrici argues that both groups of women, clients and practitioners, are under pressure to develop their work histories with only limited support and within a racialized and gendered system. However, organization workers interviewed seldom noted this parallel and proximate experience. Instead, they tended to blame, or at least judge, clients and occasionally other workers when describing current conditions of poverty and agency work; rarely would a service provider assign difficulties to decisions by those with more power and opportunity within the benefits and labor systems. This response, Henrici points out, may help the already burdened workers deal with rising requirements and diminishing funds, but potentially can limit what they do for others.

Burton and Lein then provide a conclusion to the volume. They highlight the major themes of the book against the backdrop of ongoing federal, state, and local policy changes that impact poor families.

As these authors demonstrate, the four assumptions with which this chapter begins underlie the U.S. benefits system and inspire policies and practices that confuse and constrain low-income women, their families, and those in their neighborhoods and cities who try to help them. The chapters show how women who seek aid—and those who try to give it—have adapted to "flexible" government policies and employment by remaining flexible themselves. This is particularly true for mothers who participate in Welfare-to-Work: They must both parent their children and take on paid work in an environment that offers conflicting and often confusing options for both.

Doing Without: Women and Work after Welfare Reform contributes to a broader literature that explores how individuals have dealt with global shifts in the economic and cultural context of welfare during the past decade. In these chapters, the authors consider ways in which women's post–welfare-reform choices are influenced by changes in their roles as mothers and employees (Fraser 1989; Henrici 2002; Johnson 2002; Lamphere et al. 1993; Pearce 1979; Sassen 1998; Susser 1997; see also Kazis and Miller 2001).

The experiences of women who participated in the Three-City Study have important implications for the way we think about poverty as well as for the welfare policy that we choose as a consequence. In our welfare policy, we act on our fallacies.

We act as if all citizens were equipped equally to compete in the labor market, and as if that market provided jobs that all could use to support a family. Yet H. Bell, Lohman, and Votruba-Drzal describe the workplace harassment and residential instability that women who experience domestic violence may contend with as they attempt to find and keep a job. Similarly, Skinner, Lachicotte, and Burton point out how low-income mothers of disabled children are viewed as unreliable workers when the medical caregiving of their children interferes with their workforce participation. Henrici and Miller and Lein, Benjamin, McManus, and Roy contribute to the literature that describes how entry-level jobs are those generally found by already poorer women and explains how these jobs often provide neither a living wage nor health care coverage for employees or their dependents. Worse, Angel and Lein document that such jobs often force women and children out of public health care programs, like Medicaid, when their income levels exceed program guidelines. This happens even as those jobs often add to the woman's health problems, as Henrici and Miller note.

We act as if an individual's social networks can make up the difference between what the public will provide and what a family needs to survive. Yet Bruinsma shows how poor women's social networks can be quite limited and at times completely absent when it comes to accessing resources such as child care and transportation.

Indeed, we act as if the gift of substantive aid to others, rather than poverty, is the *real* danger. This belief seems echoed by some of the caseworkers and service providers H. Bell, Henrici and Miller, and Henrici interviewed, as well as by mothers in public housing with whom Salcido spoke. In response to these fallacies, Henrici and Miller ask whether fighting poverty, as an aspect of inequality reinforced by neoliberalism, ever will become part of our national agenda (A. O'Connor 2001); the authors of this book join others to argue that it should (Morgen and Maskovsky 2003).

The beliefs about poverty that we challenge in this book have become deeply embedded in our culture and continue to guide the ways in which welfare policy is conceived and implemented. We hope this volume helps others critique these assumptions, just as low-income women help us to know better the complicated ways that poverty, gender, race, and ethnicity—and their status as mothers—operate in their lives. Such knowledge is essential to generating more sensitive, complex, and pragmatic social welfare policies in the future.

Acknowledgments

We gratefully acknowledge the funders of the ethnographic component of Welfare, Children, and Families: A Three-City Study, including: the National Institute of Child Health and Human Development; the Assistant Secretary for Planning and Evaluation, U.S. Department of Health and Human Services; the Social Security Administration; the Henry J. Kaiser Family Foundation; the Robert Wood Johnson Foundation; the W. K. Kellogg Foundation; the John D. and Catherine T. MacArthur Foundation; the Hogg Foundation for Mental Health; and the Kronkosky Charitable Foundation. We extend special thanks to everyone on our 210-member ethnographic team (for a complete list please see the project Web site, www.jhu.edu/~welfare) and the Penn State team members who produced the infrastructure, organization, and data management for the multisite ethnography. In addition, for this chapter, we would like to thank Holly Bell, Shanti Kulkami, Beth DeBlanc, and Robyn Gammill for their enormous help and fruitful suggestions.

Most of the chapters in this book developed out of papers delivered in a 2001 session sponsored by the Association for Feminist Anthropology organized and chaired by Jane Henrici at the 100th Annual Meetings of the American Anthropological Association in Washington, D.C. As the volume's editor, I am grateful to my coauthors and fellow contributors, the editors at the University of Arizona Press, and the peer reviewers, who made such valuable comments. To all, I am grateful for the time, work, patience, and encouragement they provided.

Finally, and most importantly, all of the authors wish to thank the families, community residents, and care providers who graciously participated in the project and gave us access to their lives. As we promised, we have assigned pseudonyms so that that those who helped us may remain anonymous. At the same time, we have labored to ensure that we share their words and worries as clearly, openly, and accurately as possible.

Part One **Women Looking for Work**

without a net, without a job

What's a Mother to Do?

**Laura Lein, Alan F. Benjamin, Monica McManus, and
Kevin Roy**

Researchers and policy makers have conducted considerable and
growing discussion about the types of employment experienced by
low-income mothers, particularly those leaving welfare. Less attention, however, has been paid to the substantial proportion of unemployed low-income mothers in impoverished neighborhoods, both
welfare leavers and others. This chapter draws on ethnographic data
to examine the ways in which low-income single mothers support
themselves and their families when they are unemployed and not
receiving TANF, and the implications of these strategies for both
mothers and children. It investigates the ways in which unemployment may be a single mother's response to the tension between the
growing pressure for economic self-sufficiency that is part of the
current policy shifts due to welfare reform and the primary mission
in her life—to be a good mother.

In the following sections we will explore prior research on the
employment status of many low-income women, particularly those
leaving welfare, and the inherent conflicts their situations pose for
them as mothers. We will then look at other studies that focus on
the survival strategies used by women who are neither welfare dependent nor wage sufficient. Finally, we will discuss the strategies
identified by mothers in the Three-City Study and tie our findings
into the broader themes presented in this book and elsewhere.

Irregular Employment

Under the influence of welfare reform and an unprecedented economic boom during the 1990s, large numbers of low-income mothers
left the welfare rolls, and many of them entered into employment of

some form. A growing literature on the outcomes of welfare reform has tracked the employment history of low-income mothers, particularly those leaving welfare. Studies across the country indicate that a little more than half of these women enter paid employment (Isaacs and Lyon 2000). There is also a growing examination of the types of employment these mothers experience, including large-scale studies drawing on administrative and survey data (Acs and Loprest with Roberts 2001; Isaacs and Lyon 2000) and more fine-grained ethnographic work that explores the different patterns of employment they engage in and the types of jobs they are likely to occupy (Lambert, Waxman, and Haley-Lock 2002; Lein et al. 2002). Earlier analysis of the ethnographic data from the Three-City Study (Lein et al. 2002) found that only a small minority of the study mothers secured full-time employment in a single, continuing job. The large number of employed mothers fell into one of the following patterns:

- They were almost continuously underemployed in the informal economy.
- They cycled between employment and unemployment, with the employment experiences usually including episodes of both full-time and part-time work.
- They approached full-time work by piecing together multiple jobs.

It is clear that even these employment patterns included episodes of unemployment. In fact, welfare leavers, as well as the other low-income single mothers we describe in this chapter, even if usually employed, experienced periods of unemployment or dramatic underemployment. We cannot divide our study population into those who were unemployed and those who were employed, since the large majority of the mothers experienced at least some unemployment. Instead, this chapter documents the strategies by which mothers sustained their households through periods of unemployment without TANF, rather than categorizing the families in terms of their employment status.

Mothering versus Employment: The Search for Stability

As will be repeated many times throughout this book, at the core of mothers' experiences with the labor force rests a conflict. Almost universally, mothers make mothering their top priority. Although policy makers might argue that self-sufficiency is a primary value, for the mothers we talked to, being a good parent came first. Mothers weighed the possibilities provided in the labor force against the needs of their children. The greatest needs for which they contended were for a stable and consistent home and, perhaps even more important, a way of life that was secure, providing the necessities of daily living in a regular and predictable fashion. Complementary analyses of the Three-City Study data (Roy, Tubbs, and Burton 2004; Tubbs, Roy, and Burton 2005) illustrate the strains, irregularities, and instabilities that the tension between mothering and employment can produce in low-income families. Kingfisher and Goldsmith (2001) point out that in the United States and other countries, mothers' emphasis on mothering is increasingly at odds with welfare states' emphasis on economic self-sufficiency. Mink (1998, 2002) argues that the inclusion of such pressures in welfare reform punishes low-income mothers by confronting them with a combination of tasks that are, at least intermittently, impossible.

This conflict between employment and full-time motherhood mirrors a conflict in more general social values. Low-income mothers, like everyone else in the United States, are exposed to newspaper and magazine articles, television and radio shows, and pediatricians and other professionals who emphasize the importance of consistent and sensitive maternal care for children's development, particularly during the first three years of life (Rose 1999; Skocpol 2000). This material suggests multiple and long-lasting dangers when mothers cannot spend adequate time with their children and if they cannot provide safety, warmth, and continuity in other care when they cannot be present. Balancing the responsibilities of work with the demands of child rearing creates a dilemma all the more challenging for mothers who are parenting without a partner, a situation in which a large number of the mothers in the study found themselves.

Like other recent studies, our research indicates that employment poses many difficulties for low-income mothers. Their primary access to work is to low-wage jobs with little stability, longevity, or benefits (Lambert, Waxman, and Haley-Lock 2002). While working at these jobs, which provide little flexibility, they must arrange child care, tend to the medical, social, educational, spiritual, and other needs of their children and themselves, maintain their homes, and supervise and care for their children. Overwhelmingly these mothers have incomes that hover near the poverty line (Schexnayder, Lein, and Douglas 2002), and they have little access to medical insurance, as Angel and Lein address in chapter 5 of this volume, unless they remain eligible for Medicaid (Angel et al. 2001). If they do not receive government or (rare) community-based subsidies, they depend on informal child care arrangements, since without financial assistance they are unable to afford market rates for child care (Schexnayder, Lein, and Douglas 2002). Bruinsma (chap. 2 this vol.) illustrates the costs and challenges of these informal arrangements for working poor mothers.

Only a fraction of those families eligible for child care subsidies receive them. Head Start programs, structured as education rather than child care, serve only a portion of the eligible child population in most locales. Child care subsidies concentrate on prioritized subpopulations of the poor and near-poor. Priority given to one segment of the population in need of child care may mean a shortage of care for other segments of the population. For instance, in Texas, a recent policy shift that gives precedence to families involved in programs that transfer them off welfare puts low-income working families at risk of losing the subsidies they had received in the past (Capps et al. 2001).

The Experience of Unemployment

At times, these problems become insurmountable, and women give up or lose their jobs. Other women cannot work due to their own ill health or that of a child or dependent relative (Skinner, Lachicotte, and Burton, chap. 6 this vol.). Still others decide that caring for their children themselves is of paramount importance and, given their inability to find high quality supervision for their children while they work, delay employment until their children are of school age. Some women lack the skills, education, or other assets that would allow them to hold a regular salaried position with benefits. For a variety of reasons, almost half of welfare leavers are unemployed most of the first year after welfare departure (Schexnayder, Lein, and Douglas 2002).

Studies of low-wage women's employment (Joyce Foundation 2002) emphasize the lack of stability connected to employment.

They also explore the ways in which women fill the gaps when their wages don't pay the bills and when they lose employment. Beginning with work by Stack (1974), ethnographic studies of low-income mothers (Edin and Lein 1997) as well as more journalistic work (Ehrenreich 2001) have documented the inadequacy of salaries from low-wage jobs to support a household. Such studies also illustrate the ways in which mothers and other single women juggle wages with assistance from public and private agencies and support from informal networks. A range of studies have concentrated analysis around the contrast between employment-based support and welfare-based support (Edin and Lein 1997), showing that neither is sufficient to support a household and that employment, in particular, often provides only low, undependable, and irregular income (Lambert, Waxman, and Haley-Lock 2002; Lane et al. 2001). Mothers are often dependent on assistance from others (Edin and Lein 1997; Stack 1974), and such reliance is considerably different from the economic self-sufficiency that is the ostensible goal of welfare reform.

Researchers and analysts are beginning to realize the significance of periods of unemployment in the lives of welfare leavers and other low-income women (Zedlewski et al. 2003), as well as the number and range of barriers that lie between these women and economic stability (Olson and Pavetti 1996). Lewis et al. (2003) point out that large numbers of low-income mothers sustain their families for periods with neither employment nor TANF.

Our analysis of mothers' stories for this chapter builds on prior research, as it concentrates on the ways in which low-income single mothers mobilize resources when they have little or no employment, including situations when they are neither employed nor on welfare. We explore how low-income mothers keep their families out of destitution when they cannot depend on earned income or income from public welfare. We show that just as the labor-force strategies employed by low-income mothers are complex, so too are the tactics they bring to bear when they are unemployed.

Mothers' Strategies

We now turn to ethnographic data from the Three-City Study and examine in detail four different types of strategies, often used in combination, that allowed the mothers interviewed to maintain their households during periods of unemployment. In order to develop accounts of these strategies, we worked with 154 family profiles that included the most developed employment histories and discourse about their implications. This allowed us to explore some of the ramifications of these strategies for mother and child well-being, and for the long-term prospects for stability in their households.

These strategies accounted for most of the sources of economic support used by mothers in the ethnographic sample who sustained long periods of unemployment. They included:

- Combinations of food stamps; Medicaid; Women, Infants, and Children (WIC); and disability income
- Dependence on income from another person she lived with (usually a cohabiting partner, but occasionally another family member)
- Support from someone outside the household, such as a parent, or even more occasionally child support
- A range of informal activities, including bartering, trading, and odd jobs

Although it was possible to sort our respondents in terms of their most prevalent employment patterns (Lein et al. 2002), unemployed mothers tended to use combinations of the strategies above to face unemployment. Thus, we do not assign specific patterns to individual women but rather examine the types and combinations of strategies used among our respondents. Ethnographic work, such as the study reported here, is most illuminating in examining how strategies are combined in family life and when exploring the antecedents and consequences of these strategies for the families.

Furthermore, we know from our own work and from a number of previous studies that mothers who have been on TANF at any point are likely to cycle back on to it during periods of hardship. In examining the strategies mothers use when they are both off TANF and unemployed, we see that they also had periods of time on TANF. In fact, given the low rate of payment in Texas (the site of many of our case studies), most mothers developed a range of strategies to supplement the monthly income of under two hundred dollars they were likely to receive from TANF. They continued to depend heavily on these strategies during periods when they were not on TANF.

The cases below illustrate four common strategies employed by the families. Although these mothers, like most mothers in our study, used several strategies, for conceptual clarity each case description concentrates on one of the strategies listed above.

In the first case, the mother was not employed and supported herself and her children through a combination of workers' compensation, child support, and Social Security Disability Insurance (SSDI). She also received food stamps and was eligible for public health insurance. It was this dependence on a combination of public services that allowed her to stay off welfare. In the second case, the mother substantially depended on the contributions of her coresident partner. The mother in our third case received assistance from others outside her household as an important part of her household economics. In the fourth case, the mother combined work in the informal sector with assistance from others in her network.

Other Public Support

Many mothers relied on multiple public and private programs to support themselves and their children if they did not work. Although TANF may have provided the most comprehensive support for poor mothers, women often tried to "stay off welfare" due to the stigma, hassle, and work rules that required recipients to be involved in employment or other related activities. Programmatic supports, by their nature, were piecemeal and not comprehensive: food stamps provided vouchers for food only; WIC provided nutritional supports; private emergency assistance often provided clothing or furniture. Mothers who wove together supports from these programs often did so because of unaccommodating work environments that became particularly difficult for mothers with disabilities or chronic health problems.

Julianne, a thirty-three-year-old mother of a three-year-old son, found herself in a precarious financial situation after being deserted by her husband of six years. She could not rely on the father of her child, who was under a restraining order for domestic violence. He paid only a small amount in child support after being laid off and subsequently receiving a much lower salary at his new job. Julianne, a recovering alcoholic who suffered from bipolar disorder, was also unemployed and saddled with a portion of the premium for coverage on her former husband's health insurance policy.

Although she had relied on WIC resources since her pregnancy, Julianne's experiences with other public assistance programs were mixed. For example, she reported a three-week interruption of her food stamp benefits for reasons not adequately explained to her. During the process of applying for TANF, she reported that her documents were consistently misplaced and that caseworkers were "rude . . . I just needed a little bit of help, and it wasn't there. Everyone believes in the welfare bonbon-eating mother, but I don't know anyone who fits that description." As an alternative to these programs, Julianne elected to visit a local church for food assistance and to rely on a community learning center's child care program to care for her son.

Within a few months of her divorce, Julianne secured a brief job as a homeless outreach worker and supervisor of a holding facility for men picked up drunk. However, she was hit by a truck one night while on outreach and injured her back. She began to receive $200 per month in workers' compensation because of this injury. Her income then exceeded the eligibility threshold for food stamps by $30. However, with a rent of $850/month, she still continued to rely on emergency clothing and food vouchers to make ends meet.

Her former husband's sporadic job history continued, and Julianne's child support dwindled again after he took a cut in pay. However, Julianne then received a lump-sum settlement check of twenty-five hundred dollars from workers' compensation, which she used to pay off bills. She also applied for SSDI, which she appealed upon denial. Four months later, her household situation improved a bit, because she began to receive food stamps and state-sponsored medical care. Her efforts to go to school were rewarded with the receipt of a state grant that, in addition to a Pell Grant, covered her tuition costs. She had relied on public transportation since her divorce, but with the receipt of her school grant, her uncle gave her an old car, which she used for transportation to and from school and day care.

Almost two years after her divorce, Julianne was finally approved for SSDI, which substantially increased her monthly income, to about thirteen hundred dollars per month. With this approval, she felt a sense of true financial stability for the first time since she'd been on her own. Soon after her SSDI approval, she underwent gastric bypass surgery, followed by surgery on a collapsed lung. When the monthly check was added to limited amounts in child support and financial aid for school, she was able to pay off all of her outstanding bills and purchase a car.

This case illustrates Julianne's ability to weave together support from a range of assistance programs other than TANF. In effect, she did not turn to welfare assistance because her former husband could offer substantial, if sporadic, financial support. Securing assistance from SSDI provided Julianne with the final step toward security outside of formal employment and welfare assistance. Given Julianne's severe health issues, her involvement in jobs—through formal employment or through welfare-to-work requirements—would have been limited over time. Her ability to serve as head of a self-sufficient household and to serve as a "good mother" for her child would have been limited as well. This case suggests that a range of programmatic supports is necessary for those mothers who cannot work on a regular basis in the mainstream workplace.

Living with Someone Else

Women in the study moved in and out of residences, jobs, and relationships over time. In periods of coresidence with a partner or a family member, mothers often relied heavily on the financial and material contributions of household members for sustenance. These arrangements often were short-lived, but partners' contributions could prove to be the difference in paying rent or securing food for any given month. However, coresidence was often a reciprocal relationship involving extensive emotional demands, care-work tasks, or management of household activities for multiple individuals.

Maria was eighteen and the mother of two children, each by a different father, when she joined the study. She gave birth to her first child at fifteen. When we first met her, she was on TANF, Medicaid, and WIC. She had Bell's Palsy, which she described as a nervous condition brought on by stress, and was taking medication for anxiety, stress, and depression. She had worked sporadically at both a hotel and a department store; however, she quit those jobs because she was not able to find child care during the late-evening hours she was assigned to work. She then worked briefly for a jewelry store, but again had troubles with child care.

In fact, Maria was selective in the child care she used. She once confronted day care center staff because she thought they were not changing her son's diapers frequently enough. Because she felt her children's individual needs could be met best by different programs, she enrolled them in separate day care facilities. She chose to leave jobs as well as educational programs if she could not coordinate them adequately with child care.

In part for these reasons, Maria struggled to make a living for her household. Changes in her life circumstances allowed Maria to move off both TANF and Medicaid. Although the court ordered the fathers of her children to pay her two hundred dollars a month, she received only sporadic payments from one of the fathers.

Although her relationship with her mother was sometimes strained, Maria turned to her for assistance in times of material and financial need. At one point she lived with her mother, but she left because she had difficulty getting along with her stepfather. In addition, her mother cared for Maria's children when Maria needed extra care or the children weren't able to attend their day care center. Since Maria did not drive, her mother also gave her rides to the grocery store and other places so that she could avoid having to use public transportation while also carrying packages or traveling with her children.

Maria worked only sporadically over the study period. When she was working, she earned about six dollars an hour. Maria believed that education was the route to a better job, and she had made several attempts to further her own education. Over the period of her involvement in the study Maria completed her GED, but she still felt she needed further skills and had ambitions of becoming a nurse. She also participated in job training programs, but she had to quit them when she continually was delayed picking up her children from child care.

During the course of the study, Maria became formally engaged to her partner, and they were married. She reported that he was interested in adopting her children and that he participated in raising them. Maria described her relationship with her husband as both emotionally and financially supportive: "When something's wrong, I'm there to comfort him; as well as when I'm upset, he's there to comfort me." Maria reported that they didn't "fight over money, but we do stress about it—paying bills." Maria's plans for the future included wanting to move with her husband to a duplex and eventually to their own house. However, she also maintained her own bank accounts and planned on getting a job so that she would be independent if something were to go wrong in their relationship.

Six months into her marriage, Maria's life was in transition again. Her husband had been arrested for failing to report to his parole officer. He was sentenced to jail for about six months. At the time of his arrest, Maria expressed frustration but was committed to trying to restabilize her life and the lives of her children. Although angry and disappointed with his arrest and jail term, she was resigned to the difficulties this would introduce into her household.

During this time, Maria learned about a work preparation program that included training, job placement, and case management assistance with other life issues. However, Maria was concerned that she might not be able to meet all the requirements of the program. She already had difficulty keeping up with her responsibilities to her children and her household.

Although Maria drew on multiple strategies to support her household, she clearly relied upon the contributions, both material and logistic, of her coresident husband. However, even when she spoke enthusiastically of their partnership, she recognized the fragility of the relationship, and thus was reluctant to become overly dependent on him. His arrest confirmed how important it was that she maintain her own resources for supporting the household. Significantly, Maria's account highlights the degree to which care and concern for her children competed with the time and energy she could have devoted to retaining employment and continuing her education. Mothering activities included time spent with children, care and attention to discipline, oversight of the facilities caring for her children, and attention and supervision when others were caring for them. As mentioned, coresidence may relieve some of the concerns over financial resources, but it may complicate mothering requirements, as women are obligated to manage household and care-work tasks in larger families.

Support from Nonresident Others

Some mothers were embedded in extensive networks of extended kin and friends. When unemployed mothers experienced financial and material needs, these networks often stepped up to support them and their children. The most reliable support seemed to come from the mothers' own parents and immediate family. Younger mothers in particular received support from nonresidential family members, often in recognition of their efforts at self-sufficiency. Nonresidential provision of transportation and housing, as well as of food, money, and child care, was often short term but flexible, allowing mothers to cope with crises that arose while living in conditions of poverty. In this way, mothers' participation in and nurturance of close, reciprocal relationships with family and friends was a crucial element of surviving unemployment.

Frankie grew up in San Antonio in a neighborhood that included a number of relatives: a beloved grandfather and grandmother, a protective uncle, and a warm and nurturing mother. During the time we interviewed Frankie, her grandfather was hospitalized for a week; she commented that even if his illness were serious, he probably wouldn't say much about it, because "he's the type who doesn't like to make a big deal." Her grandmother was the center of family life, responsible for family holiday celebrations. During the time we worked with Frankie, her grandmother died, at age ninety-seven. She also described her uncle with pride and affection: "He's real cool; he's really nice. He's the one who helped me and my mom and my sister when my dad, when he beat my mother up." Frankie spoke of her mother with pride and affection: "She's real nice and caring and giving, and she's real generous; oh, my God, she's generous." Frankie lived with her mother for a period after her child was born, and prior to that with her uncle.

Before she had a child, Frankie had worked in many retail jobs, including time in a store, in fast food, and in telemarketing. Although her husband felt differently, Frankie wanted to return to work. Frankie had been receiving TANF for almost a year at the beginning of her involvement with the Three-City Study, but she left welfare during the first year and was not recertified for either Medicaid or food stamps.

Although Frankie's husband worked, he was not a secure financial resource for the family. He earned five hundred dollars every two weeks, but, as Frankie pointed out, a great deal of that money was removed, partially to repay debts from an earlier period in his life. Furthermore, he owed almost one thousand dollars in fines: "Right now he has warrants for his arrest. . . . They're speeding tickets." He was heavily in debt with student loans and also gambled habitually.

Frankie commented: "He does not give me cash. He buys things that I need, or he'll pay things, he'll take over payments." Frankie found it lonely living in a subsidized apartment after living in her mother's house when her child was an infant. "It [living in her own apartment] was different, because you had to pay all the bills. It was hard. You have to pay your own bills, your own food, everything. You were on your own. It was lonely. It was sad."

Furthermore, her housing situation was precarious. Frankie and her husband lived in public housing, and the housing authorities recommended that she not list her husband on the lease for her apartment. She felt they wanted to be able to remove him from the premises should he cause a problem. They also advised her not to include his income, because then her rent would increase, and that increased rent would need to be paid even if he left.

Neighborhood yard sales were, for Frankie, an economical means of obtaining household items and clothing, as well as a source of additional money when she held her own sales. After her sister's truck was wrecked, Frankie found it more difficult to hold them. Frankie had used her sister's truck to prepare for and participate in yard sales, and she could not keep up with this activity when the truck was no longer available.

Despite these active economic strategies, Frankie was heavily in debt, responsible for regular payments on delinquent bills, and had a very poor credit rating. She described receiving frequent calls from bill collectors. Frankie noted that her family bought things they shouldn't have: "That's just who we are. We're poor. People don't want to admit it; that's why they buy all these fancy things, and they end up in debt. They just want to have, have, have." Sometimes, as a final strategy, Frankie and her husband sold some of these items to a pawn shop.

Even though Frankie lived with her husband in their own apartment, she relied extensively on family members with whom she did not live. They provided emergency housing, transportation, child care, food and money when needed, and emotional support. Their assistance was a critical component of how Frankie supported her family.

In particular, short-term nonresidential supports helped Frankie survive circumstances that threatened the health and stability of her family: precarious housing, sporadic financial contributions from her husband, and heavy debt. It is difficult for low-income mothers to move on and off public support programs like TANF or food stamps, given eligibility requirements and case-processing demands. These types of supports reduced Frankie's and other mothers' dependence on the unreliable and inadequate resources provided by public programs and filled in during periods when they were not receiving public assistance. However, mothers often could draw only upon supports from nonresidential networks for specific items and for short periods—and because such networks were primarily comprised of low-income households, they often were strained.

Networks and Odd Jobs

This fourth strategy involved mothers who were active in providing in-kind services that supported their children. Many women were committed to volunteer work in churches, day care centers, and community centers, all of which allowed them to access important resources for their families. Often these in-kind activities were required of mothers who took part in networks of reciprocity. Other women worked hourly, seasonal, and short-term jobs for cash.

At the beginning of the study, Lori lived in a large public housing project with her two children, a six-year-old and an eight-week-old. The children had different fathers. The older child's father was involved in his child's life through caring for him on weekends and attending school functions. Lori talked with him regularly about any problems that came up with their son. In contrast, her younger child's father did not want to be involved and had not even seen their child. Lori knew several of her neighbors and was close friends with one of them. One of Lori's sisters lived nearby and regularly helped Lori with child care. Lori also saw her mother every few months, but her mother was mentally ill and often difficult to deal with, particularly when she did not take her medication. Lori saw other relatives less frequently.

Lori had dropped out of high school after cutting classes for a while. When she was nineteen, she completed her GED. She wanted to attend college and earn a degree related to business practice. She hoped to settle into a more regular full-time job as her children got older.

Lori received both Medicaid for her children (but not herself) and food stamps, but she did not use TANF. In fact, she had never been on welfare. Her six-year-old was in school, but Lori cared for the baby herself. During the study period, Lori applied for and was awaiting a court order for the baby's child support. Her older child's father listed their son on his medical insurance; however, Lori continued to use Medicaid after determining that the private insurance covered far less than Medicaid did.

Lori spent her weekends working two ten-hour shifts on Saturday and Sunday at a local flea market. She worked at a booth selling beer and sodas. Her sister watched her children when she worked and when her son's father was not available to do so.

Lori was anxious to get a steady full-time job. With the help of her older son's father, she interviewed at a bank, but was unsure whether she would be able to accept a steady job there because of the hours required. As she told her ethnographer: "I am a little depressed, because I might not be getting the job at the bank after all." In the end, she was unable to accept the job offer, since the supervisors there wanted her to begin work at 5:30 in the morning five days a week. In order to be in the office by 5:30, Lori would have had to leave both of her sons at day care before 5 a.m.—considerably earlier than most child care facilities in her area were open. None of Lori's friends or family were available to help take care of the children in the early morning hours and transport them to day care. She continued to hope for a job with regular hours from 8:00 a.m. to 5:00 p.m.

Like most of the mothers we met, Lori's employment decisions revolved around her children's well-being. Unable to find steady work that coincided with her child care, she continued living "paycheck to paycheck," working weekends at the flea market because her son's father could provide child care during that time.

Discussion

Many of the mothers in the ethnographic study struggled to maintain the values of self-sufficiency *and* good parenting. When they could not find a pathway to good parenting through employment, they joined the almost 50 percent of welfare leavers who do not hold jobs. This chapter adds to what we know about what these mothers do, how they spend their time, how they bring into their families the goods and services they need, and how they care for their children.

The situations of mothers raising their children with neither the benefits of employment nor TANF for at least some period of their lives illustrate the importance of multiple resources in the lives of low-income mothers. By exploring four common strategies of unemployed mothers, we demonstrate the role that other resources play in impoverished families' lives and the degree to which low-income mothers, in spite of efforts to enter the labor force, continue to remain dependent on other resources. Our cases demonstrate that these resources are at least as irregular and impermanent as welfare or the kinds of jobs most readily available to low-income mothers. Almost all of the mothers, except the very young or the very ill, had a work history and aspirations to reenter the labor force. For example, despite significant barriers, Maria participated in job training and looked forward to employment. Unemployment appears to be a transitional condition that mothers cycle through, between periods of employment and, sometimes, public assistance.

Clearly, mothers leaving TANF are not seamlessly transitioning into economic self-sufficiency. In this chapter we have built on earlier work (Edin and Lein 1997; Lein et al. 2002) that describes how difficult it is for single mothers to support their families on low-wage work. Many strategies used by unemployed mothers also are used by employed mothers in combination with wage work. During periods of unemployment, these strategies occupy a more central role in their families' maintenance.

Mothers combine different strategies to keep their families going. Julianne, the first mother, was probably most reliant on a single strategy—other public services. Due to her disability, she was eligible for perhaps the most consistent and supportive of the cash transfer programs, SSDI. With this, child support, and other public and community services, she was able to sustain her family life. The other three mothers combined strategies. In addition to her use of informal employment, Lori also drew on public services and the assistance of family members.

Although these stories illustrate mothers' resourcefulness and resilience, it is important to appreciate how fragile these strategies can be. As we see in Frankie's case, partners' contributions are welcome but not consistently available. She was unable to plan for a secure future from her partner's overall financial stability or income. Not only were her partner's earnings irregular, he could also could have been arrested or unemployed, hence her dependence on the contributions of others outside her household. This type of instability has implications for children in low-income families. The rhetoric of welfare reform enforces the urgency and primacy of economic self-sufficiency as a requisite for both good parenting and good citizenship. Some reports say that children raised in welfare-dependent families do not fare as well as other children, and that mothers who do not become economically self-sufficient are not performing well either as mothers or as citizens. Mothers are aware of these evaluations and of how they are seen in the public eye, and this creates even more pressure on them (K. Newman 1999, 2001).

The fact that almost half of the people who have left the welfare rolls did so without entering the labor market (Isaacs and Lyon 2000) is a basic conundrum of welfare reform policy. Ethnographic data here and elsewhere throughout this book highlight some of the central challenges of the policy. In addition to the stories presented here, Henrici and Miller (chap. 3 this vol.) detail the mismatch between the skills that many former TANF recipients bring to the labor market, the skills required to succeed in that market, and the life circumstances that keep many TANF recipients from even getting on the first rung of the economic ladder: The jobs they find do not sustain them and their families. As Salcido (chap. 4 this vol.) illustrates, housing-program supports often require mothers to raise their children in a dangerous neighborhood. Angel and Lein, in their work on health insurance (chap. 5 this vol.), point out that having a job often means decreased access to health care. Furthermore, service sector jobs require flexibility in child care duties that that many mothers cannot achieve. Bruinsma (chap. 2 this vol.) and Skinner, Lachicotte, and Burton (chap. 6 this vol.) reinforce, with their accounts from mothers from the ethnography and disability studies, the reality that caring for children is work for mothers, particularly if the mothers or children are ill or have special needs. However, the mothers interviewed for the Three-City Study worked hard at the seemingly contradictory tasks presented by welfare reform. The challenges these mothers face and how they cope with them will be played out in subsequent chapters and in the public arena as welfare reform unfolds.

flexible families

Low-Income Women Negotiating Employment Opportunities,
Wages, and Child Care Needs in San Antonio

Beth H. Bruinsma

The most recent reforms to welfare in the United States focus on
how to facilitate the participation of women in the labor force. In
February 2003, the hour requirements for work and work-related
activities were increased for welfare recipients, mandating that recipients spend forty hours a week engaging in work-related activity.
Changing welfare policies in the United States indicate much more
than a movement to reduce individual dependency on governmental
support; these policies also index shifting constructions in women's
roles and definitions of work (Kingfisher and Goldsmith 2001). Although care work and domestic labor were initially recognized as
socially valuable work and supported by welfare policies (Nelson and
Paredes 1984), proponents of U.S. welfare reform posit full employment as the key to family self-sufficiency and prioritize women's
roles as potential wageworkers. Implicit in these reforms to welfare
policy is the anticipation that women will turn for assistance to
marriage and the support of a male breadwinner instead of to the
state. Despite this impetus, the number of households headed by
women is increasing in the United States, and a disproportionate
number of them are low income. Without adequate economic and
social capital to supplement services and resources formerly sustained by welfare benefits and employment, women and their families are now increasingly at risk of becoming more impoverished
while working than while receiving benefits. For women with young
children to care for, securing reliable, affordable, and flexible child
care is crucial to whether or not they sustain workforce participation
while maintaining their parental roles.

In response to ongoing discussions on the intersection of wom-
en, poverty, welfare reform, and wage labor, this chapter highlights

ethnographic material from interviews conducted with low-income Latinas and European American women relevant to these debates. Concentrating on eight women negotiating their emerging roles as worker-parents in San Antonio, I attempt to describe how some low-income women contend with their responsibilities as caregivers alongside welfare reform and the subsequent prioritization of poor women as potential wage laborers. These experiences, as related to me in consecutive monthly interviews between 1999 and 2002, represent the arduous attempts and frustrating setbacks of women who are negotiating their roles as mothers and wageworkers.[1] Although the situation of every family connotes a distinct experience with welfare reform, this longitudinal fieldwork in San Antonio points toward the idea that long-term employment is contingent upon many factors that sometimes overwhelm the social and economic resources available to a family.

In addition, this ethnographic research on welfare reform indicates that child care responsibilities intersect and conflict with the emerging prioritization of women as workers and that child care concerns significantly influence the ways women talk about their expectations of work and their perceived social networks. In the context of interviews, women repeatedly expressed the experience of "being all alone" with "no one to count on but me" for child care while they worked or looked for work. I suggest that these narrative expressions of self-reliance and self-sufficiency imply that when and if these women do receive help from family, friends, or neighbors, informal assistance does not completely replace formal benefits or services. Low-income and working poor respondents identify the social networks available to them as unable to provide economic, emotional, or child care support because these networks are tenuous, already strained, or simply unavailable for reliable and sustained assistance. As Portes and Landolt assert, "Contrary to the expectations of policy-makers, social capital is not a substitute for the provision of credit, material infrastructure, and education" (Portes and Landolt 2000, 547).

Individual responses to collective concerns for meeting financial, emotional, and care needs for a family vary according to individual experiences and often change across time. Although some women embrace the prevailing sentiment that work represents economic independence and an opportunity to "do better" for oneself and one's family, other women resent it, react against the valorization of "workfare," and point to the futility of trying to function as a self-sustaining single parent and wage laborer while raising young children. Above all, child care is a prevailing concern among all working mothers and a factor that every parent must initially contend with before they can imagine themselves as workers. Careful consideration of these women's voices adds emphasis to the necessity for affordable, accessible, and flexible child care options for women who are able and willing to work, and, conversely, to the desires of some women to delay working until it is emotionally and economically feasible.

Choosing to Work

Working is, above all, one decision out of the multitude of choices that women must contend with as they weigh the well-being of themselves and their dependents against receding public services and family benefits. However, the range of possibilities out of which a poor woman chooses whether or not to work is circumscribed by the available material and social resources, her personal experiences and aspirations, and larger social factors such as the current economic demand for wage labor. Additionally, in this volume, Bell, Lohman, and Votruba-Drzal (chap. 7) describe domestic violence, and Skinner, Lachicotte, and Burton (chap. 6) discuss disability in low-income families as significant barriers to employment. Recent anthropological literature has reformulated perceptions of poverty as a gendered experience that must be critiqued in the context of changing social structures, communities, and globalizing trends (Abramovitz 1996; K. Newman 1998; Peña 1997; Schneider 2001). Kingfisher and Goldsmith (2001) present neoliberalism as an emerging "cultural system" characteristic of contemporary capitalism, which exists both as a discourse and as a tactical system that fosters the privatization of services and production through free market exchange (Bourdieu 2002; Cleaver 1997). Practices and discourses characteristic of neoliberalism, such as welfare reform, have subsequently recast women in the role of "gender-neutral worker-citizens" (Scott in Kingfisher and Goldsmith 2001, 716), which stands in contrast with previous conceptions of women as primary caretakers first, and breadwinners second.[2] Furthermore, neoliberal practices favor flexible organizations and individuals that can successfully compete in a free market economy by fluctuating with market demands for wage labor. The advantage of flexibility as a strategy will be salient in the following discussions of child care and working women.

One effect that neoliberal practices have on the distinctive identities of women is that differences between individuals and social groups are obscured, resulting in the collapse of previously gendered categories of caregiver and worker and the subsequent prioritization of wage labor over unpaid activities such as caregiving. The collapse of differences between wage laborers ultimately results in the disregard of all other activities positioned inside "the realm of reproductive and unpaid labor" (Kingfisher and Goldsmith 2001, 717). In this way, the significance of activities such as child care and mothering are depreciated and, eventually, silenced in the public discourse that surrounds work and welfare. However, within welfare reform, low-income women must still continue parental duties alongside the emerging emotional, social, and economic demands to become self-supporting workers—heads of household for their families.

Although neoliberal capitalist praxis and discourse obfuscate gender differences, "poverty knowledge" (Goode and Maskovsky 2001) in the United States constitutes poverty as a gendered and individual predicament, with the state functioning as a final, yet temporary, recourse for individuals who have exhausted all other opportunities for support. The shifting objectives in the public assistance system from AFDC to PRWORA and TANF now emphasize the transitory nature of contemporary public assistance and the necessity of work for welfare recipients. In addition, and perhaps more alarmingly, children have been displaced, rhetorically as well as officially, from the foreground of the recently restructured benefits system, despite the rhetoric that many changes to policy, such as the added emphasis on two-parent families, are in fact invested in child development and well-being.[3]

In keeping with welfare reform policies, which emphasize work and family self-sufficiency, there is considerable pressure for low-income women to meet all the obligations placed on them by caseworkers, employers, children, and, more implicitly, American social structures. However, not all women respond to these social and economic pressures in the same ways. Women may have diverse attitudes toward work and family that vary across time and place. Segura (1994) found that U.S.–born Mexican women living in the United States are more likely to identify with American ideals that venerate women's domestic roles and to express ambivalence toward women's economic roles, whereas Mexican women living in the United States do not view work and family as conflicting spheres. Similarly, "ethnic" women and their families have been thought of homogeneously as having extended and stable kin networks that support their participation in the workforce. However, individual narratives such as the following comment from Veronica, a young woman of Mexican American and European American descent, destabilize this position. At one point during the project, Veronica lived in the same subsidized housing complex as her mother and younger siblings. When I asked Veronica if her family members were available to care for her son while she worked, she exasperatedly replied: "Everyone says why don't I ask my mom. Well, my mom is not the kind of person that—she's not going to help me out. I have to pay her every single time—fifteen, twenty dollars, even if it's just for two hours." What is more, assumptions about women's kinship and support networks efface structural barriers to workforce participation, such as low wage rates for women, increasing child care costs, and access to education.

As table 2.1 illustrates, several factors are involved in the experience of moving from welfare to work for one woman. The obstacles that Veronica experienced included obtaining and utilizing child care subsidies as well as undergoing intense periods of domestic violence that precipitated a total disruption of work, child care arrangements, and, finally, welfare benefits. In chapter 7 of this volume, Bell et al. explore further the relationship between domestic violence and workforce participation among welfare recipients. Simply put, the transition from welfare to self-sufficiency through employment is not a seamless process.

However, it is important to note that for all of the women referenced in this chapter, access to subsidized child care is related to attaining and maintaining employment. Table 2.2 illustrates Lori's experiences with work, education, and child care. A twenty-eight-year-old European American mother, Lori works full-time during the week and part time at a flea market each weekend. She has completed some college courses toward a business degree and now works for a financial corporation. During interviews, she often commented

Table 2.1 Work-related Activities and Child Care Arrangements for Veronica, 1999–2002

Variable	1999			2000	2001		2002
TANF	—	—	Yes	—	Yes	—	Yes
Job training/ Education	—	—	—	—	CNA[2]	—	—
Employment[1]	$8	$8	—	$7	—	$7	—
Child care subsidy	Yes	Yes	—	—	Yes		—
Reason for Leaving Employment	Job hours extended beyond available child care			Domestic violence precipitated absences from work and termination	Subsidized care arrangements did not meet work hours		Waiting for child care subsidy

[1] Amounts represent hourly wage
[2] Training for a Certified Nursing Assistant degree
Abbreviation: TANF = Temporary Assistance to Needy Families

on the subsidized child care she received from the Texas Workforce Commission. At one point, she asserted: "If it wasn't for CCMS [Child Care Management Service], I couldn't work. . . . I couldn't pay the day care, plus rent. . . . Most of the time, I work Saturdays, too. . . . I need extra money because, you know, for groceries and stuff around the house."

Lori's daughter attended day care during the week while her son attended school. Her son's aunt received a subsidy to care for both children each weekend. This assistance allowed Lori to work more than full-time. Lori and her children recently moved out of a public housing complex and into a new subsidized house, where Lori has the option to apply her rent toward the mortgage. Working as much as she was able and moving toward her goal of home ownership were two components of Lori's desire to "do better" for herself and her children. Yet a second job was necessary for Lori to make ends meet, and groceries were still considered "extra" for her household. Lori's experience highlights the fact that self-sufficiency for a single parent may require subsidized child care and a sustained period of working more than full-time.

Table 2.2 Employment, Education, and Child Care Experiences for Lori, 1999–2002

Variable	1999	2000	2001	2002
Employment				
Weekend	$8/hour	$8/hour	$8/hour	$8/hour
Full-time	—	—	$8/hour	$8/hour
Education	Junior college	Junior college	—	—
Child care	Subsidized child care	Subsidized child care	Subsidized child care	Subsidized Subsidized

Flexibility, Work, and Child Care

Oliker (2000) notes that the ways women care for their dependents are changing. She asserts that "in the absence of a social safety net or wage-earning partner, single mothers now must provide financially for their children or risk losing them" (169). Unlike many mothers, single women receiving TANF do not have the option of limiting their work involvement or work hours. Poor single women, unlike middle-class women or women in dual-parent households, are not as "free to trade their job or income opportunity for flexibility to meet domestic needs" (Oliker 2000, 169) if they expect to meet all their family's basic needs. Hence, individuals with inflexible schedules, limited job skills, or tenuous social networks are at a disadvantage, whereas individuals and organizations that offer the most flexibility and resilience are favored by contemporary corporate culture (Martin 1994). Flexibility is becoming a constitutive and discriminating factor working upon all individuals today, and it is increasingly being used as an exclusionary criteria or requirement for social and economic advancement.[4] In Veronica's case, limited child care opportunities and volatile domestic partnership left her with little latitude to secure and maintain employment even though she had acquired the appropriate job training and certification to work as a nursing assistant.

However, flexibility in employment can be strategically practiced when women have access to low-cost and reliable child care as well as to viable employment opportunities. Women who have friends and relatives who can provide child care and other forms of support have more latitude to decide whether to work or delay employment until all their children are of school age or older. They also have slightly more options for employment, as they can usually increase their potential work hours beyond those offered by formal care providers. Hence, their access to informal care networks places them in a more flexible situation than mothers who have few social resources to supplement their child care needs. Oliker points out that "the same job opportunities will look very different to a mother who has help with babysitting and one who does not" (2000, 173), and, frequently, flexible and reliable child care determines whether a job is an opportunity or an impossibility.

Despite various obstacles, some women positively frame the prospect of working as a means to individual and financial independence that will allow them to feel as if they are "doing better" for their children and themselves. Indeed, most welfare recipients actively counter prevailing conceptions of them as lazy or dysfunctional, sometimes criticizing and distancing themselves from neighbors and kin whom they perceive as unmotivated to "do better" for themselves. The desire to "do better" is intimately connected to providing their children with material resources and a better place to live. However, poor and working-poor women with young children unanimously cite child care as one of the many factors related to the possibility of meeting their own goals toward work as well as the expectations of caseworkers and members of the public sphere. Often a woman's opinions about work are paired with an expectation for state assistance with child care and household expenses. Women frequently speak to the futility of single-handedly negotiating work requirements and parental responsibilities. Karen, an articulate European American respondent and mother of two young daughters, expressed her frustration at attempting to work and meet the child care needs of her preschool-age children. Karen stated that the difficulties arranging child care around her employment prospects had been "a nightmare . . . I just passed a job by last week. It was a second-shift job, like from 3:30 to 12:30 a.m. I couldn't do that. . . . And it paid pretty good, but it was second shift. I wouldn't have anybody to watch them at night. Plus they are in school, and I want them to continue to go to school. I wouldn't have anybody to pick them up that I would trust and rely upon. . . . So what was I going to do? I just told them I couldn't do it." Karen, like Veronica and many other low-income women, was often put in a stressful predicament when she conducted a job search. As Lein et al. describe in chapter 1 of this volume, low-income women are often underemployed and spend periods cycling between employment and underemployment. Both Veronica and Karen had skills and job opportunities, but, for them, taking a job was impossible without reliable child care.

Encouragement from caseworkers to rely on kin for child care may only compound a mother's frustration with the effort to meet expectations of self-sufficiency. As K. Newman (2001) contends, welfare workers' anticipation of kin support rests on an assumption of traditional roles of elder women as caretakers, not as working women. Recent ethnographic work illustrates that, with the implementation of PRWORA, older women are being drawn into the workforce, either for the first time or after an extended pause (Edin and Lein 1997; K. Newman 1998). Veronica completed her certification as a nursing assistant in a program sponsored by the Texas Workforce Commission in 2001.[5] However, it was a struggle for her to find a job that made use of her new skills and accommodated her five-year-old son's school schedule. Even though she lived near her mother and frequently spent time with her family, Veronica couldn't count on her mother to help her with child care because her mother already worked full-time to support Veronica's three school-age siblings and to supplement her Social Security benefits. Veronica explained: "I don't have any family support for them to help me watch my son. My mom works from eight in the morning till 9:30 at night. The only other people that are here are my two sisters that are in high school and my younger brother. So, as far as family support, I don't have nobody to watch him. If I did, I wouldn't be on TANF. I'd be out there working and going to school at the same time." There were positions available for nursing assistants during the daytime, when her son attended preschool, but, Veronica stated, "The shifts are from 7 a.m. to 3 p.m. . . . And they don't start breakfast at school until 7:30. . . . So I guess I'll have to keep looking for one that starts at eight. . . . And there's nobody that I know that would watch him for that amount of time, every day."

Thus, Veronica could not rely on her mother to watch her son before and after school each day, so she continued to look for work and a child care arrangement she could afford. Her experience illustrates the unintended consequences of welfare reform described by K. Newman (1998) and Kingfisher and Goldsmith (2001) on women who are expected to draw upon informal care provided by family, friends, and neighbors. Seminal work by Stack (1974) highlights the complex social networks between women and other female kin within and beyond the nuclear family. This is demonstrated as more and more women who previously cared for other children in their home as part of a complicated informal exchange network are required to perform wage labor outside their home and make arrangements for the care of their own children. This is not to say that social networks are no longer an important support system for low-income women but rather that these networks are increasingly unable to provide consistent and low-cost child care necessary to sustain women's work efforts.

Meyers, Brady, and Seto (2001) point out the increasing demands for formal child care providers and child care subsidies as women of all ages enter the workforce. The demand for subsidized child care increases concurrently with the number of women redirected into the workforce. In San Antonio, many mothers commented that child care subsidies are often depleted long before the end of the state's fiscal year. To cope with the rising demand on finite and already scarce subsidies, women are encouraged to draw upon resources that they feel their family members cannot or should not be expected to provide. However, although many low-income women I interviewed agree with the premise of welfare reform and the significance of employment, they still expect the state to subsidize what they and their social networks cannot. Some women even noted that they applied for TANF specifically to receive secure subsidized child care while they searched for work, with the incentive that they will be able to maintain this subsidy after they begin working.

Within welfare reform, all individuals are held to the tenets of self-sufficiency through employment regardless of gender, ethnicity, socioeconomic position, or personal circumstance. What is more, the emphasis on work operates from the assumption that women's kin are available and willing to provide support (Oliker 2000, 182). Thus gender, along with class and ethnic differences, is elided from emerging public policy discourse about working women. Some respondents reacted against demands to work made by caseworkers and welfare reform policies, resisting the pressure to embrace their roles as potential workers. Lucia, Ysenia, Sonia, and Veronica described their struggles to arrange child care around work schedules and their subsequent resignation that they would "just have to wait until they [the children] go to school."

Child care limitations, combined with the available transportation, educational, and employment resources, are some of the persistent causes that these women cited for abandoning expectations of working, at least temporarily. Sonia had only worked twice, for a few weeks each time, in the past two years. She cited the stress of working and raising four boys, combined with the absence of any sustained social support, as her reason for not maintaining her jobs in seafood and barbecue restaurants. Ysenia worked intermittently as a security guard on weekends in various places around San Antonio, and she relied entirely on her mother-in-law or estranged husband to watch her four-year-old son during court-ordered visitation times. However, Ysenia became increasingly concerned about her son's well-being when he spent time alone with her husband and his girlfriend, so she was reluctant to leave him in their care beyond the visitation period. These factors, combined with the fact that she was unable to secure a job in her desired position as a security guard during the abbreviated weekday hours when her son attended a Head Start program, contributed to her lagging motivation to look for a job until her son was enrolled in kindergarten in the fall, when he would have a longer school day and the possibility of after-school activities.[6]

Hochschild's (1995) critique of the cultural expectations of individual success and the idealized construction of the American dream is salient to ongoing debates about welfare reform and anticipated family self-sufficiency. The rhetoric of the "American dream" is continually at work in the lives of poor and working poor women through recent welfare reform policies. *Personal responsibility* is a term that resonates with Hochschild's postulation of the third tenet of the American dream, which challenges all individuals to live up to their potential for success. The shift in rhetoric from welfare to "work opportunity" rearticulates the dominant paradigm: All individuals should be offered equal access to the necessary circumstances to realize success. Moreover, the initiation of time limits for welfare benefits and services reinforces the notion that if, given ample opportunity to work and achieve self-sufficiency, individuals still fail, then it is only a result of their own lack of desire or ability to improve their situation. Thus, poverty in the United States is constituted as an individual shortcoming, not as a persistent by-product of structural or economic conditions, which reinforces the idea that individuals, rather than institutions or social structures, should be the focus of welfare reform.

It's important to note that Hochschild also maintains that governmental policies are the primary course to ensure "'that everyone, regardless of ascribed status, family background or personal history' can pursue their dreams" and "have 'the reasonable anticipation of success'" (1995, xiii). As I listened to low-income women in San Antonio speak about their experiences negotiating public assistance and working, Hochschild's words fell flat. Nevertheless, the theme of personal success through work and education prevails not only in political rhetoric but also in the views of some women. In contrast to the reluctance of some women to enter the workforce, Lori, Karen, Nora, and Barb, all mothers of preschool-age children, had well-developed employment histories and supported the idea that it is "better" to work or complete their educations than to be full-time mothers relying on TANF benefits and social networks for support. Additionally, all these women had plans of home ownership, and Nora and Barb were already pursuing that objective. Working and maintaining child care was part of their plan to provide for the long-term needs of their families. However, all respondents asserted that reliable child care was essential to their goals.

Formal Child Care and Flexibility

Although acquiring subsidized or affordable child care is initially important, women must still contend with stringent schedule restrictions when considering work opportunities. Providers and preschools often strictly enforce policies regarding pickup times and payments. Mothers operate under extreme fear and intimidation about returning for their children by a certain time at the end of the day. Karen, a mother of two preschool-age girls, described her experience at a Head Start center and at a YWCA, where late-pickup penalties ranged from fines to reports to caseworkers to, in extreme cases, the termination of a child care subsidy. Being released late from a job by a manager or missing a bus can be ruinous to a parent's day care arrangements. Hence, there is an inherent contradiction at work on poor mothers trying to negotiate employment and formal child care arrangements. This points to a central contradiction for low-income working mothers: A woman must remain flexible in order to optimize her chances for employment, yet she is not allowed the benefit of flexibility within all other aspects of her life in terms of children's schedules, child care provider's hours, and work responsibilities.

Martin's conception of flexibility (1994) also offers many prospects for thinking about social processes at work in the lives of women in San Antonio. While women must negotiate what they perceive to be rigid welfare policies, they must also maneuver every day in numerous ways, shifting between various and overlapping identities as single parents, employees, students, and survivors as they struggle to "make it" and meet the expectations of caseworkers, employers, friends, and families. Although flexibility as a strategy for survival is practiced out of necessity, women ultimately express a desire for a return to an imagined unbounded period of stasis, which they articulate in terms of financial and emotional stability for their families.

Choosing Care

As welfare reform policies mandate, all recipients are initially evaluated for their projected ability to work, but child care responsibilities (as well as care for elderly or disabled kin) do not exclude an applicant from work requirements. As Skinner et al. discuss in chapter 4, this fact makes it particularly difficult for women with disabled children or family members to maintain employment. Within welfare reform, caregiving is constructed as a temporary, private problem, not a long-term, public concern. Nor is parental child care prioritized in the same way that wage work is for welfare recipients. As a result, limited amounts of subsidized funds for child care have been made available to women, and time limits for welfare benefits reduce opportunities for women to be primary caregivers to their own children.

However, many respondents do indeed consider parenting young children as work, which is why they desire to delay wage work outside the home until their children are old enough to attend school. When faced with work requirements and time limits to benefits, many low-income women emphasize the necessity for sources of formal child care arrangements that will allow them to work. Arrangements with subsidized and affordable day care providers are articulated in contrast to informal arrangements with friends or relatives, which usually occur in the context of a reciprocal exchange, initiating a series of obligations for mothers that are financially and emotionally taxing.[7] In some cases, these costs outweigh the perceived benefits of working. Furthermore, for some women informal child care arrangements are not even perceived as available or possible.

Negotiating child care and working are very difficult for women who arrived in San Antonio more recently. Although some women, such as Veronica, had kin networks available, albeit unwilling or unable to help, Karen, a thirty-six-year-old mother who recently moved to San Antonio, had no kin networks on which to depend for child care when she worked. Karen had no relatives or friends in San Antonio other than members of her partner's family, and she repeatedly identified herself as "all on my own" with "no one to depend upon" where child care was concerned. Karen had worked temporarily as an office assistant and as a cashier and had participated in the required programs under the Texas Workforce Commission. Nevertheless, she felt that her options for work were acutely reduced by her availability between the weekday hours of 7 a.m. and 5 p.m., when her daughters attended a charter preschool near the public housing complex where they lived. She stated that she needed more help with child care to get on her feet again. She was willing to pay for child care, but she needed a job before that would be possible. In the event that she did find full-time or part-time employment as a cashier or in an office, she doubted she would be able to spare more than eighty dollars a week for child care, at least initially, which was about half the cost of care for two children by a licensed provider.[8]

Table 2.3 presents a brief sketch of Karen's most recent struggles to attain economic independence through employment. As with other women, Karen's life had been punctuated with various periods of domestic violence and residential mobility throughout San Antonio. These facts made maintaining child care arrangements and employment difficult for Karen. Although she had some post-high school education and experience in the construction industry, the tight labor market in San Antonio, when compounded with her ongoing need for flexible and affordable child care, made it difficult

Table 2.3 Periods of Employment, TANF Receipt, Residential Mobility, and Subsidized Child Care for Karen, 2001–2003

	2001				2002			2003	
TANF	—	—	Yes	Yes	Yes	—	Yes	—	
Employment[1]	$12	$12	—	—	—	$8	—	Americorps	
Subsidized child care	—	—	Yes	—	Yes	—	—	Both children in preschool	
Domestic violence	—	—	Yes	—	—			—	
Residential mobility	TX	TX	FL	TX	Southeast San Antonio			Northeast San Antonio	Southwest San Antonio
Reason for leaving employment		Laid off			Could not afford child care at night			Still with Americorps	

[1] Amounts represent hourly wage
Abbreviations: FL = Orlando, Florida; TANF = Temporary Assistance to Needy Families; TX = San Antonio, Texas

for her to locate work that paid as much as the twelve dollars per hour she had earned as an administrative assistant for a construction company in 2000.

Despite her need for affordable and flexible child care, Karen could not count on her partner's relatives for help. In exchange for a few hours of child care, she was obligated to several weeks of requests for services and errands from the family. Child care for her daughters before and after preschool hours was not, in Karen's estimation, "worth" persistent requests for groceries, errands, and money. Karen felt that she could not rely upon her partner's family to help even when they offered or agreed to care for her daughters because "they only help when they expect something else in return. Which puts more pressure on, which really isn't much help. . . . They either expect money, or the favors they expect take more hours. . . . The favors they expect are time-consuming. . . . If they watch the girls for four hours, they expect twenty hours worth of favors. . . . At times, it's just too much." When employment opportunities occurred outside her daughters' preschool hours, Karen was left with no resources to fall back on for care.

As Edin and Lein (1997) explain, informal arrangements may be available to women, but usually at a cost. Following from Portes and Landolt's (2000) discussion of social capital, Karen's and Veronica's narratives evidence the consequences of social ties, where the motives of donors must be considered when receiving a gift or service, and the possibility of excessive requests for repayment must be considered alongside the positive attributes of social networks. Child care is almost always part of a reciprocal relationship in which money or services will be expected in return, sometimes at a greater cost than women feel the child care is actually worth (Edin and Lein 1997). From this perspective, working becomes socially and financially costly for many women.

In conjunction with this idea of reciprocal relationships, interviews with Veronica and Karen also suggest that the social networks available to poor women for assistance with child care are themselves experiencing financial stress. Although Veronica's mother or Karen's partner's relatives may be available to help with child care, they are also themselves in need of resources. These women's experiences support Mink's position (1998) that caregiving is work, which is precisely why formal child care providers exact money for care from those who can afford to pay for it.

However, financial subsidies for family and friends who do provide much-needed child care for working mothers have allowed some women to take weekend and evening jobs to support their families. Lori completed her associate degree while receiving subsidized child care and now works full-time during the week as a customer service representative and fifteen hours each weekend at a local flea market. Her caseworker helped her secure subsidized funds for child care, and the funds were sent directly to an aunt who needed income and agreed to care for Lori's children on the weekend. Lori described the arrangement with her relative in this way: "I need it, and they don't have any day care facilities open for the weekends. And they said it could be an aunt or uncle of the child. . . . His aunt wasn't doing anything, so I said, 'Do you want to babysit?' . . . She's going to make pretty good money. She's going to make almost what I make a month off of that."

But this arrangement was satisfactory for Lori only "as long as we get along [her son's father, the aunt, and herself]. . . . Because that's it. . . . If we get into an argument . . . she's not going to watch my kids." Lori feels that her son's aunt "only does it for the money; that's all right, I guess. She needs a job; she needs to make money herself." Lori would have preferred to make an arrangement with a close friend's mother, but the subsidized funds were restricted to a close relative. As Lori's experience illustrates, child care is work that even next of kin expect to be compensated for, and subsidies that are flexible for mothers to use at their discretion with relatives provide necessary and flexible child care options for mothers who work during the hours when most child care facilities are closed. However, as Lori, Karen, and Veronica show, state-subsidized informal arrangements are restricted and often emotionally stressful for mothers, and thus, formal arrangements frequently emerge as more desirable.[9]

The reliability and long-term availability of child care arrangements are crucial factors for mothers who work or are looking for work. Although it may be difficult to find a day care facility that meets the temporal, financial, and emotional requirements of everyone involved, mothers feel that they can at least depend on formal arrangements over time if they meet the established rules and financial requirements of those who provide child care services. Since most respondents emphasize that they have no family or friends available to provide care consistently at the same time each day or for months at a time, they feel that if they can afford to pay for it, a day care center or individual who is paid an established fee will at least be reliable; thus, the respondents may work indefinitely.

Frequent and sudden relocation also contributes to women's desires for and the necessity of formal child care providers to accommodate their financial and scheduling needs. From the cohort of eight women that I discuss in this chapter, all but two moved at least once during the two-year interview period. Moving to a different neighborhood may position families out of the immediate reach of networks of neighbors, friends, and kin that they may have developed around their previous residence. As table 2.3 illustrates, Karen moved four times in three years, and one move was to another state before she moved back to San Antonio. Moving, working, and parenting can sometimes be so time consuming that it takes many weeks, even months, to establish contacts with new neighbors, and any prior informal child care arrangements may dissolve.

Lori and Sonia's families were friends and neighbors for about two years, continuously exchanging babysitting, food stamps, and car rides until Sonia moved from the public housing courts where they both lived and into a privately managed apartment complex. Sonia and Lori still remained friends, but Sonia's new apartment was several miles away on the outskirts of San Antonio, and she did not own a car or drive. Still, Sonia's youngest sons occasionally spent the night at Lori's home, and Lori gave Sonia rides to the store whenever possible, but both felt the loss of a convenient and trustworthy child care option.

In contrast with the situations I have just presented, women who do receive sustained assistance with child care from family members have more opportunities to work and are able to use their earnings for expenses other than child care. Nora, a Mexican American mother of three school-age girls, had a younger sister who lived with her and cared for her daughters while she worked at a convenience store every night. Additionally, Nora's sister took all of her nieces to live at her home in Florida during the summer of 2003 so that Nora could work even more and save money toward a down payment on a home.

When I met Barb, a twenty-nine-year-old European American mother of three daughters, she was working forty hours a week at a San Antonio shoe factory. Barb had weekends off, and her mother and stepfather lived with her in a house trailer that Barb owned. In exchange for a place to live, Barb's mother, who was temporarily unable to work, cared for her eighteen-month-old granddaughter and school-age granddaughters during the day while Barb worked. Additionally, her mother babysat for other children in their trailer park in exchange for money, using some of her earnings to help Barb make the land payment. Barb described this arrangement in the following way:

> My mom helps me with the housework and with the girls in exchange for staying here. . . . I let her move in with me because, you know, my mom has helped me with all three of my kids. I was fourteen when I had my oldest daughter. So, you know, my parents really helped me out a lot. So when they lost their apartment . . . in exchange for having to find a babysitter, I let them move in here. My mom takes care of the kids when they get home from school, takes care of her [Barb's youngest daughter] during the day, and she cleans my house, and she has supper done for me a lot of times when I get home. So, my mom helps me out a lot for me letting her stay here.

Barb's family arrangements allowed her to work full-time and make payments on her house trailer while her daughters were being looked after in their own home. In this situation, kin support for child care promoted a woman's entry into the work force and contributed to her ability to continue working.[10] Thus, it was affordable for Barb to work and meet her child care needs, as well as to direct her extra income toward owning a home.

However, the return of older women into the workforce has resulted in the erosion of social support networks for some women like Barb. When I first became acquainted with Barb, her mother, Pam, was unable to work, positioning her and her husband in need of a place to live. Even before Pam was reemployed, Barb asserted her desire to secure formal day care for her youngest daughter so that she could relieve her mother from her child care responsibilities and, more importantly, because she felt that her arrangement was "temporary" and contingent upon her mother and stepfather's necessity for a place to live and her mother's pending return to work. However, she said, "Every time I call, my caseworker just says that they don't have any openings, or there's a freeze on it. . . . To me, it feels like my caseworker don't help me try to get day care."

After-school care for older children, especially adolescents, is an essential child care arrangement for some mothers. Keeping school-age children "out of trouble" is a dominating concern for all parents in central San Antonio, and some mothers want to make sure that their children are supervised after school and not "running the streets." After-school programs are popular among low-income families with elementary- and middle-school children in central San Antonio. However, one of the drawbacks of after-school programs is that they follow the school calendar, leaving women to fall back on their own resources to supplement supervision during weekends, holidays, and summers.

Prioritizing employment may push more women toward decisions in which such child care arrangements are not perfect choices but the best solutions out of a narrow range of less appropriate alternatives. While some children go to child care centers after school and during school vacations, despite protests (Sonia's older sons "don't like it, but they have to go"), women like Karen are forced to make difficult choices about work and child care. She feels she often has no alternative but to leave her daughters in the care of a neighbor she does not approve of or with an alcoholic partner for several hours between the time preschool ends and she returns home from work.

Men and Caregiving

Although some respondents asserted that biological fathers and partners should help provide or pay for child care, for many women this was not a possibility. Karen expressed the desire for her partner, a man of Mexican origin, to help her watch her children, but she countered that "because of his culture, the man is not accustomed to taking care of children. He is good with them, and he will feed them, but when it comes to long-term care, I would not leave them with him during their waking hours. . . . During their waking hours, there is just too much to do, and he is not equipped. He is almost fifty years old, and he stands by the Mexican culture that the men don't take care of kids." Thus, Karen only expects her partner to watch her daughters for brief periods of time, and not consistently, either. Many women I interviewed involved with Latino or Mexican men do not expect them to provide sustained and reliable child care, and they invoke culture and gender as barriers to caregiving.

This is not to say that fathers, even nonresidential ones, never spend time with their children or assist with child care. Some women were able to arrange work during the weekends when fathers had court-ordered visitation periods with their children. Lori and Ysenia were able to use weekend visitation times to substitute for the absence of available or affordable day care. However, this is only possible when fathers take care of all of a woman's children, including children they are not biologically related to, as in Lori's case. Therefore, another complication with informal child care by kin and fathers arises for mothers who have children by multiple partners and cannot expect their families to care for them.

As more welfare recipients contend with time limits, informal child care arrangements will most likely become more scarce and more costly to women who rely on them while they work.[11] Recent qualitative analyses support the idea that with the withdrawal of public benefits, families are increasingly expected to turn to their available social resources to sustain themselves (S. Bell 2001; Edin and Lein 1997). Although some poor families do sustain themselves with organized and mutually beneficial networks of support, other families have fewer reciprocal systems of exchange, allowing some individuals to be drained by unbalanced exchange relationships. Still other families must function without the asset of economic support from others. This does not mean that they are totally estranged from kin and friends, but that these people are also economically strained and themselves in need of assistance.

These interviews with women in San Antonio illuminate the multifaceted and complex nature of situations and options poor or working-poor families find themselves maneuvering within in terms of kin support, work, and child care. Kin support cannot be assumed as a universal child care option for poor mothers. Grandmothers, aunts, and sisters fulfill multiple roles, often with children and jobs of their own. Consequently, these relatives are often also economically strained and increasingly seek wage labor or require that child care be compensated for with wages.

Although wage work for all low-income mothers remains the focus of welfare reform, the San Antonio women also demonstrate the desire and necessity for formal child care options to support their roles as mothers. Subsidized child care is an essential albeit scarce resource for working poor mothers. As Veronica, Lori, and Karen's experiences indicate, informal arrangements are tenuous and costly to mothers, and the family and friends that are willing to assist with child care are themselves in need of income and subsidized services. If mothers cannot afford to pay acceptable wages to or do favors for friends or relatives, they cannot expect to rely on these arrangements for consistent or long-term support. The situations of these women speak to the notion of "mobilization of ties" (K. Newman 1998, 772) that distinguishes between who one knows and on whom one can actually count for support. Although Veronica and Karen may have kin and friends to call on for other forms of support, none are perceived as willing and able to provide child care assistance.

Additionally, there is often a lack of child care providers near residences or workplaces that accept children who pay with subsidized funds. Whereas Mulroy (1995) and Edin and Lein (1997) demonstrate that low-cost and easily accessible child care is essential to mothers who must work, I emphasize that flexibility and reliability are also key components to the child care needs of working mothers. Women are often able to locate employment options as retail, food service, or health care workers, and these jobs frequently require that employees remain flexible to work available shifts that change from week to week, not only during hours when day care facilities are open. Women such as Lori, Karen, and Veronica who have skills and experience in retail or health care are willing to work, but they first need to secure affordable, dependable, and flexible child care arrangements. Furthermore, kin cannot—nor should they—be the only option for child care assumed by welfare policies.

This preliminary research indicates the complex nature of women's needs and desires for child care and the tenuous relationship of low-income families, welfare reform policies, and employment opportunities. It also augments our understanding of women's experiences as those women struggle to improve their social and economic situations. Although mothers are directed toward work to meet time limits for benefits and to achieve financial self-sufficiency, the experiences of some women in San Antonio suggest that child care needs are directly related to whether work is feasible or affordable. Furthermore, families without relatives and friends to supplement subsidized child care are doubly burdened by work requirements and child care needs. Recalling the words of Mink (1998), it is essential "to make work pay" by creating flexible relationships between women and policy so that families may transition not only off welfare but out of poverty as well.[12] It is also crucial to think critically about the social consequences of emphasizing "work first" for families to be sure that we are not situating a family's physical and emotional well-being at a lower priority than a parent's earning potential.

Acknowledgments

I would like to recognize Megan Watson, Emily Leventhal, and Melissa Biggs-Coupal for conducting some of the initial interviews with families and for introducing me to some of their respondents. I also wish to thank Jane Henrici, Holly Bell, Laura Lein, Lillie Salcido, and Melissa Biggs-Coupal for their comments during the development of this chapter.

Notes

1. This research constitutes a portion of the ethnographic work conducted within Welfare Reform, Families, and Children: A Three City Study at the San Antonio site.

2. Kingfisher and Goldsmith (2001) highlight the side effects of neoliberal rhetoric and policies, which at once create new, empowered spaces for women and have several detrimental effects on the way gender and individuals are dealt with in public policy.

3. Susser (1997) discusses the phenomena of increasing work expectations and decreasing child care assistance within the 1996 welfare reform policies.

4. Martin describes this trend toward privileging flexibility in terms of the human immune system and corporate culture, citing these entities as just two of the sites where "new versions of old hierarchies are being put forth" (1994, 232). The human body functions as a metaphor for society and a site from which social analysis can be interpolated. From Martin's work, we can garner then that culture, like capitalism, constrains individuals by prizing flexibility as an empowering quality that all Americans must contend with every day to meet demands pressed upon them by the social ideals of individuals as workers, parents, and consumers. However, whereas Martin maintains that flexibility is now advancing as a compelling force for corporations, workers, and bodies, Jennifer Hochschild asserts that "separatism and rigidity seem to be gaining ground" in U.S. society, threatening the ideology of the American dream. Hochschild follows an impressive and exhaustive agenda in her aspirations for inclusiveness (1995, 8) in evaluating the American dream along the axes of class, race, and gender, in *Facing up to the American Dream*.

5. The Texas Workforce Commission is the agency that coordinates services and programs to facilitate local workforce needs in Texas. According to the TWC web site, the organization maintains that individuals "must assume personal responsibility for making decisions about their lives and must be accountable for their actions" and that the agency is committed to becoming a "flexible and learning organization."

6. Head Start is an early child development program administered by the Head Start Bureau, and more broadly by the Department of Health and Human Services, which serves low-income families and children ages five and younger to enhance school readiness of young children.

7. In *Making Ends Meet*, Edin and Lein demonstrate that almost all informal child care situations involve the exchange of money or services and, thus, are not "free" (1997, 125).

8. In 1999, according to the Texas Association of Child Care Resource and Referral Agencies Web site, in Bexar County (where San Antonio is situated) the average price of weekly full-time child care for one infant or toddler was eighty-two dollars; the average price for the same amount of care for a child of preschool age was around seventy dollars. These averages consider the costs of care in child care centers as well as private homes.

9. Presser and Cox (1997) substantiate this point, documenting the prevalence of low-wage or undereducated workers with non-standard work schedules, and, subsequently, their desires for formal child care arrangements to meet their needs.

10. Hao posits the price-of-time hypothesis, in which some form of coresidence or income support reduces the price of a woman's household time through assistance with housework or child care, thus reducing the cost of job searching or working and promoting her ability to continue working. (1994, 163).

11. In "Tyesha's Dilemmas," K. Newman (1998) describes how welfare reform affects the intertwined lives of welfare recipients who reside together and exchange child care responsibilities.

12. This preliminary research also supports assertions for amendments to initial welfare reform policies such as those proposed by Patsy Mink. Mink proposed a bill that would shift the emphasis of welfare reform from that of reducing the caseload of welfare recipients to a focus on decreasing the number of families living in poverty. Increasing funds available to states for child care, education, and job training were part of Mink's proposed bill, a treatment of which appeared in Caroline Polk's article (2000) circulated online through *Womenenews*.

work first, then what?

Women and Job Training after Welfare Reform

Jane Henrici and E. Carol Miller

Job training and career development services to help families locate sustainable employment receive unequal support within different states and cities. Very limited help is available with qualifications, but comprehensive packages for women to learn skills and gain education are few and underfunded.

The Texas state government and the private businesses with which it contracts operate a set of programs to aid poorer families within an overall approach that is well represented by its campaign name, Work First. As the analyses by H. Bell (chap. 8) and Henrici (chap. 9) discuss, ethnographic research within the city of San Antonio indicates that private, as well as public, agency workers and those seeking benefits have distinct and sometimes conflicting motives, incentives, and definitions of success in their involvement with Work First. The amount of money or time that service providers and low-income families invest in programs to help individuals become employed can vary, as can the outcomes.

On one hand, the Texas Workforce Commission (TWC), the state agency responsible for oversight of the network of public workforce development services throughout Texas, received multimillion-dollar performance bonuses for its welfare reform work (Texas Workforce Commission 2001, 59). On the other hand, poor women with young children who seek aid in San Antonio report that they are told to find a job immediately regardless of its quality, and without a thorough assessment of needs or a concrete plan in place to facilitate the attainment of long-term financial self-sufficiency and sustainability for the entire family.

In between these two poles are service providers who report that, although they are adapting, utilizing creative problem solving, and responding with some success to current political and workforce demands for "flexibility" in themselves and in their clients, the legislative provisions have "set us up for failure." Also in between are a few women who state that they have found help from such agencies both in terms of immediate employment and larger goals for themselves, but that they need more if they are to continue to work.

Federal Legislation

The structure of the workforce-development service-delivery system affecting job training agencies and their workers is complex. So are the lives of the women and children affected by the programs and their constraints, as Lein et al. and Bruinsma (chaps. 1 and 2) point out. However, as this chapter and those of H. Bell and Henrici (chaps. 8 and 9) describe, a bridge between those complexities is unlikely.

The confluence of the federal-level legislative mandates of the Personal Responsibility and Work Opportunity Reconciliation Act (PRWORA) of 1996 and the Workforce Investment Act (WIA) of 1998 required the implementation of a radical social experiment. The intention was to subvert, then replace, the existing workforce-development and social-welfare-policy paradigms and structures.

In the most general terms, PRWORA newly highlighted individuals and work, eliminated automatic entitlement for welfare benefits, and devolved responsibility for implementation to the states. The declared objective of these policies was to enhance flexibility in order to address the needs of local contexts. PRWORA put a sixty-month lifetime limit on cash assistance to an individual caring for children and required evidence that the person had a job or an acceptable reason not to work.

The Workforce Investment Act, meanwhile, required states to streamline and coordinate workforce and skill development services into a universal "one-stop" service-delivery administration model. Programs were to be "comprehensive" and "client-centered" (Bass 2000). The act removed states' service delivery responsibilities. The law created a system in which Local Workforce Development Boards "contract locally with other provider organizations." These boards now "bear most of the responsibility for delivering Welfare-to-Work services" (Perez-Johnson, Hershey, and Hershey 1999, 13).

The Welfare-to-Work grant provisions of the Balanced Budget

Act of 1997 piggybacked onto PRWORA. It focused on ensuring that those in impoverished areas with markedly low skills would find employment. The Welfare-to-Work plan identified the existence of structural barriers to employability, such as a lack of transportation or child care, as well as "the serious personal and skill deficits with which many participants will enter employment" (Perez-Johnson, Hershey, and Hershey 1999, 32–34). The Balanced Budget Act authorized the allocation of three billion dollars to be distributed by the U.S. Department of Labor to states and local governments for assisting the hard-to-employ in finding salaried work.

Subsequent to the Balanced Budget Act, the Welfare-to-Work and Child Support Amendments of the Consolidated Appropriations Act of 1999 were enacted to allow more flexible eligibility to enable broader participation in programs. These amendments represented a response to feedback from early program evaluations about overly "restrictive criteria" in the initial legislation (Perez-Johnson, Hershey, and Hershey 1999, 44). At the same time, the 1999 amendments stipulated that program participants were limited to six months of job training before seeking employment.

The Department of Labor Appropriations Act of 2001 stated that agencies that received grants to implement Welfare-to-Work programs could "extend the period of performance of their grants up to five years from the date of the grant award" (U.S. Department of Labor 2001, 2). This additional layer to the legislation was in response to the delays occurring when putting Welfare-to-Work programs into practice (Perez-Johnson, Hershey, and Hershey 1999, 37).

All together, this incredibly intricate federal legislative scheme encompasses the publicly funded strategies and services aimed toward the declared goal of a family's financial independence. Some of the types of workforce assistance around the United States include internships; subsidized on-the-job training; unpaid work experience, or volunteer work; job readiness training; GED and English as a Second Language classes; job placement assistance; training programs for the development of specific professional skills, licenses, or certifications; mentoring; and adult literacy and rudimentary math education. The legislation also allows states to use their block grants or matching funds to provide other services that might support work participation, such as assistance with transportation, clothing, child care, and job retention (Negrey et al. 2002).

All of this federal legislation follows, with certain compromises, political and economic models of privatization and limited government support for social services. Implementation required drastic reorganization at every level to make that fit. Certain public and private agencies have disappeared since the mid 1990s, whereas others have expanded, and concomitant shifts in the larger U.S. economy have added to these effects.

Local Implementation

Texas activated its version of welfare reform and the Workforce Investment Act "one-stop" service delivery model in 1995, putting in place Local Workforce Development Boards before the 1996 federal deadlines. In Texas, the process of translating new service paradigms and mandates into concrete procedures and implementation at the local level appears to be at least as salient as policy language in terms of affecting client outcomes. Finding service gaps is part of any major administrative change; the restructuring in Texas is exponentially more complicated. In addition to significant paradigm shifts, the privatization of workforce-development service delivery involved the administration of workforce centers by inexperienced contractors. Those charged with oversight have found convoluted communication and accountability channels (Cruz 1999, 93; Rossi, Freeman, and Lipsey 1999, 44; Texas Workforce Commission 2000, 3). However, Work First requirements of families have not made allowances for problems and delays due to changes; such difficulties might hinder a program's potential as well as a trainee's success, but the expectations and requirements remain in place as though programs and individuals operate within an established and well-developed system.

In practical terms, the initial response of TWC to this complex transition was to rely upon two primary performance measures: (1) a reduction in the TANF caseloads, and (2) success at job placement by workforce-center contractors for all clients, including those who were not Welfare-to-Work participants and who might have been much easier to assist with employment. The Work First mandate, officially announced in November 1998, had in fact been in place throughout Texas years earlier (Texas Workforce Commission 2000, 49). Meanwhile, the myriad legislative tenets that were aimed at providing a more holistic and comprehensive approach to helping families were not as evident.

Even when a comprehensive approach is utilized, long-term success with job training reportedly requires that the training be ongoing and flexible. Variables that can affect the outcomes of training programs include the availability of stable, living-wage jobs with benefits as compared to the number and skill level of potential applicants.

Other significant factors are the availability of affordable support services, such as transportation and child care. These services are often not available at times that fit into the schedules of the "hard-to-employ" who may have, for example, multiple medical appointments; Skinner, Lachicotte, and Burton (chap. 6) note how that particularly can affect families with disabled children.

In spite of such risks, researchers conclude that job training programs that undertake the broader effort have a better chance at success than do narrowly focused programs. Case studies around the United States indicate that comprehensive packaging has a greater chance of functioning for families, particularly if the programs include a flexible approach to diverse needs and abilities (Friedlander and Greenberg 1997; Grubb 2001, 286; Holzer 2001, 233; Negrey et al. 2002).

According to ethnographic data from Welfare, Children, and Families: A Three-City Study, the workforce-development service-delivery system in San Antonio has been in flux, as administrators and workers attempt to incorporate the more complex principles of the legislation. However, this shift has not resulted in a wider and more holistic set of services or job training programs for the state, but rather one that is even more restricted.

Currently, training is largely limited to job readiness (such as résumé preparation, clothing suggestions, and interview tips) and vocational supports for the hardest to serve (whether in the form of subsidized jobs or job searches). This arrangement appears to be less a catalyst for career advancement toward self-sufficiency and, with few exceptions, more about redirecting women away from either cash assistance or subsidized education (Lafer 1994; 2002; 2003; Plimpton and Nightingale 2000). This suggests that the existing set of changes cannot function without even more reform within the public-private service delivery network, its guiding legislation, and the greater spheres of social policy as they relate to public education, community planning, and urban and economic development.

As described in the Introduction to this volume, we interviewed low-income women, workforce development service providers, and other community members on topics related to the impact of welfare reform from January 1999 to December 2002 as part of the Three-City Study. For this chapter, we used ethnographic data from both the San Antonio Family and Neighborhood Studies. In the latter, we could find a pattern of the Welfare-to-Work workforce development service delivery system that is, even for those trained as professionals within it, tremendously complex and constantly evolving.

For the Family Study, poor women and their families provided us with eleven hundred interviews and observations from which to pull a sketch of their lives. Interviewed families were selected for general income level and distribution among racial and ethnic identities and neighborhoods, rather than for job training involvement. However, family members and researchers talked about job training, primarily within interview protocols concerning training and education, work experience, and child care, although the topic sometimes appears within other interviews as well. Approximately half of the families were receiving cash assistance at the time of recruitment, the other half not, but individuals in both sets changed their welfare status during the course of the research project, and this and other life-course adjustments could affect whether they were required, or wanted, to participate in Welfare-to-Work job training.

Of the seventy-seven families we interviewed across San Antonio over the four years following welfare reform, only sixteen caregivers, or roughly 20 percent, presented themselves as having participated in formal job training within the Welfare-to-Work programs. This low percentage seems an artifact of the emphasis in Texas on sending all applicants directly to seek employment regardless of education or experience level. Of those sixteen women reporting job training experience, most talked about seeking it as an element of obtaining other assistance, such as referrals to jobs that paid more than their current work or regular and subsidized child care, rather than for the content of the training. Only two of the women interviewed who took part in job training expressed satisfaction with it as a form of employable-skill development. Nevertheless, the other forms of assistance obtained through job training participation were critical to families' subsistence and should not be ignored when considering the significance of supported training programs. In other words, we found that women participated in Welfare-to-Work job training programs more often where those programs were tied to subsidies and cash assistance, even if the programs could not be said to be completely comprehensive or, perhaps, of much aid toward finding and keeping jobs.

We conducted interviews and observations in apartments, stores, and agency offices. We found that the lives of San Antonio low-income women and their children often include unsteady and discontinuous cycles of employment, underemployment, and unemployment; public benefit receipt, denial, and independence; and intrafamilial and extrafamilial provision of supportive services, such as child care and transportation; and times of adapting to a lack of support or resources. One African American woman interviewed for the Three-City Study in San Antonio described her use of public assistance in this manner:

> I am what you call "the working poor." Only difference between me and [that other girl] is that I was smart enough to go to [a federal housing development] and not to the regular rent. Because regular rent, you just cannot do it. If you lose your apartment—I did it before! You lose your apartment, that's it! You're evicted! Whereas here, they'll work with you, you know. If you're not with someone that's income-based, if you're not with an apartment that says, "We go by your income," Honey, you're good as . . . unblessed! And there's a lot of women who are sweating it out. They're working very hard, they're paying . . . child care. . . . But if you're not smart enough to go toward income-based—people are not aware of this. Women are not aware of this. They've got so much pride. They don't know—you go to a place that says "Income," you know, 'cause these men try to make you feel bad, especially the ones that are running the world. They should know that this little child thing that you get once a year from taxes? That's not diddly-squat! When you're trying to take care of child care and everything else during the month. Nobody tells them this. Nobody told me that. I didn't know it. I knew nothing about WIC when I had [her first child]. I thought it was welfare. I have a job. A lot of these women are like, "Stay away from welfare." That's how I was. Anything not to go to welfare—"I've got my pride."

If they can, and have learned what services might help them supplement their wages, San Antonio women with children after welfare reform typically must piece together what they can of the elements necessary to making it day by day. Like other poorer families elsewhere and in other periods, they do this within variable circumstances, with a mixture of concerns, and with varying degrees of well-being. Family and Neighborhood Study respondents in San Antonio overwhelmingly informed us that the Work First mandate was successfully implemented in Texas to the extent state planners intended, and that women with children seeking aid did not necessarily find jobs.

Training Difficulties

Although the study methodology does not offer a representative sample of the San Antonio population of Welfare-to-Work clients, or of job training service providers, patterns in our interview narratives raise some compelling questions. As will be discussed, these patterns show how the myriad legislative tenets aimed at providing a holistic, comprehensive approach to facilitating economic empowerment and financial self-sufficiency for clients with significant barriers to success seem peripheral to the Work First system in Texas. Where there is job training, it is not embedded within a responsive set of resources, or fully funded, or given priority. The programs are incomplete and as such cannot be comparatively evaluated; at most, details concerning the experiences of providers and clients in the programs can suggest features for improvement toward their completion.

Meanwhile, we found that certain individual service providers were very aware of this paradox. They identified for us a need for continued collaboration among workforce centers in order to form a support network for families of interacting agencies. Conversely, the fact that most caseworkers focused in their practice almost exclusively on rudimentary and brief job-readiness training, rather than on a full set of educational and aid programs, might indicate that these providers believe in minimal intervention. Regardless of individuals' theories about what will best serve their clients, reward strategies of agency administrations encourage all caseworkers to select short-term measures within Work First. For training programs actually to meet existing legislative standards toward developing women caregivers as salaried workers, providers told us that a constellation of mutually supportive services and resources would need to be in place, as well as agency stimulation to use them.

From the view of the trainees, most of the women with whom we spoke found their job training generally unhelpful in obtaining substantive and sustained employment. The Family Study respondents concurred with the Neighborhood Study respondents: Women who took job training as part of Welfare-to-Work also indicated that, if the training programs had been consistently part of a wider range of resources, the success might have been better.

First, as noted, short-term job readiness training and job placement assistance is more common within Work First than job training services that provide concrete vocational skill enhancement or credentials. Most aid seekers received minimal assistance and accepted jobs regardless of their quality and without a comprehensive assessment of the seekers' short- and long-term needs.

In fact, low-income women with young children in San Antonio expressed satisfaction if they could then keep their wage employment, since that possibility depended on them locating reliable and convenient child care and transportation, maintaining the health of their children, and acquiring the funding to support those circumstances. One woman felt trapped by her son's illness and her lack of care for him while he was sick:

> But [the caseworkers at a job training program] don't know that I have, that I went, that I didn't work that over there in the new job [as a motel housekeeper]. They don't know. But they might tell me something, how come I didn't get that job. 'Cause see, the day care don't take care of my kids when they're sick. They can't. . . . [Pointing to one of her children] I want him to get better so I could go work, 'cause if I go work, they're going to call me from day care: "Go and pick him up." They're going to call me, call me, every day to pick him up. And I cannot go and pick him, because, cleaning in a motel, you can't leave your job.

Second, and an issue linked both to course content and lack of additional support, is the fact that for those who do receive either job readiness or skill enhancement services, the investment of time, money, or other resources creates more financial hardship than already existed, without providing financial sustainability in the long term. Some clients that received skill enhancement services even incurred a debt burden that exceeded reasonable financial gain, and since student loans may be counted as income, temporary cash benefits are even lower, which in turn creates a new financial strain.

One African American respondent explained why she would not try Welfare-to-Work training and education programs:

> I've seen so many people get job training and get those loans. My sister did that, and she got a loan, and she got a job working at the place she went to school at. I can remember her taking her income tax. It's this thing TANF have you going to, and you learn how to go on job interviews and write résumés and all that. And she was saying, "Don't go to those schools." Because they don't give you money or nothing. They just train you and give you a uniform and bus ticket to something. You can't make it on that.

Another woman's physical health suffered from the type of training she was assigned. After she was hurt lifting heavy boxes while participating in a job-training program, she had to quit and lost the assistance she had received while on it. She had to "have my mother come to clean my house and everything. I stayed like that for two weeks. I hated it. I couldn't do nothing, not even open a door." In subsequent years, she required medical treatment for her condition.

A third problem is the lack of flexibility among most programs, despite a range of backgrounds and levels of familiarity with the subject matter among low-income women. One mother took two sets of courses offered at a facility and felt ready to move to a more advanced program but was told that if she did not fully complete the rudimentary classes at the first institution she would be denied child care, despite having been assured she could keep it if she continued with her education. Since she had in fact been certified as having completed one of the classes at the first agency program and would have to first pass a test before being accepted at the other agency, she considered herself making a logical advancement. The service provider's response to her situation seemed illogical by contrast because "they want you to work, they want you to succeed and stuff, so how come they want you to go to the 'career readiness'? It's dumb. I don't get nothing out of it, you know? I already know what they're doing." That level of class, she said, made her feel "like a little fifth grader."

Related to this limitation is a fourth obstacle, which is that many agencies are underfunded. Consequently, service providers can be limited in the types of training they give and unable to teach their clients skills such as searching the Internet. Instead, agency programs concentrate on teaching skills such as résumé creation before sending trainees to jobs for which résumés are no longer needed. Describing her experience as not very useful, one mother told the interviewer: "[At the job training] we were putting clothes, we were separating the clothes, toys, stuff that the people donated—we were standing up for eight hours. That was doing a lot of damage to my legs. Because you only really get an hour break. And that wasn't helping me. And then they had us outside in the heat. I was working eight hours; it would come out eight hours a day."

Or an agency might give training that particular women could use, but lack the resources for the additional assistance she needed to become employed. Following the same training described in the quote above, a European American woman thought she had benefited from the experience, but was frustrated because it was not enough: "[The agency] helped me with the program and got me the job and everything, but then they said they couldn't help me with day care. . . . They helped me with bus tickets and everything and took me to my interview, took me to go to the drug test and everything, and they said they couldn't help me with day care [once her training was complete]." As caseworkers and women seeking aid both know, unless the children are older a mother without child care cannot find and accept wage employment (for more discussion of this issue, see Bruinsma, chap. 2). Multiple service providers identified the issue of their own agencies' limited resources as the way in which the system "set[s] us up for failure."

Finally, a fifth factor to consider is that the existing pool of organizations in San Antonio contracted by workforce centers to provide job-training services may have disparate impacts on communities within the city based on such characteristics as ethnicity, age, or ability to be successful in a formal, mainstream organizational setting. Some existing organizations emphasize aid to those of a specific ethnicity, and some policies are implemented in ways that favor the young and those who can succeed in more formal institutional settings, such as community colleges. Other aid seekers may be at a disadvantage under this scheme.

In contrast, where at least a partial array of services was available for families, some participants reported to us that they felt great satisfaction and stimulation of ambitions they would need to support themselves and their children. The same parenting and readiness classes that had been too basic for her neighbor were useful for another Mexican American respondent, who managed to stay through all of them and thus receive uninterrupted child care. When we asked her if she thought the training had been useful, she answered, "Yes, very. We went [to spend time in a national insurance corporation]. That was so insightful. You have to act a certain way. You can't be the same way you are around your friends that you are when you're trying to look for a job or when you go into the interview."

One San Antonio nonprofit organization that has received attention for its reported success in several areas, including job training, is the city's Industrial Areas Foundation's Project Quest (Warren 1998; K. Newman 1999). Although only two of the women we interviewed had the requisite starting education level and one- to two-year time commitment to complete a Project Quest training program, those two told us that they valued their experience and the help. One woman interviewed twice with Project Quest before being accepted into the program, and with her Welfare-to-Work subsidy did not need a student loan, as others did. She told us that she was excited about her training: "Project Quest pays for your tuition, your books, and they'll help with like your utilities and in some cases they'll help people get clothing."

This woman chose to train specifically for microcomputer data entry. Data entry is an example of nontraditional training that many trainees and caseworkers apparently believe to be of great value toward long-term and higher pay employment, despite lack of evidence (Negrey et al. 2002, 96–97). In fact, since Project Quest directors will not allow staff caseworkers to place their graduates in jobs that pay below a living wage ($7.10 at that time in San Antonio), it is probably the commitment of the organization itself, and of the employers with which it has made arrangements, that improves chances for stable work for poorer women, rather than merely the type of training provided and acquired. Furthermore, as has been stated, without the overall package of help that an organization must provide, such as child care and transportation, and the ability of the woman to take the time to train despite health concerns of her own and her children and the other many barriers to complete a program, any type of training remains incomplete.

Another respondent, a European American, also said that she had learned a great deal both from her training and from subsequent community college classes that she had then taken as part of her Welfare-to-Work. She told us that she hoped to finish with her preparation within a year after the interview. "It may be in December, because I have to repeat a business math course." What kind of job do she want? "Anything that pays over five-fifty. I want to get a good decent job to where it has great benefits, a pension plan, all the whole nine yards. Because I don't want [my child] doing without. I don't want her to want for anything."

Meanwhile, a specific caseworker even within the most limited of programs can respond individually to different education or experience levels among clients, even to the point of skipping the "readiness" classes, and help a woman with children receive cash benefits as well as other needed support while she develops skills beyond the rudimentary or repetitive. In other words, despite the fact that this combination of evaluation, flexibility, and tailored resources directed at assisting a family into self-sufficiency is part of the Welfare-to-Work mandate, it seems that provision of that combination is the capricious, or perhaps compassionate, exception rather than the standard rule. One mother interviewed stated that she received day care:

> Because I was going through the Texas Work Force, and they put me through the CCMS [Texas Child Care Management Service subsidies]. My Texas Workforce caseworker wanted me to go, either go back to school or go through classes to go look for a job. I already went through all that. . . . They weren't going to send me to go look for a job, and they told me to go to school for my GED. They said "I'll give you six months, and see if you get it by then; if not, if you need more time, I'll give you more time."

The current service delivery scheme has moved the locus of responsibility from the state to the local and even the individual level, but it is unclear whether neoliberal privatization and competition in this constrained market will produce enough positive change to justify the radical restructuring. Our most recent conversations with families in June and August 2002 show that, of those who took job training as part of Welfare-to-Work and who remained available for interviewing, twelve of the sixteen were either unemployed or employed in the same type of work they had found before training, with no marked pay or benefit increase.

Two of the women who did have employment had been sent by TWC caseworkers to Americorps, through which one succeeded in keeping a steady and supportive job that was likely to continue past her commitment period. The other had re-enrolled in a higher level Americorp position for which she had long-term career plans. Another woman was interning as a medical technician while completing her high school equivalency. The fourth was happily employed in a clerical position with a large corporation and coworkers she found agreeable, received benefits, and had been able to move with her children to be closer to the job and provide financial aid to others in her family. These last two women both received their current employment in connection with the training and subsequent education they received through Welfare-to-Work support.

Training Debates

Much of the existing literature on job training argues that it tends overall to be of little long-term help for participants unless it is part of a larger set of services, and even then an ability to respond to varying conditions and demands among families is required for training to be effective (King 2004). Our analysis of the San Antonio data from the Three-City Study supports this conclusion, suggesting that before job training can be of at least temporary assistance to low-income women it must be part of mixed sets of services; however, a flexible and comprehensive package of services is generally unavailable to women there.

In the universe of all possible intervention strategies to provide a safety net for women with children, for which income and access to some minimum standard of resources or quality of life is constrained by any of a variety of factors, job skill level is significant for those who do not own or control other forms of capital. With PRWORA, the Workforce Investment Act, and current reauthorization plans for welfare reform, the United States has a legislative and appropriations strategy that demonstrates willingness to provide aid so that women can have access to a range of options for preparing and training with the goal of employment. Predictably, the U.S. implementation scheme is fairly minimalist. The mandate seems to be to provide assistance to those who need it, with the least burden to those who are otherwise successful in the economy.

Strategies previously implemented, such as those under the Job Training Partnership Act (JTPA) and the Comprehensive Employment and Training Act (CETA), focused on immediate access to job skill enhancement programs, presumably to try getting everyone to a minimal standard of education and training before guiding clients into the workforce. Neither of these programs concentrated on the particularly complicated and constantly changing lives of welfare recipients. Evaluation of the outcomes of these programs met with minimal or at best mixed success in terms of the intervention translating into increased success in the job market. In terms of larger community issues, such as actual job creation and efforts to reach women with a range of needs, CETA's level of funding and its implementation apparently had the potential to make long-term effects had it continued (Morgen and Weigt 2001). However, if training programs were not fully funded in poorer neighborhoods and implemented in combination with a constellation of other services such as child care and housing subsidies, many failed to help participants (men and women) gain and keep stable employment.

The strategies under PRWORA and the Workforce Investment Act appear to be a reaction to this limited success. The logic appears to be, "If it didn't work to give training up front, let's mandate work initially and build practical experience in the job market, and worry about enhancing education and vocational skills later." The issue again is one of outcomes for aid seekers. Texas initially achieved success in mandating work in the booming economy at the time of implementation, but evidence of long-term success at facilitating sustainable financial self-sufficiency for clients is not convincing. Furthermore, assessment of whether implementation schemes disproportionately favor or handicap certain groups remains insufficient, although earlier research on prewelfare reform systems suggests that women of color benefited marginally more than others. However, more studies that examine training and race and ethnicity are needed (Browne 2000; Holzer 2001; Pérez and Muñoz 2001; Reskin 1999).

Employment for the women who seek government aid is central

to the current assistance system of the United States. However, the devolutionary character of that system is such that the situation has become one of "Work first, but then what?" Study observations reveal the inconsistent nature of access to resources and work and the demanding and complicated schedules encountered by the women and families with whom we have talked and spent time as their children aged and prepared for preschool. Our observations revealed limited use of job training services that could raise income and advancement in the job market for women with children. Given this picture, it appears unlikely that the current workforce development intervention scheme—even given time to mature and become more efficient and integrated after radical restructuring—will meaningfully translate into the purported attainment of financial self-sufficiency and sustainability for the hardest to employ.

Without appropriate emphasis on the individuals and families seeking assistance and an evaluation of the long-term self-sufficiency that they claim or actually have, block grant funding that allows flexibility between services also allows providers to mandate work first without considering long-term needs. Women with greater needs are, in fact, those who are neglected. In all, the likelihood of this strategy leading to sustainable financial independence seems low, given the predictable obstacles in the lives of low-income families.

Do we value providing aid to low-income families to attain some minimal standard of living? What do we require of the poor for receipt of aid, and why? What tenets do we use to help us prioritize the distribution of funds? Are we willing to tolerate implementation schemes that have disproportionate impact on groups that we otherwise define as needing protection from discrimination based on factors such as race, ethnicity, age, and gender?

If we require the poor to prioritize work over other elements required in a holistic approach to well-being, exactly what sacrifices does this demand? Are sufficient supports in place to ensure that all families have access to some minimal level of well-being, as defined by access to resources such as child care, health care, housing, transportation, and food, and to relationships and a lifestyle that support some minimal standard of functional physical and mental health? Does an implementation scheme that translates into unpredictable access to basic supports curb client motivation and willingness to make such sacrifices?

Workforce development programs as implemented after welfare reform in San Antonio have little potential to diminish the range of obstacles that impoverished women face. Service providers and local Workforce Development Boards may, in fact, have been set up for failure. As an alternative, U.S. society should begin to invest funds for more comprehensive social assistance for low-income women and their families, as our analysis of the ethnographic material from this study in San Antonio suggests.

Part Two **Climbing over Walls**

looking for home

Welfare Reform and the Illusion of Prosperity

Lillian M. Salcido

The thought of one day owning a house, or even renting an apartment without assistance, is a common dream shared by a group of Mexican American mothers from San Antonio, Texas, who are in transition from welfare to work. They aspire to live in a place that is safe, where their children can play and feel at ease. In interviews with women living in some type of subsidized housing as a part of Welfare, Children, and Families: A Three-City Study from 1999 to 2002, each expressed how having a home of her own would significantly improve the quality of her family's life. Welfare reform's rhetoric of self-sufficiency promised what they believed to be a second chance to improve their families' fates by making them productive members of the workforce. Through a "sense of place," these women desire a more middle-class lifestyle. This means referring to the place they live as "home" rather than "the ghetto." However, it seems unlikely that any of these women will ever be able to make the leap from single welfare mom to homeowner. Although all the women who participated in the larger study may share the dream of one day having their own home, this chapter will focus solely on the experiences of a group of women and their families with whom I spent time.

Most poverty research pertaining to Mexican Americans deals only with recent immigrants and migrant populations and lumps Latinos with other people of color. These studies tend to address Latino populations as homogeneous and assume that they all share a common experience. Such viewpoints also assume that the lives of low-income Latinos are identical to those of other low-income people of color. The qualitative ethnographic research with which I worked on the Three-City Study, at this date still being processed and analyzed, has attempted to go beyond those limitations and look at women of distinct Latino identities and some of their diverse experiences with poverty in the United States.

Looking for "Home"

When these women talk about the concept of "home," precisely what do they mean? How does being poor, single mothers affect their perceptions of what they consider a "good" home? An analysis of Latinos and housing issues will give insight into these questions.

Latinos have among the highest homeowners' occupancy rates in Texas (Acuña 1988). According to Rodolfo Acuña, home ownership among Latinos is higher in Texas because "Mexicans are more segregated and, until recently, fewer lived outside the *colonia* [neighborhood]" (Acuña 1988, 428). To the participants in this study, a home of one's own was imperative. Further research is needed to determine the significance of home ownership among Latinos in Texas, as well as whether this factor contributed to these women's desire for their own place.

Ruth Sidel's work focuses on the life perspective young women have about family, work, and the contemporary roles of women in society. Latinas were among the women Sidel interviewed, and her analysis is consistent with the perspectives I observed. She contends that, regardless of their class, race, ethnicity, or education level, the women want a piece of the "American dream" (Sidel 1990). These young women have middle-class desires for a career, material wealth, and success, but hold on to "symbols of identity and security in an era of fragmented family life, insecure, often transient relationships, and vanishing sense of community" (Sidel 1990, 223). Sidel's thesis, that mainstream culture's aspirations have an influence on those from the lowest income level, who are among some of the most marginalized from the dominant culture, resonates with an examination of single mothers and welfare reform. Aside from the issue of perceptions about housing and homes, there needs to be more research about Latinos and the U.S. benefits system in general.

In their book, *Welfare Racism*, Kenneth Neubeck and Noel Cazenave assert that the term *welfare mothers* evokes one of the most powerful racialized cultural icon in contemporary U.S. society" (Neubeck and Cazenave 2001, 3). The authors employ the term *welfare racism* to underscore how single black mothers became synonymous with the word *welfare*, and also how: "[I]n our conceptualization of welfare racism, attitudes refer to a set of negative beliefs and judgements about welfare recipients that often manifest themselves in racist stereotypes" (Neubeck and Cazenave 2001, 36). Since World War II, "highly punitive, racially subjugating welfare policies have been employed as part of a process of racial control in response to a variety of real or perceived threats posed to white racial hegemony by racially oppressed groups." Although these authors focus on welfare racism's impact on African American women, their analysis holds true for the single Latina mothers I observed in San Antonio.

According to journalist Jason DeParle of the *New York Times*, since PRWORA was implemented in 1996, "White recipients are leaving the system much faster than Black and Hispanic recipients, pushing the minority share of the caseload to the highest level on record" (Neubeck and Cazenave 2001). Although Latinos were becoming a greater portion of those who need government assistance, there continues to be a dearth of welfare reform studies that specifically address Latina mothers and their children. Patricia Zavella suggests that studies of Latinos of all income levels should focus on specific regions of the United States: "To understand whether there are significant numbers of citizens versus undocumented immigrants, note the gender compositions and labor market opportunities of migrants and settlers, and pay attention to salient features of race relations, including discrimination against those with distinct racial features and how their meaning changes over time" (1996, 372). A regional approach gives a distinct understanding of Latinos in the southwestern United States.

Mexican American Women and their Children in San Antonio

The Three-City Study examines, with a combination of quantitative and qualitative research methods, the effects of welfare reform over several years in Boston, Chicago, and San Antonio. According to Zavella: "Each Latino group has its own history in different regions of the country, where particular structural processes—conquest and subordination, waves of migration and settlement, the specific nature of industrialization and urbanization, and discrimination toward racialized others—have produced particular configurations of segregation and economic vulnerability" (1996, 372).

The San Antonio site offers a different regional perspective from either Boston or Chicago because of both its southwestern geographic location in the United States and its proximity to the Mexican border. Although there are Latina participants in Boston and Chicago, their histories differ from those of their San Antonio counterparts. A number of Latinas in the Chicago and Boston areas are immigrants from Central and South America and the Caribbean. In contrast, San Antonio is historically Latino. Many of the Latinas who participated in the project in San Antonio are second- and third-generation women whose families migrated to San Antonio as refugees of the Mexican Revolution, during the Great Depression, or after World War II.

What the San Antonio study participants share with their counterparts in Boston and Chicago is a history of impoverishment that continues to keep them on the lower rung of the economic ladder. Although unemployment rates remained relatively stable during the economic boom that coincided with the implementation of welfare reform and other changed benefit systems, the jobs created in San Antonio's strongest industries, tourism and health care, were largely low skilled and service oriented and were typically low wage and without benefits. Since the majority of San Antonio's population is Mexican American and 19.4 percent of that population is low income, the scarcity of living-wage jobs for Mexican Americans in San Antonio is a factor in their increased involvement with the benefits system.

Unemployment and underemployment of San Antonio's Mexican Americans have a profound impact on their children. A nationwide study conducted by the Children's Defense Fund after the implementation of PRWORA found that the people most affected by the welfare law were children living in households headed by single mothers. The report stated, "The number of children living below one-half the poverty line rose by 26 percent from 1996 to 1997 . . . [and] was especially high for Latinos/as (12 percent), followed by blacks (10.7 percent) and whites (9.5)" (Neubeck and Cazenave 2001, 219). As the proportion of minority welfare recipients increases, so does the need for additional study of groups such as Mexican Americans in San Antonio.

Housing and Self-Sufficiency in San Antonio

Welfare reform ended the federal guarantee of support for poor families. Finding and keeping paid employment is now a requirement for receipt of cash assistance called Temporary Assistance for Needy Families (TANF). In addition, there is now a five-year lifetime individual limit on receiving that aid. Proponents of this legislation argued that poor families would become "self-reliant," going off the welfare roles through participation in the workforce. This premise would have some validity if there were a sufficient number of jobs that were stable and paid enough to enable former welfare recipients to make it on their own (Piven 2001; Schorr 1997). Yet the women who participate in programs set up as part of PRWORA and related self-sufficiency efforts are constantly being challenged to "tough it out," to stay in compliance with a strict set of rules and to work at unstable minimum-wage jobs in order to guard against losing their benefits. Those Mexican Americans in San Antonio who progress toward their goal of self-sufficiency do so only if they find assistance and subsidies for child care, transportation, and housing (for more about the need for child care subsidies in particular, see Bruinsma, chap. 2, this vol.). However, as with other forms of aid, government-supported housing and housing subsidies are gradually disappearing from the already fragile safety net for low-income people.

PRWORA's key provisions are work requirements and time limits. Federal block grant money to each state also allows spending to help women find jobs through child care and transportation subsidies. Prior to welfare reform, gaining access to health care coverage through Medicaid was one of the primary reasons many women went through the trouble of getting welfare cash even in states where only low monthly payments were provided. Medicaid has now been "de-linked" from cash help so that poor children and pregnant women can at least get health care even if the caregiver is employed.

Meanwhile, housing assistance to poor families is funded from still other federal and local agencies. In 1998, two years after it passed the more extensive welfare reform law, Congress passed the Quality Housing and Work Responsibility Act, which transferred control of housing programs away from the federal government. The devolution of low-income housing program was not as sweeping as the overall transformation of the federal welfare system. Thus, the transformation of the housing benefits system in the past decade has received less commentary than other aspects of welfare reform (Sard and Bogodon 2003). Several studies have observed that the housing assistance system is undergoing transformations that are similar to the changes in other aspects of the welfare system, but the process of change has been slower in this area (Newman 1999; Sard and Waller 2002; Swartz and Miller 2002). In fact, however, the cash and housing programs overlap. Newman (1999) maintains that almost half of households with children living in public housing in the mid-1990s were AFDC recipients.

What little research exists suggests that housing problems for poorer families will only get worse. In the past, the prevailing view has been that there was enough housing to accommodate the nation's demand. However, the availability of affordable rental housing for low-income households has decreased in the last decade (Mulroy 2002). The effects of private market forces are significant for low-income households because Section 8, a government-subsidized program, depends on an abundant supply of rental housing. An April 2002 policy report by the Brookings Institution indicated that "[b]etween 1995 and 1998, the number of households receiving federal rent subsidies declined as a result of the demolition of public housing, the expiration of federal subsidy contracts for more than 120,000 privately owned units, and the lack of federal funding for any new housing vouchers" (Sard and Waller 2002, 3). However, simply because the households that received help declined in number does not mean that the members of those households all found suitable or affordable places to live. Unlike the pre-1996 AFDC recipients studied by Newman, few families receiving TANF also receive housing assistance because federal housing programs serve only about a quarter of the eligible households, and few states contribute enough resources to maintain or build more housing.

Although the overall condition of the San Antonio Housing Authority's (SAHA) housing stock is rated highly on the Public Housing Advisory Score (a federal measure of housing authority performance), as is a small portion of its larger housing developments, many units are located in neighborhoods with large poverty concentrations. Life choices are greatly compromised when occupants live in a public housing complex. Tenants often fear leaving their apartments after dark, making it difficult for women to work a second- or third-shift job. Neighborhood quality can vary greatly between public housing complexes and Section 8 housing. Alicia, a mother of three, viewed her move out of public housing with mixed emotions: "It's better [living in a duplex in an economically mixed neighborhood] than the courts. The courts, they have a lot of shooting, a lot of drugs. And here so far I haven't seen that yet."

These mothers, like generations before them in San Antonio and other cities, had misgivings about living in public housing developments, since the buildings are usually located in inner-city neighborhoods plagued by crime and violence (Edin and Lein 1997). Cultural geographer David Harvey has argued that location can have an effect on "opportunities and life chances of the residents of different areas, redistributing 'real income' and exacerbating inequalities between social classes" (McDowell 1999). The participants appreciated having an affordable place to live, but some of the women felt that the milieu of the public housing developments was a less-than-desirable place to raise children. As Lina, a mother of three small children, observed: "There are always cops around, like for people trying to break in. Just yesterday, there was a man trying to break into the corner house [apartment]. They caught him as he was about to tear the screen . . . and they said that he was a sex offender before, and they didn't know if he was trying to break in to steal [or] because there was, like, four kids there." Lina had lived most of her life in public housing. She would have liked to move to the Villa Veramendi complex, where she grew up, so that her children could go to the same elementary school she attended as a child. She was living at the Alazan-Apache complex because it had the only opening available. Although she dreams of one day "getting a house, having everything for my kids, and having a good job," she believes that the best she can hope for is to transfer to another public housing complex, one in which she would have a better support network of family and old friends.

Some women move out of the public housing developments and into apartment buildings or single-family homes by qualifying for Section 8 vouchers. U.S. Department of Housing and Urban Development (HUD) eligibility criteria define "affordable rent as 30 percent of a household's monthly income" (Mulroy 2002). Elizabeth Mulroy contends that many families who qualify for housing subsidies have incomes that are much lower than HUD standards. Section 8 housing is not very different from the public housing developments these women are trying to leave, but it often offers a respite from the noise and high crime of the public housing complexes. Upon approval, which in some cases can take two or three years, finding a suitable Section 8 house can be an arduous endeavor for the prospective tenant. According to Alicia "[b]ecause I was on Section 8, I only had so many houses [from which to choose]. They give you a list, and half of those houses had already been taken. This was the only one." Section 8 tenants are at the mercy of the list. Selectivity over criteria such as good schools, accessibility to parks, shopping and transportation is in many cases not an option.

Sonya, a mother of six, had been living in public housing in the Wheatley Courts, on San Antonio's historically African American east side, for five years. Several authors have noted that people of color are more likely than whites to have been "sanctioned-off" welfare programs for rules violations (Neubeck 2002), and Sonya's situation illustrates this trend. She was beginning to see the toll public housing was taking on her children. She had worked at Sonic, a fast-food restaurant, for a few months and seemed to be progressing toward some job stability and steady wages. Then all at once, she lost her child care because of a misunderstanding. Instead of taking the children to day care, their father was keeping them at his home, and they missed the maximum number of days allowed. Then she lost her job because she had problems getting along with her boss. Suddenly she was back where she started, applying for TANF and beginning once again the tedious process of looking for work and child care. During the few months it took to get back on her feet, she received Medicaid as health coverage for her children and food stamps as well as housing assistance. However, because of a problem with her TANF application, she had no cash income. She got money by giving plasma. Once I saw her scratching a large, dark bump on her arm, and I asked if she was still giving plasma: "Yes. That's why I'm itching it, because I've got to go back tomorrow."

After a few months without a job, she started job training classes and was able to get her children into day care with subsidies through the Welfare-to-Work system. Her son's promotion to middle school motivated her to make some changes. Sonya worried that the bigger middle-school boys would pick on Bobby, who was small for his age. She discussed with school administrators the possibility of having him repeat the fifth grade; instead, they passed him on to the sixth grade and recommended putting him in special education classes.

Frustrated by the outcome, she felt her only hope was to move out of the neighborhood as soon as possible. At the time of the interview, a Family Self-Sufficiency (FSS) coordinator from Wheatley Courts was trying to help Sonya get an emergency Section 8 housing placement so that she could move to private apartments on the north side of town that would accept government payments:

> It's called Oak Manor [Apartments] . . . The kids would go to, like, Alamo Heights schools or, like, Northeast Independent School District [with more desirable schools] instead of the San Antonio Independent School District. Because, really, Bobby's been doing that school since kindergarten, and he was doing real well, but then. A lot of it has to do with where we live, because he sees his little friends not doing what they're supposed to be doing, and he figures, "Well, I can get away with it, too." Mom's not going for that!

When I spoke with Sonya at our last interview, in August 2001, she was still waiting to hear if she would receive a Section 8 voucher.

The condition and maintenance of the housing has also been an issue. If the tenant's door or window breaks, she must pay for the repair or replacement. Often tenants end up paying for materials to do their own repairs, as well as fees for the repairs they cannot perform themselves. When they can't afford the repairs, many of the families become vulnerable to the outside elements, as well as to break-ins by vandals and burglars.

Another concern participants had with their current housing conditions was the need for a "quiet place." The din of the housing complexes is sometimes loud and distressing, leaving children fearing for their safety. As the mother of three children, Alicia expressed how, even though the public housing complex was more like home because of the sense of community she felt with her neighbors, moving to a Section 8 duplex on the east side of San Antonio was preferable. "There was too much gangs and stuff like that. Here there's not. So far I haven't seen any gangs or anything like that. It's real quiet."

In Sonya's complex, cars drove around at four or five in the morning with their radios blaring:

> I mean, you could hear it coming all the way down the street, and there's a Cadillac out there in the back, and I woke up because I kept coughing, and then I hear the boom, boom, boom, and at first I thought somebody was knocking on the door. I look

out the window, and they've got the trunk open with those big old boom boxes. They were just hanging out . . . at five o'clock in the morning. These people really got on my nerves. It's bad enough that I didn't want to get up this morning.

Sonya still dreamed of living in a house. She was hoping she would qualify for a Habitat for Humanity home: "They have a thing called Habitat for Humanity that I have looked into, but they said that I would have to donate so many hours. But right now the only thing I've got on my mind is getting a job." Unfortunately, a follow-up of Sonya's situation a year later found her living in the same public housing apartment, having lost her employment as a fast-food worker.

In addition to the services provided through relevant state and state-contracted agencies that accompany cash benefits, SAHA provides social services through its federally funded Family Self-Sufficiency program, along with housing help. In the housing FSS program, as in TANF Welfare-to-Work programs, clients agree to educational and income goals, although in practice San Antonio caseworkers of the former program have placed more emphasis on education. A GED is the minimum educational goal to which clients can aspire within FSS. The income goals, meanwhile, are set at a point where the family would reach ineligibility for cash assistance and housing subsidies.

Family Self-Sufficiency coordinators assist families by obtaining services to help them realize their goals. They help with day-to-day problems such as childcare and transportation. Originally an incentive in the form of an escrow account established for participants at the time of enrollment was built into the program to keep clients motivated to stay on track. If clients reach both their educational and income goals within a five-year period, they gain access to these funds. As clients' incomes increased, so would their monthly rent payment, with amounts above their original rent placed into their escrow accounts (H. Bell 2000). In theory, clients would accumulate a substantial amount, possibly as much as fifteen thousand dollars apiece in escrow, and they would be able to use the money as a down payment on a house. In practice, only one participant I interviewed had accumulated anything (about three hundred dollars) in her account. None of the women was likely to ever use the program to attain the goal of self-sufficiency for which it is designed.

A survey of 1,039 public housing authorities, or PHAs, with at least 250 units conducted by William Rohe and Rachel Kleit found that "larger public housing authorities were more likely to have active FSS programs than smaller authorities. . . . [They also cited] a lack of interest in the program by potential participants, understaffing, and a lack of job opportunities when participants graduate as large problems" (Bogdon 2001, 166–67). These issues were also common in San Antonio.

Two of the mothers I interviewed participated in the FSS program. They lived in the Alazan-Apache Courts, in which FSS participation was mandatory (H. Bell 2000). Melanie and Mandy are sisters. They both attended San Antonio College, and each was working toward a credential for interpreting for the deaf. Mandy, at twenty-four years, had four children ranging in age six years to six months. Melanie was the youngest in the family, at twenty-two, and had a two-year-old daughter. They saw their present situations as temporary. The fact that Mandy had more children than Melanie made her situation seem more tenuous than that of her sister. Having to maintain a GPA of 2.0 or above to keep her financial aid and work-study funding only added to her load. Meanwhile, studying at home was difficult, since she took her four children to different day cares and schools. In the spring of 2000, she lost credit for a math class because her professor had to drop her. She worried about how she would be able to keep up her challenging schedule and finish her degree: "He dropped me. I got strep throat and I had to be out, since it was contagious. I had a doctor's note, too, so I let him know, and then after that it was just problem after problem. It's so hard to balance work with the kids and with school. I'm afraid they'll just cut me off, and I have no idea where I'm gonna go when my contract at Alazan runs out."

Mandy had qualified for Section 8 just before she moved to the Alazan-Apache, but she decided to remain in the development because her family would benefit from the services offered by the FSS program. She perceived the program as a step up from being on TANF. Mandy's perception of welfare recipients was much the same as the public's: women who are lazy, deviant, and dangerous (Hays 2003). She talked about the struggle she had to endure to prevent her banishment from the "nicer area" of the Alazan-Apache Courts:

> That's what has been keeping me going, is going to school, doing like my routine, working, and you know. And I have to, so I [can] keep this place here also. If I don't work or go to school, then I

have to be put in the ugly area [of the Alazan-Apache Courts] where it's just pretty much welfare people, and I'm on welfare too, but I'm doing something. And over there it's just welfare and they're just gettin' their, you know [check]. . . . Then after I finish here, I get the escrow. I have money accumulated here. I have about three hundred dollars accumulated already.

Since participation in FSS is mandatory at the Alazan-Apache housing development, it was not clear how accurate her reading of the situation was. But the women living in the "ugly part" of the Alazan-Apache Courts were doubly stigmatized: as stereotypical "welfare queens" and because they had to live in the unsightly apartments.

Mandy hopes to move from subsidized housing to a house in a better part of town, but her dreams are fading. After she took the summer off to have a baby, Juan, conceived unexpectedly after a botched tubal ligation, Mandy lost her work-study job because her abusive husband, Pete, often interfered with her work. Unable to complete two of her college courses since Juan's birth in midsemester, she was planning to start school again and was looking forward to getting back into a routine: "I need to be in a routine. I've got to get things in order again so I can make up for the time I took off when Juan was born." (For a more comprehensive look at the effects of domestic violence on work in transition from welfare to work, see chap. 7 of this vol.)

Her sister Melanie saw the FSS program as her ticket to a better life. Every time we met, no matter how bad her situation seemed, she talked about how much she hoped her life would change materially once she was able to finish her program and go to work. Melanie struggled with depression, which often made it difficult for her to keep up with a demanding schedule. When I raised the issue of her depression, Melanie talked about how she would benefit from counseling of some kind to deal with problems that stem from her childhood, but said that her mother thought she just needed prayer:

But it's like, yeah, Mom, that's fine for you, but I'm in my shoes, and you live in my shoes and [only then] can you understand what I go through day by day. My insurance will cover it [the therapy], but the thing is, you know, my mom, I still think I'm a little kid when it comes to my mom, because if she doesn't condone it, I just feel really, really guilty . . . even if I am an adult and I am on my own.

In another interview, Melanie confessed that she feared if she were to seek counseling the state would take her daughter away from her. "You never know what the repercussions of getting counseling [are]. I'm afraid that they might take Ella away from me, and I can't risk that."

Melanie's strategies to achieve her goal of self-sufficiency were always changing, but her latest plan, to join the Air Force, was one that helped motivate her.

> Well, I have always wanted to join the military, but I just didn't think that I could hack it, and I was talking to one of the girls in my American Sign Language class, and she's in the Air Force. I'm a single mom. I can't really do that. Just talking to her. . . . She's a single mom also, and I thought, "Maybe I can [do it] if she can." I'd like to be a linguist . . . [and if I] score good on the entrance test, which is something that I definitely want to study for . . . I've heard the higher you score on the test, the better housing you get. And housing to me is really important, and if you're an E-4 [in the Air Force], I believe, and up, you can have a house on base. And that's my main goal.

It was a constant struggle for Melanie to maintain her grades, care for her child, and do her work-study job. She was always looking to ease the pressures of trying to make ends meet.

The experiences of Mandy and Melanie illustrate how programs such as FSS intend to offer some means of extra support to their participants, but many times fall short of meeting the challenge of the unexpected predicaments families encounter. Amy Bogdon's assessment of self-sufficiency programs finds that although it is too soon to know if they will be a success, they do show some promise. Bogdon cautions that programs such as FSS may be used as an alternative to work requirements and time limits imposed by TANF, which could leave "already understaffed [programs] . . . oversubscribed, further limiting their effectiveness" (2001, 171).

Melanie and Mandy's living situation was affected by another policy initiative, the Hope VI program. Alazan-Apache Courts, where the sisters lived, is one of the oldest housing developments in the nation, built in the 1930s, and is being updated largely with federal money as part of a renowned remodeling project. As it renovates each housing development, SAHA empties it by sections and inhabitants must find other homes. In order to change to an even greater extent the living patterns of the former housing development residents, SAHA set up Section 8 arrangements within neighborhoods distant from the central city. San Antonio Housing Authority caseworkers then provided the Section 8 vouchers to the former development dwellers and told them to look elsewhere for apartments with landlords who would take government payments as rent. Soon after, the housing authority demolished the old buildings and built new ones that contained fewer but larger apartments oriented more toward privacy and safety than the originals, which included some small independent houses. As part of the national effort of HOPE VI, the SAHA projects at Alazan-Apache have the mixed results of eliminating some of the dangerous housing while, in the name of providing opportunities, destroying whole communities and their members' support for one another (Swartz and Miller 2002).

Critics of programs like HOPE VI are doubtful that such efforts will reap positive outcomes. Jeff Crump contends that such programs are designed to "move the recipients of public and assisted housing aid into the low-wage, contingent labor market" (Crump 2003, 185). Anthropologist Cheryl Rodriguez's research into the policy and political impacts of HOPE VI found that, in the case of some poor African American families in Tampa, Florida, almost 80 percent of the women and their families relocated to neighborhoods that were more distressed (2003). Although a few of the residents benefited from HOPE VI, the program also in essence destroyed a community by displacing hundreds of relocated families to blighted neighborhoods. Rodriguez viewed the HOPE VI program as poorly planned, haphazardly administered, and, in some cases, viciously implemented (Rodriguez 2003).

Ironically, the participant with the highest hopes fell further than anyone else I observed. Eva had lived for about three years in the aging buildings of Lincoln Heights Courts, another housing development on the west side of San Antonio. Unlike Alazan-Apache, Lincoln Heights is historically African American. A petite, vivacious mother of five children, Eva suffered from depression, which sometimes interfered with her ability to function well. At the time of our interviews, Eva was taking antidepressants and sleeping pills. She also came from a family that had a history of drug and alcohol dependency. Although she did not like the housing complex where she lived, Eva liked the fact that she and her family live in the general neighborhood where she grew up. Emotional and material supports for emergencies were often just around the corner. Nevertheless, when she was having problems paying her rent, she went to SAHA for some assistance:

> Well, you know, I needed a lot of assistance as far as SAHA, because I'm behind in my rent a little bit, so they recommended SAHA to me, and this lady came over and did an evaluation. She gave me tons of referrals for clothes and household items, one for the Bexar County Housing for rental assistance, one also for Project Quest. Project Quest is an organization that is actually training people for five weeks to become a certified nurse's assistant . . . and [a] referral for trying to get the kids into cultural arts centers.

She had yet to take advantage of any of these referrals when we met two months later. Eva's situation illustrates the fact that programs related to housing assistance can also be at the whim of those it seeks to help. In Eva's case, her depression and use of medication seemed to affect her willingness to seek out assistance and work with potentially beneficial programs. When doing our six-month follow-up interviews, we were unable to find Eva. On a recent visit, I saw her walking in the west side of San Antonio. Shortly after I stopped visiting her, Eva became dependent on cocaine and subsequently lost custody of her children.

In this chapter, I have shown how Mexican American single mothers in San Antonio are for the most part simply getting by, and I have described their housing situations on the road to "self-sufficiency." Although the issue of housing is evidently critical to these women, it often sinks far down on their lists of priorities. Unless these women get some kind of subsidy, whether from the government or a private charity, what they consider a desirable place to live and raise a family remains beyond their reach. It is clear that, along with financial safety nets and credits, realistic methods for women to obtain higher salaries and subsidies for continued education and "real" job training must be in place before these women will ever have a chance at self-sufficiency and their dream of home ownership.

Notes

Author's Note: This chapter, in contrast to others in this volume, focuses on the racial and ethnic identities of the women (Henrici, Lein, and Angel, Introduction), therefore, I use the terms *Mexican Americans, Hispanics,* and *Latinos/as* interchangeably to reflect how these women identified themselves (see also, Henrici, chap. 9, this vol.).

the myth of self-sufficiency in health

Ronald J. Angel and Laura Lein

Data from the Three-City project illustrate the impact of health and poverty policies on low-income single mothers in our three cities. These mothers' experiences as they seek out dependable health insurance and health services illuminate the weaknesses in U.S. health care policy and the implications of those weaknesses in the lives of low-income families. In this chapter, we first present an overview of the history and current status of health care policy in the United States. We then present findings from the Three-City Study survey data to illustrate the degree to which families experience unstable medical insurance and care. We show here that many families that include both children and adults do not have health care coverage. In addition to the survey, the Three-City team collected more detailed ethnographic data on a smaller sample of families. Data from two of these cases demonstrate how it is that families in which a parent is working and who are less dependent on public services find themselves at high risk of having to go without health insurance and, as a result, occasionally without needed health care. These data make it clear that the full range of health care needs of poor families cannot be addressed with our current patchwork system of public and private coverage. We argue that only comprehensive national health insurance can provide adequate health care to all citizens in a fair and equitable manner.

The United States is alone among the highly developed nations in its failure to offer universal health care coverage to its citizens (Esping-Andersen 1990; Hicks 1999; Weir, Orloff, and Skocpol 1988). Whereas such coverage is an integral part of citizenship in the nations of Europe, Americans expect families to assume responsibility for their own health insurance. The failure of all attempts since the Truman administration to extend coverage more broadly and the recent resounding defeat of the Clinton health plan attest to the weak support for universal health care even among working-class Americans. Universal health care plans appear too socialistic in a political culture that still resists the intrusion of big government into the market or into the lives of citizens. Of course, the resistance to universal coverage does not applied to all groups. Once a person reaches the age of sixty-five he or she enters a different domain in which Medicare coverage is available to everyone (Angel and Angel 1997; Myles 1989; Weir, Orloff, and Skocpol 1988). For working age adults and their families, employment is the primary source of coverage.

The fact that Medicare is available to all older individuals, albeit at some cost for some services, highlights a fundamental dilemma in American social welfare policy generally, and health care policy more specifically. The elderly comprise a predominantly white and middle-class population. Since the introduction of Social Security and the guarantee of an adequate retirement wage, poverty has shifted from the old to the young (Angel and Angel 1997; Myles 1989). The old are a politically powerful and vocal group able to further their own interests. The working-age poor and children in families below or near the poverty line cannot. Their vulnerability is compounded by the fact that in the United States the poor are disproportionately female, young, and either African American or Latino. Whereas Social Security and Medicare are universal citizenship rights that carry no stigma, cash assistance, food stamps, and Medicaid, the next largest national health insurance program after Medicare, are targeted to the poor and bring with them the stigma associated with what Americans view as the personal failure of poverty.

Work and Health Care Coverage

America's failure to adopt some version of universal health care coverage for groups other than the elderly reflects not only a suspicion of big government, but also a preference for market solutions to social welfare problems (Esping-Andersen 1990; Hicks 1999). In the United States, that has meant a health care system that is private and financed by the purchasers of health care. Since World War II those purchasers have been primarily employers who offer their employees health benefits in response to generous tax incentives (Hacker 2002).

Until quite recently, when rising health care costs began affecting the degree of coverage offered by many employers, this system has been a success for the middle-class families it has covered. It has worked to assure high-quality care and maximal choice in providers and health plans. For the working poor and those who are not employed, it has been a disaster. Jobs in the service sector rarely offer benefits, including health benefits, and private coverage on the open market remains prohibitively expensive. The unemployed, of course, have no access to health insurance unless they qualify for Medicaid or some other special program. Very few poor adults do.

The result of this approach to health care insurance in the United States is an inevitably inequitable system in which members of the middle class are guaranteed access to high-quality health care, whereas the poor must rely on an incomplete system that covers some individuals but not others. It is a system that provides reasonably comprehensive coverage to young children and poor pregnant women but provides only incomplete coverage to older children and no coverage to most poor adults. As our ethnographic data reveal, even though the poor qualify at times for private health coverage through work or for Medicaid because of low income, their health care is sporadic, incomplete, often expensive, and difficult to obtain. Poor families are disproportionately likely to contend with a variety of circumstances that increase their health risks, including unsafe working conditions, elevated stress, environmental toxins, neighborhood violence, and lack of access to primary health care. As a consequence, the children and adults of these families are plagued by health problems that make the goal of self-sufficiency through work extremely difficult (Edin and Lein 1997; Link and Phelan 1995; Mullahy and Wolfe 2001). Skinner, Lachicotte, and Burton (chap. 6, this vol.) illustrate the added burden that lack of access to universal health care creates for families where either caregiver or child has a disability. The need for consistent access to health care for a person with a disability means that some families will not choose to forfeit Medicaid coverage by entering the labor force. The ability of families, with and without identified disabilities, to cope with the elevated health risks of poverty is undermined by this incomplete health care financing system.

Self-sufficiency obviously requires education and job skills, but it also requires health and vitality that make economic and social mobility possible. Our current health care financing system fails because of widening gaps in access to care that end up sapping the productivity of those in greatest need, while leaving them with limited and undependable services. The goal of welfare reform is to encourage employment and self-sufficiency, but often poor families find that when they leave the welfare rolls for jobs in the service sector they are worse off, particularly regarding health insurance, since even with transitional Medicaid they can lose their access to health care coverage.

Health Care Coverage in the Three-City Study

The Three-City Study findings are consistent with data from the most recent Current Population Survey (CPS) that show minority children depend heavily on Medicaid (table 5.1). They also confirm that Mexican American children are at elevated risk of having no form of health insurance. In the Three-City Study, 8 percent of non–Latin American, white, African American, and other Latin American children were uninsured at the time of the survey. Only 5 percent of Puerto Ricans reported no health insurance. In comparison, more than one-quarter of Mexican-origin children were uninsured (26 percent), a figure supported by the findings of the CPS. The Three-City Study, though, provided more detail and insight than the CPS into the role of state policy on Medicaid coverage for children of different ages. The differences among Boston, Chicago, and San Antonio were striking at every income level below 200 percent of poverty, the income level that defines our sample. Among the poorest families, those with incomes below 100 percent of poverty, 82 percent of children were covered in Boston and Chicago, but only 64 percent in San Antonio. It is in this below-poverty-line income range that Massachusetts and Illinois have introduced greatly expanded optional coverage. Among families with incomes slightly above the poverty line, San Antonio lags far behind Boston and Chicago. In families with incomes between 150 percent and 199 percent of poverty, only 5 percent of San Antonio children receive Medicaid compared to 40 percent in Chicago and 23 percent nationally. Texas has chosen not to extend coverage beyond what federal law requires, and the impact of this decision on impoverished families is clear.

The CPS and the Three-City Study survey data clearly demon-

Table 5.1 Selected Type of Health Insurance Coverage for Persons Younger Than Eighteen Years by Race and Hispanic Ethnicity, 2001

Type of coverage	Non-Hispanic White	Non-Hispanic Black	Mexican American	Cuban American	Puerto Rican
Private/Employer (%)	80	53	42	58	47
Medicaid (%)	15	38	35	27	42
None (%)	7	14	26	18	11
Total number (in thousands)	44,378	11,227	9,314	270	987

Source: U.S. Census Bureau, *Annual Demographic Supplement* 2002, and unpublished tabulations for Hispanic subgroups.
Note: Respondents were asked to indicate all forms of coverage that applied and could indicate more than one source. Figures include only the most common forms of coverage. Because some respondents reported both Private/Employer and Medicaid coverage, columns can sum to more than 100 percent.

strate the dependence of poor families on Medicaid. Yet many poor children who appear to be eligible based on income do not participate in the program. Survey data gives us no real clue as to why, nor does it reveal the degree of insecurity in coverage and its lack of continuity, one of the standard indicators of the quality of one's medical care. Through our interviews we found that, although some children in a family might have private or Medicaid coverage at some point, coverage is often lost when a parent becomes unemployed or when Medicaid eligibility lapses. For most poor families, periods of coverage are followed by periods with no coverage. In addition, family coverage is often incomplete; although at any one time, some children are covered, at the same time, others were not. This incomplete coverage presents parents with serious challenges in insuring their children's health, and this challenge contributes to instability in employment and family routines.

Examples from the Three-City Ethnography

Mothers and children may be ineligible for a number of reasons and for different reasons over time. Marriage or cohabitation with a partner reduces the possibility for public health insurance. Although the partner's income may move the family above eligibility for public services, the partner's job likely offers health insurance only at high cost and or in limited ways, if at all. Similarly, as a single mother strives for more continuous employment, she herself becomes less likely to be eligible for insurance coverage. As her earnings move upward toward the poverty line—and even above it—the family may remain impoverished and she is unlikely to have dependable insurance coverage for herself and her children.

Marriage and cohabitation, then, minimize the likelihood of full health care coverage for a family, as does employment in a low-wage job. Because access to health insurance is situational and tied to the specifics of household structure and employment, it can be easily lost. Even families who have reasonably complete health insurance coverage face the reality that the insecurity in their lives includes the continuing possibility that changing circumstances will leave them without complete coverage.

Two examples below illustrate this continuing fluidity in family lives. Winette, the mother in the first example presented below, keeps trying to hold a job, often struggling through periods without health insurance. As we last see her, Winette is working on applying for public assistance, and no one in the household has health insurance. Meanwhile, Lydia struggles to support her household, sometimes with and sometimes without health insurance. As we leave her, she has acquired health insurance for her family through her manufacturing job. As important as this health insurance is for Lydia and her family, she recognizes that it is only as stable as her employment.

Winette is a mother who, in a six-year relationship when we first saw her, had no health insurance. Then, after fleeing her partner, due to abuse, she continued to have considerable periods of ineligibility for medical insurance as she moved from one job to another in an effort to keep her earnings relatively stable. None of her jobs offered health insurance, but her earnings kept her above the level of eligibility some months. Furthermore, her movement from one job to another made it more difficult to document her earnings and her eligibility.

Winette feels good about her employment record, scattered though it is. In fact, as she proudly explains, once she left her abusive husband, she "always got another job before the next pay check" in her effort to maintain steady employment. She never missed more than one month's pay in a transition. However, only her youngest children have had health insurance during the period since she left her partner.

Winette dropped out of high school when she had the first of her four children to move in with her child's father, with whom she lived for the next six years and considered her husband. He then fathered two more of her children. During the first four years of her marriage, she stayed at home taking care of her children and depending on her partner's support. During this period the family had no health insurance because her partner's job did not offer this option. She received prenatal care during her first pregnancy at a local clinic that offered a special program for pregnant teenagers. She and her partner paid for her care during her succeeding pregnancies, which lead to the medical debts typical of many of the families we studied.

After four years of staying at home with her children, Winette began working at a series of fast food jobs, and then returned to her schooling, first achieving a nursing assistant certificate through a state agency, and then joining an Americorps program through which she gained her GED. She began what would become a succession of jobs, working first for a local nursing home, and then at a child care center. Neither her partner's nor her own job provided health insurance, and their combined earnings continued to keep them and their children ineligible for Medicaid (the state Children's Health Insurance Program [CHIP] was not yet available in Texas).

During this same period, her partner became increasingly abusive. Finally, she left, moving briefly out of town, where she took a job in a cookie factory. Without the resources from her partner, without eligibility for public services in this new community where she had no residential history, and isolated from her family, she found that she could not manage the physical work in the un-air-conditioned bakery. After a fainting spell while on the job, she returned to San Antonio, where she found an apartment and resumed her work in the child care center. Although the center offered partial health benefits, she could not afford her required employee contribution, so she and her children went without health coverage. However, the child care center offered her reduced rates for her own children, an important benefit that allowed her to work regular hours. Furthermore, during this period, her wages, since they were not now combined with her partner's, were low enough that her youngest children were eligible for Medicaid.

However, she soon moved to a new job, drawing on her health care certification, and began employment at a nearby nursing home. While working at the nursing home, she could choose between two different tracks, one offering lower wages and access to some benefits, the other offering higher wages and no benefits. Needing the higher hourly wages to support her household, she chose to work in a no-benefits labor "pool," as she describes it. However, her higher wages made her income-ineligible for the subsidized child care she had enjoyed for a period, and she no longer had the reduced-cost child care that went with her child care center employment. Unable to pay for child care, she changed her hours to a forty-hour weekend, working one eight-hour shift and two sixteen-hour shifts, during which time her aunt could watch her children.

Her higher wages also cut her and her children off from Medicaid eligibility. At this time, her youngest child was diagnosed with asthma, and she herself began to have a series of problems with her teeth. Since none of them had health coverage, neither she nor her child received regular treatment. She was trying hard to register her children in the new state Children's Health Insurance Program (CHIP), which targets children of the working poor, but had not succeeded in mastering the eligibility forms. Furthermore, she had no information on any source of help for herself.

Family health insurance is not only a matter of eligibility, although eligibility is certainly a key issue. Mothers must also recognize the eligibility criteria for the various kinds of health care available to them. They must have the time and energy to pursue the insurance for which each household member is eligible. They must sustain periods when their inability to provide appropriate documentation or to meet with an eligibility worker leaves them or their children without health insurance. Winette, above, is still struggling both to identify and to apply for the health insurance for which she and her children may be eligible. Meanwhile, ongoing medical conditions are treated only sporadically.

Even when a mother is able to secure health insurance for her whole family, such coverage often follows a period of more limited coverage, and it is based on relatively fragile employment or only those services she has been able to identify, as is the case with Lydia. Lydia is a Mexican American immigrant to the United States who arrived as a child and had her own first child at the age of fourteen with the man she eventually married. She was married two years later and had a second child. She started working almost as soon as she became a mother, but at odd jobs, such as selling snow cones from a cart and helping her husband with his construction work. These jobs were interspersed with periods of unemployment, due primarily to her difficulties in finding and keeping child care. As a mother who was never on TANF and often employed only part time, she did not have ready access to child care subsidies, and as an immigrant without a large family of her own, she did not have an extended helping network to depend on, either. Neither she nor her husband had access to health insurance, but Lydia was covered by Medicaid for her first pregnancy, and her children have been covered by Medicaid for a good part of their lives.

Although her children maintained their medical coverage with Medicaid until relatively recently, Lydia herself lost her coverage shortly after her first pregnancy. During the next years, and through her second pregnancy, neither she nor her husband had health insurance. They obtained health care through CareLink, a San Antonio program that allows families to pay off medical debts at a rate determined by their financial situation. Lydia was assessed for a rate of payment at twenty dollars each month, which she thinks of as the cost of her health care.

However, Lydia's situation has changed in the last several years, as her children became old enough for school-based programs, and she could take on full-time work. She took a job as a temporary line worker in a manufacturing plant, and has stayed there for the last several years, advancing first to a permanent job and then to a supervisory position. Now, with wages well over minimum wage (although under ten dollars per hour), and with health insurance coverage for her family, she has rejoined her husband, from whom she was estranged for several years. With their joint resources, they have moved to a better neighborhood. Her only concern right now is the stability of the company for which she works. Manufacturing jobs have become rarer in San Antonio as plants have closed down or moved elsewhere. Although Lydia feels fortunate to have her job, she is not sure how long she will keep it. Even with her current health insurance, she is still paying the medical costs accumulated through the CareLink program when she had no medical coverage.

Mothers like these often deal with complex situations in which they have been able to acquire health insurance for some members of the household, but not for others, or for a period of time, but not continuously. In some cases, medical conditions go untreated. In other cases, families assume debts in order to purchase needed care, as in Lydia's case.

The ethnographic accounts add three important dimensions to the issues raised by large-scale data sets and the Three-City survey itself. First, they show that health insurance for low-income families is seldom stable. Families' eligibility and access to services changes over time. In only a handful of our families was health insurance for all members of the household continuous over periods of more than a few years. Although some household members, particularly children, might be eligible for Medicaid for much of their childhood, they eventually age out of their coverage, at ages depending on household income. Parents who were employed might need to pay increasing proportions of their income for employer-provided health care. The instability of jobs in the service sector also contributes to fluctuations in the access to employer-provided health care. As the story of Winette illustrates, women in relationships marked by episodes of domestic violence are even more prone to residential and employment disruptions (see Bell, Lohman, and Votruba-Drzal, chap. 7, this vol.), which helps limit their access to health care.

Second, mothers without health insurance may become seriously ill as medical conditions go untreated. Mexican Americans in San Antonio are at seriously elevated risk of diabetes and its consequences (Stern et al. 1984, 1992). Diabetes will create ever more serous problems for those women who do not receive regular treatment and medical oversight. Their ability to sustain a healthy pregnancy, to continue employment, and to be active parents depends on careful monitoring of the disease. Diabetes is not, of course, the only health problem facing low-income mothers. They suffer from all of the leading causes of death associated with poverty (Mullahy and Wolfe 2001). Such conditions, untreated, affect a mother's household. Overall, when mothers lose their ready access to health care, they are at increased risk, and their risk becomes a household risk. One mother from the ethnographic study described a series of difficulties she faced in managing her diabetes as she gained and then lost medical coverage. Even when she regained medical coverage, it often entailed a change in physician, and her treatment was interrupted. Skinner, Lachicotte, and Burton (chap. 6, this vol.) discuss the cascading effects of mothers' untreated medical conditions when they try to manage the care of a child (or children) with an identified disability.

Third, irregularities in health insurance cause multiple problems that magnify each other. Again, as Skinner, Lachicotte, and Burton detail in chapter 6, mothers often lose time at work when they are the primary caregivers for children with chronic illnesses or special needs —both conditions potentially exacerbated by a lack of health care. Lost time often translates into job loss, as the jobs held by low-income mothers rarely offer sick days or personal days for family crises. Health levels are compromised when job loss leads to food insecurity, eviction, and virtual homelessness for some of these families.

Employment Does Not Mean Self-Sufficiency in Health Care Coverage

The core goal of welfare reform is, of course, to foster self-sufficiency through employment. In reality, the only achievement is that almost half the families that receive cash assistance have been dropped from the rolls. Very few have become self-sufficient and even fewer have become self-sufficient in terms of health care coverage. Without Medicaid, working families must depend upon a seriously inadequate health care safety net. Our data show that employer-based coverage for children increases when a family leaves welfare, but employment hardly leads to health care self-sufficiency for the vast majority of low-income families (Angel et al. 2001). Within six months of leaving welfare, only 9 percent of children are covered by a parent's health plan; after a year, only 27 percent are covered by an employer-sponsored plan. Since Medicaid coverage drops at the same time, from 91 percent for those off less than six months to 69 percent for those off one year or more, coverage remains incomplete.

These findings and the dramatic drop in the welfare rolls occurred during a decade-long economic expansion, and even then many poor families and children had no health insurance coverage. Since our study ended, the economy has worsened significantly and the employment prospects of poor families have deteriorated. The working poor can possibly find work, but very few are able to find employment that provides health care, especially for the entire family. Consequently, when low-income families do manage to arrange for health insurance coverage, it is unlikely to be stable or long lasting. It remains in place only as long as a job lasts, or as long as the family meets the frequently changing eligibility requirements of a public program. The low-wage service sector depends on cheap labor, and health care benefits are anything but cheap.

The Medicaid Marriage Penalty

A clear secondary objective of welfare reform, and the stated desire of George W. Bush's administration, is to encourage marriage. Yet when it comes to Medicaid coverage, our data once again corroborate previous research that shows a clear marriage penalty. Given current policy, children in two-parent households are at higher risk of being uninsured than children in single-parent households (Rolett et al. 2001). Rather than rewarding marriage among the working poor, the rules for Medicaid eligibility penalize marriage. Indeed, our data indicate that if a male is present in the household the probability that the children will be covered by Medicaid decreases. As our ethnographic cases show, the ability of low-income families to maintain health insurance, particularly in two-parent households, depends on the possibility of finding the kind of job that carries health insurance. Once acquired, the insurance is only as stable as the job itself. Families are caught between two unstable ways of acquiring health insurance: either they are eligible for means-tested poverty programs, the criteria for which have been changing, or they acquire health insurance through their employment, which is only as stable as the job itself and may demand a high shared cost on the part of the employee.

Thus, most low-income families experience periods when at least some members of their households are uninsured. These periods are costly in many ways. Families go into debt; families deal with untreated medical conditions; families spend their scarce resources of time and energy trying to find and keep medical insurance.

The Future of Health Care Coverage for the Poor

The Three-City Study demonstrates the pervasiveness of health problems among the poor and makes it clear that because of the complexities of access to health care, as well as its soaring cost, self-sufficiency in health coverage is truly a myth. Even as Americans do their best to maximize market solutions to the problem of health care financing, the reality that health care is beyond the reach of all but the most affluent citizens and the fact that many employers do not offer coverage require states to play a central role. In 1998, less than one-fifth of all health care expenditures were paid directly by consumers; private employer-based policies covered another third. Almost half of all expenditures were covered by direct public expenditures, including payments by Medicare and Medicaid (Levit et al. 2000). Even middle-class Americans face the threat of bankruptcy as the result of unanticipated medical expenses (Sullivan, Warren, and Westbrook 2000). The Three-City Study data show that for single mothers and working-class couples even routine medical expenditures are more than they can afford.

There is no doubt that the state's efforts to provide health care can be effective and that they can reach families who would otherwise simply do without the care they need. The Three-City Study clearly illustrates how important Medicaid is to poor families. The parents in our study went to great lengths to obtain it for their children and they clearly appreciate its value. In the absence of Medicaid these families would have virtually nowhere else to turn except to charitable organizations whose capacity to respond is clearly limited. Since the study began, new state initiatives to extend Medicaid and the introduction of CHIP have reduced the number of children without health insurance (Kenney, Haley, and Tebay 2003). A particularly welcome aspect of this improvement is that it has been concentrated among children in families below 200 percent of poverty and among Latin American and black children, the segments of our population in greatest need.

Such improvements are encouraging, but despite these recent gains millions of eligible children remain uninsured (Hill and Lutzky 2003). If the most that we can produce as a society by way of extending health coverage for children and adults is incremental improvement in existing programs then millions will, in all likelihood, remain uncovered or incompletely and sporadically covered. The real danger we face is that as a result of the recent economic downturn these incomplete programs will be cut back rather than expanded. As we found in the Three-City Study, even while coverage for poor children is improving, coverage for poor adults, except during pregnancy or for serious and debilitating illness, is virtually nonexistent (Long 2003). If anything, the situation of adults has worsened as the parents of low-income children lose whatever public coverage they had as the result of welfare reform and as employers cut back on coverage as the result of the economic downturn (Kaiser Commission on Medicaid and the Uninsured 2003). Again, tinkering with existing programs will not address the health care needs of adults.

The decade-long economic boom of the 1990s did not benefit all Americans equally. Even in good times, minority Americans, single mothers, and even many nonminority families find it difficult to get by. When the economy sours, their precarious situation becomes worse. The poor are subject to a double jeopardy: they are at elevated risk of poor health because of the poverty and occupational disadvantages they face, and they have uncertain access to complete and adequate health care. In this way, lack of access to health care joins the list of other challenges to family self-sufficiency that we explore throughout this book. These challenges include disability, insufficient housing, inadequate child care, domestic violence, and lack of education or skill preparation for the workforce. The data from the Three-City Study, which includes delineation of the impact of health and health insurance problems on the lives of poor families, indicate the critical importance of resolving our nation's health insurance dilemma. We are in desperate need of a system that provides low-income, as well as middle-class, families with secure and continuous health insurance and access to health care.

the difference disability makes

Managing Childhood Disability, Poverty, and Work

Debra Skinner, William Lachicotte, and Linda Burton

This chapter draws on ethnographic research with forty-two families in San Antonio, Chicago, and Boston who had at least one child with a disability to describe the dilemmas that caregivers face when dealing with poverty and disability within the context of current reforms in public assistance programs and policies. These families' experiences highlight how programs and policies configure their lives and point to ways that both poverty programs and disability agencies could change to support these families' moves toward economic security.

The links between poverty and disability are well established. Disability can be caused or made worse by environmental and social conditions associated with poverty, and disability can create economic problems that place families in impoverished situations (Garbarino and Ganzel 2000; Lukemeyer, Myers, and Smeeding 2000; Seelman and Sweeney 1995). The prevalence of both child and adult disability is higher among families in poverty. For example, in 1996 the rate of disability for children age three to twenty-one living at or above the poverty line was almost 6 percent, compared to 11 percent for children below the poverty line (Fujiura and Yamaki 2000). Other studies conducted before the 1996 welfare reforms indicated that 11 to 17 percent of families receiving welfare benefits had at least one child with an activity-limiting disability (Loprest and Acs 1996). The 1999 nationwide Survey of Income and Program Participation (SIPP) showed that 44 percent of TANF beneficiaries reported having physical or mental impairments, three times the rate of the non-TANF population (U.S. General Accounting Office 2001). Among adult beneficiaries, major depression, a significant barrier to work, alone may affect 25 percent or more of adult women caregivers

(Danziger et al. 2000; Lennon, Blome, and English 2002), and other forms of disabling conditions may reach even higher prevalence (Johnson and Meckstroth 1998).

Despite these statistics, critiques of welfare reform—both from advocates of policies that set time limits on benefits and link them to work participation and from those who critique welfare regulations as forms of punishment and surveillance—have for the most part omitted from their discussions cases of poor families caring for members with disabilities or chronic illnesses. Similarly, most research studies of welfare recipients and welfare reforms have not specifically examined disability or illness for the unique differences those conditions may make to low-income families' ability to maintain work and permanently leave the welfare rolls.[1] With few exceptions (Earle and Heymann 2002; Meyers, Glaser, and MacDonald 1998; Meyers, Brady, and Seto 2000; Smith et al. 2002), disability and illness are typically viewed as only one barrier to work among others that create a category of "stayers" or "the hard-to-serve." As a result of these omissions, there is little awareness among researchers, policy makers, and frontline workers of how intersections of disability, poverty, and the policies and programs that relate to each affect families who must on a day-to-day basis manage disability in contexts of limited resources.

There has been concern among some policy analysts and disability advocates that welfare reform may more severely impact families that have a disabled member (Ohlson 1998; Rosman and Knitzer 2001).[2] There are a number of ways that public assistance programs and disability can converge to affect these families. First, welfare reform uncoupled, or "de-linked," eligibility for TANF from that for Medicaid. Formerly, AFDC beneficiaries were automatically eligible for Medicaid, but now individuals must qualify for both programs separately. Families who are not eligible for enrollment in TANF, or who leave TANF, are often not aware that they may still qualify for Medicaid. Indeed, a number of studies have shown a decline in the number of families receiving Medicaid or any form of health coverage once off TANF rolls. Guyer (2000) reports that half the women who leave the welfare rolls lose Medicaid coverage shortly thereafter, and the Three-City Study found that the longer a family had been off TANF, the less likely it was to be covered by health insurance of any kind (Angel et al. 2001; Angel and Lein, chap. 5, this vol.). (See

Greenberg 1998 and Mann et al. 2002 for statistics on health care coverage after welfare reform.)

More specific to families of children with disabilities are the reforms that link Medicaid, TANF, and the Supplemental Security Income (SSI) Cash Assistance Program. To qualify for SSI, children under eighteen must have a physical or mental condition or conditions that can be medically proven and that result in marked and severe functional limitations. The Social Security Administration has issued a medical "listing of impairments" that serves as the basis for determinations. The 1996 welfare law narrowed this list. Maladaptive behavior was eliminated as a qualifying condition, as was the individual functional assessment, which had qualified children in the past. As a result of this more restrictive eligibility standard, about 60 percent of the 245,737 cases on which a redetermination was completed were deemed ineligible under the new criteria (Committee on Children with Disabilities 2001). Families whose children do not qualify or are terminated can appeal if they have the knowledge, persistence, and resources to do so, but in the meantime they are without benefits (Rosman and Knitzer 2001). One major concern of advocates for children with disabilities is that families that are already financially strapped will fall further into poverty with the loss of SSI benefits and will be less able to provide appropriate care for their children with disabilities. Even though the Balanced Budget Act of 1997 required states to reinstate Medicaid coverage to children who received SSI benefits before 1996, there is great concern that many children will lose Medicaid if they lose SSI (Ohlson 1998; Rosman and Knitzer 2001).

Other major issues for TANF beneficiaries who have children with disabilities are the work requirements and time limits, and exemptions to these, as set out in states' TANF programs. States vary in whether they allow exemptions from time limits or work requirements if the caregiver has disabilities or is caring for a disabled household member. In the majority of states (twenty-eight), caregivers of a child or adult with a disability are not exempt from the time limit and, presumably, will need to enter the workforce once their TANF benefits end (Center on Budget and Policy Priorities 2000). As for the states in the Three-City Study, Texas exempts these individuals from work requirements but not from the sixty-month lifetime limit for TANF; Massachusetts allows exemptions from the time limit for disability, illness, or caring for disabled family members; and Illinois has no exemptions from the time limit, and only caregivers of a child under one year of age or individuals sixty or older are exempt from work requirements. Disability status per se is not regarded as grounds for exemption from work participation but may be considered as a medical barrier to work and warrant a temporary exemption (Center on Budget and Policy Priorities 2000). Nationally, a GAO survey found that 27 percent of county TANF offices exempted clients from work participation but not from the lifetime time limit on receipt of benefits (U.S. General Accounting Office 2001). These exemptions from work requirements but not time limits are problematic in that individuals may not gain the experience or training that would help them obtain and maintain work once their benefits end (Lennon, Blome, and English 2002).

Policy analysts have speculated regarding how recent reforms in public assistance programs might impact families, especially those dealing with childhood disability (Ohlson 1998; Rosman and Knitzer 2001), but as yet there is only limited empirical research that documents the impact of reforms on families with members who have disabilities, and even fewer accounts of the realities and complexities of these families' lives from an ethnographic perspective. Our findings from the Three-City Study ethnography present some of these complexities.

The Families

In the ethnographic component of the Three-City Study, forty-two families were recruited in the three cities specifically because they had a child under eight years of age with a moderate or severe disability. Twelve of the families were African American, fourteen European American, and sixteen Latin American. Most of the forty-two primary caregivers (81 percent) were the children's biological mothers. About one-fourth of the caregivers were married, and the remainder were never married, divorced, separated, or widowed. Only one-fourth of the caregivers were working at the time of recruitment, mostly at part-time and low-paying jobs with no benefits. All forty-two families had household incomes below 200 percent of the federal poverty line (in 2001, the federal poverty level for a family of three was $14,630 per year, or $1,219 per month). At the time of recruitment, twenty-two households received TANF, and five were former beneficiaries. Of the forty-two children, twenty-six received SSI at the time of recruitment, and three others were approved for SSI benefits during the course of the study. In addition, more than one-quarter (twelve) of the caretakers reported having a disability, defined for adults as a condition (disease, disorder, or injury) that limits their ability to perform major life activities, including work and child care. Over the course of the project, a majority of the other caregivers reported mental health problems (for example, depression and anxiety), chronic health problems (for instance, arthritis, diabetes, and cancer), or learning disabilities (for example, dyslexia) that, although not always disabling, caused them some difficulty in carrying out daily activities. Five caregivers received SSI for their own disability at the time of recruitment, and one other qualified for benefits during the study. Ten of the households had other children or adults with a disability. Thus, almost half of the households had two or more persons with disabilities and three-quarters received SSI payments for at least one member. Forty-four percent of all the households received both SSI and TANF support.

Defining Disability

In defining disability for this study, we were confronted with a number of possibilities. At the federal level alone there are more than forty different definitions (Westbrook, Silver, and Stein 1998). For this study, we recruited families with children whose disability might make a difference in their caregivers' ability to work or otherwise comply with TANF requirements. Criteria for inclusion were that families have a child eight years old or younger with a moderate to severe disability (for instance, moderate to severe delays in cognitive, communicative, behavioral, motor, and/or adaptive skills). We purposively included a broad range of disabilities to represent children who have different needs and thus present different issues for families (for example, autism: high-impact behavioral issues; Down syndrome: significant cognitive delays and possible health problems; spina bifida: high-impact medical problems; and cerebral palsy: physical and perhaps cognitive delays).

The children's diagnoses included cerebral palsy, Down syndrome, seizure disorder, severe ADHD, significant developmental delays, visual and hearing impairments, spina bifida, Pervasive Developmental Disorder, autism, chondrodysplasia punctata, various syndromes (for example, Kartagener syndrome, Angelman syndrome, and Cri-du-chat syndrome), severe asthma, and other involved medical conditions (for instance, congenital heart problems, brain damage, and lung disease) that resulted in developmental delay and disability. More than half the children had multiple disabilities.

Although the families had different histories and stories to tell, they had many experiences in common because of having a young child with a disability. First and foremost, families found that caring for a young child with a disability was a full-time job. The health care needs of these children were extensive. The children's medical histories often included hospitalizations, operations, medications, and the use of specialized equipment for feeding, mobility, or communication. Some of the children had significant mental health disorders that called for behavioral interventions and medications. Other children had physical disabilities and developmental delays that required medical, educational, and therapeutic interventions. Since the needs of the child with a disability are often profoundly evident, most families had a heightened sensitivity to having to work harder to facilitate their child's health and development. There was an immediacy and often an emotional and moral urgency to caring for the child, sometimes on an hour-to-hour basis, standing by as needed for emergencies and procuring necessary services and resources.

Caring for a child with disabilities necessitated building routines around child care; piecing together and navigating a network of medical, therapeutic, educational, and social services; and being "on call" to deal with the child's medical or behavioral problems. The majority of caregivers spent a great deal of time and effort locating and scheduling specialists and intervention services for their children. It was not unusual for a child to have a host of therapists, doctors, and teachers, and for caregivers to have numerous appointments every week with these and other specialists. For example, Delores, a thirty-year-old European American mother, was the main caregiver of three children when she joined the study.[3] Her two-year-old son, John, had gastrointestinal problems, seizures, and allergies, and her three-year-old daughter required leg braces for an undetermined problem. Like many of the caregivers, Delores had health problems as well, including seizure disorder, partial paralysis, and recently diagnosed cervical cancer. When we recorded her activities for the month of November 2000, we found that Delores met with her children's therapeutic specialists, educators, doctors, and dentists twenty times. Ten of these meetings were at home, where early interventionists came to provide counseling and physical therapy for John. The other ten appointments were at one of seven locations in the city—two Head Start programs, two hospitals, one early intervention center, one health clinic, and one dentist's office. Managing her children's services as well as her own disability made it difficult for Delores to maintain a job.

For the families of children with moderate to severe disabilities or chronic illnesses, concerns about health care access and quality were paramount. Finding and utilizing health care services took time. Time was also needed to access social services. Services generally did not come to these families; they had to seek them out and piece them together. Services were not granted immediately; families had to demonstrate that they were eligible, and they often had to go through the process over and over again. Each visit to human services, whether medical or social, included hours of waiting time. For some of the families, weekly routines often included a succession of offices and waiting rooms, as well as efforts to locate the transportation needed to arrive at offices. Families had to marshal and allot their time, energy, and emotions carefully.

Caregivers had to manage not only the specialized health care needs of their disabled children but also the numerous tasks related to daily home and school routines common to all families. Many of them did so in spite of their own disabilities and poor health. A significant proportion of the caregivers among the forty-two families had a variety of physical and mental ailments, including cerebral palsy, Sjögren's syndrome, neuromuscular impairment, sickle-cell anemia, epilepsy, diabetes, arthritis, cancer, depression, anxiety, bipolar disorder, and post-traumatic stress disorder. One-fourth of the caregivers had conditions that were disabling enough to curtail their daily activities and ability to work outside the home. Only a few mothers felt that their health was good.[4]

It was not only physical conditions that affected families. For a majority of families, mental health issues were also a concern. Most caregivers were highly effective at meeting their families' needs and demonstrating strength and resourcefulness in the face of multiple challenges, but these efforts took their toll. Caregivers talked of being constantly worried and feeling overwhelmed and stressed. A majority mentioned having bouts of depression.

Leticia, a Mexican American mother whose seven-year-old son, Roberto, had been diagnosed with Pervasive Developmental Disorder, provides an example of this intensive labor and its emotional cost. Roberto was in a special program at school, where he received some services. Leticia told the interviewer, "Roberto is a very, very difficult child." She sought out special training on how to care for him in the home, and she attended a mothers' support group that provided information and emotional support on issues that involve her children. Leticia told the interviewer, "So many people work together for me," and she named the therapists, counselors, teachers, physicians, pediatrician, psychiatrist, nutritionist, and social worker who worked with Roberto. She also talked about SSI, food stamps, and Medicaid as providing crucial resources. Managing all the appointments and paperwork put stress on her and other family members. Leticia said that she sometimes felt depressed and wanted to run away, but she continued her efforts to help Roberto.

Marjorie, an African American mother of four children, three of whom had special needs, also talked about the strain she was under from caring for her children with few resources or social supports in place and from dealing with her own post-traumatic stress disorder and cervical cancer:

> I just been kind of down, you know, because I guess reality has hit me that until my kids are older I can't do—there's nothing I can do, you know? And I got so much stuff in my head that I want to do. I can't do it. I don't have child care, you know? No family up here. Nobody that I know. So what can I do? You know, even trying to get a part-time job, I can't even do that. And that's kind of hard. . . . . It's been kind of depressing.

Marjorie's case points to another theme that was common among the families: Caregivers neglect their own health for the sake of their children. For many months, Marjorie neglected seeking treatment not only for her enduring psychiatric disorder but also for cervical cancer. She said that treatments left her too exhausted to watch her children. At one point, her doctor wanted to hospitalize her for pneumonia, but she had no one to care for her children and could not obtain emergency child care funds, so she recovered at home. In spite of multiple health problems, Marjorie spent a great deal of effort managing her children's services and took justifiable pride in her parenting, but some days she just did not have the energy to deal with everyday routines.

Caregivers' priorities were simple: Children's needs came first. And caregivers were better able to meet their children's needs than their own, due to the insurance coverage and special services for children with disabilities. All the focal children had health coverage, with Medicaid their predominant insurer (thirty-seven out of forty-two focal children were covered solely by Medicaid; four had Medicaid and private insurance; and one child was covered entirely by private insurance). As a result of this coverage, abetted by early intervention and special education services, these children were, for the most part, getting the medical, therapeutic, and educational services they needed. Although some families on Medicaid experienced scheduling difficulties and long waits, or sometimes felt discriminated against as "Public Aid" patients, overall, most mothers gave positive evaluations of the care their children received from a variety of specialists whose services were reimbursed by Medicaid (Skinner et al. 2002).

The caregivers themselves, even if insured, seldom took the time to attend to their own health care needs, nor could they afford the copayments for doctor's visits. The eleven mothers not covered by any form of health insurance rarely visited a doctor. Both groups of caregivers tried to pay any out-of-pocket costs for their children, but they often would not buy medicine for themselves. Some mothers would not take prescription drugs, either because they could not afford them or because the side effects made them too sleepy to care for their children. Others refused operations or other medical treatments because they felt they could not take time away from their child care duties.

Although it is not surprising that mothers of any income level make sacrifices for their children, this strategy is more detrimental to those with limited resources, who must make tough choices allocating those scarce resources. Postponing health care turned out to be counterproductive when the caregivers' health deteriorated to a point that it affected everyday activities, including caring for their children.

Intersections of Welfare Reform, Disability, Work, and Caregiving

As Bruinsma and Bell argue in chapters 2 and 8 of this volume, welfare reforms have created a shift in focus from mother to worker. One concern raised by professionals who work with young children with disabilities is that if the caregivers of these children enter the workforce, they will have less time to devote to caring for the children and locating and managing the therapeutic, medical, and educational services the children need. Thus, the children may receive fewer services, and their development may be less than optimal (Ohlson 1998). Caregivers in this study often acted as case managers for children of theirs with disabilities. They saw accessing services and caring for their children, including those with disabilities, as their primary responsibilities. Caregivers worried about who would tend to their children's medical needs and manage the services should they return to work.

At the end of the study, few TANF beneficiaries had been able to get or keep full-time jobs. Even if the child with a disability was in child care or a school setting, caregivers felt as though they were still "on call" for medical and behavioral emergencies. Balancing work and child care is difficult for any family, but it is especially difficult for low-income caregivers of young children with disabilities. Several mothers lost their jobs over the course of the study because of having to miss work to handle their children's needs; their employers were unwilling to grant them time off from the job. For some families with children with disabilities and chronic health conditions, expectations set out in welfare policy or held by caseworkers are unrealistic and potentially detrimental to children with special needs (see Bell, chap. 8, for caseworkers' pressure on mothers to return to work). Emily's situation highlights the dilemmas faced by caregivers of young children with severe disabilities who cannot get exemptions from TANF time limits or requirements for work participation.

Emily, a European American mother, lives in Illinois, a "universal participation" state that officially grants no exemptions from the five-year time limit for receiving TANF benefits. Over the course of the study, Emily cared for her young daughter, Suzy, who had severe visual impairment and developmental delay. Emily received a total of $711 per month from SSI and TANF and an additional $150 in food stamps. Most of the money went for rent. Emily was in constant financial distress, losing utilities and phone service on occasion and borrowing heavily from her sister and mother to buy food at the end of every month. During one observation, Emily's TANF caseworker (a self-sufficiency caseworker who works with the "hard to serve" cases) told Emily that her TANF clock was ticking and that she would need to find work. Emily explained to her caseworker that she had to be at home for the numerous therapists who came to the house daily to work with Suzy. She also had to take Suzy to three other sites for educational and therapeutic services. The caseworker told Emily that she should rearrange the therapies so they were all in the morning, find child care for Suzy in the afternoon, and go to work. Emily explained that one therapist could only come in the afternoon and that she could not find child care that she trusted. The caseworker asserted that Emily would not be exempted from the time limit and urged her to be creative in finding child care. Emily reported being under great stress from these dilemmas. She decided to go back to school to learn to be a chef and planned to work when Suzy was old enough to be enrolled in a school-based child care program, but she was worried about being able to keep a job because of Suzy's health care needs. She wanted to leave TANF, but she stayed on for the medical insurance. She, like so many of the mothers, was worried about losing Medicaid for Suzy if she went back to work, and she was certain no private insurance company would cover Suzy because of her preexisting medical conditions.

As this case exemplifies, full-time or even part-time employment presents dilemmas for many caregivers of children with disabilities, especially those with children who need full-time care (see also Bruinsma, chap. 2, regarding challenges to finding reliable child care). Caregivers in this study who were not working wanted to go back to work at some point because they felt they would be better off financially and personally. No caregiver expressed a desire to remain on welfare, and most said they would rather be employed if they could find trusted child care. However, in all three cities, there were few slots in child care centers for children with moderate or severe disabilities. Even if some type of child care was available, caregivers trusted few people to provide the specialized care their children needed. Some caregivers feared that their children would be abused or mistreated by child care providers and would be unable to communicate this to them. Caregivers who managed to work usually had trusted family members available to provide specialized care for their children or were able to enroll them in school-based programs compatible with their work hours.

Child care was more of a problem for families of younger children with disabilities, since children three years old and older are served by the public school system.[5] However, school as a child care provider is not always the answer: Children get sick; mothers are called to school for children's medical crises and behavioral problems; work hours and school hours often do not coincide, so children still need before- or after-school care; and schools close down for a number of days during the year when caregivers must work. What caregivers needed was dependable, safe, and appropriate child care for children with special needs and a flexible and understanding workplace that would allow them to take off work when necessary.

Also, as Emily's case indicates, caregivers fear losing health care coverage for their children if they leave TANF and go to work. Caregivers who returned to work were seldom offered or could afford health care benefits through their workplace. Choosing between work with no or limited benefits and staying on TANF and Medicaid was a major decision for some families. However, not everyone was exempt from time limits, which meant the decision to get off TANF was made for them.

Race and Disability

In analyzing families' experiences with childhood disability, caregiving services, and work, we looked explicitly for differences by race/ethnicity. Although individual caregivers sometimes interpreted their experiences with social service workers in racial terms, for example, when they perceived differential or preferential treatment depending on the ethnicity/race of the recipient and provider, and although they reflected on wider contexts of racism, the families in the disability study were more apt to describe their opportunities and barriers in terms of disability and poverty statuses, policies, and programs as enacted locally. Having a child with a disability and having limited resources necessitated entering the worlds of early intervention, special education, Medicaid, TANF, and SSI. These spheres are not free of racialized practices, but more salient to caregivers were the ways in which these programs positioned them and responded to them as poor and disabled. Having to negotiate these worlds and dealing with childhood disability with limited resources may create more similarities than differences across families from diverse racial/ethnic groups. We found no discernible differences in caregiving and advocacy practices; access to social, medical, or health services; or work status related to ethnicity/race (Skinner et al. 2005).

This three-year ethnographic examination of low-income families with children with disabilities highlights several important points that should be considered in current debates and future reforms in TANF, SSI, and other public assistance programs.[6] Being the primary caregiver for a child with disabilities entails more than caring for the child in the home. It also means accessing and managing the child's educational, therapeutic, and medical services and being on call if the child gets sick or exhibits problematic behavior. This full-time devotion is valorized in middle-class women who are expected to sacrifice paid employment to provide in-home care for their children with disabilities (McKeever and Miller 2004). But the expectations are different for poor mothers. As feminist scholars have pointed out, welfare reform, before and after the 1996 act, has embodied a devaluation of the parental care done by poor women. It has been less about "work" and "self-support," and more about establishing the "discipline" of work and the habits of good workers in both adults and children who have not raised themselves to that ideal (Mink 1998; Schram 2001). Women are framed by TANF policies as workers first, and defined as good mothers if they have jobs. Their care and service management is not always recognized as work. It is no wonder that caregivers responded to this framing by asserting their competence as parents and the value of their children as worthy of care. In their words, as in the truly impressive case management they performed for their children, women in the study reclaimed the position denied them. One woman put it emphatically: "Nobody knows, but no matter what, I know that I'm a good mother and that's what counts. That's what counts to me, that I've done everything that I'm supposed to do." The women saw themselves as good mothers, which meant that their children rightly came first in their concerns and actions (Limoncelli 2002; compare Seccombe 1999).

Full-time and even part-time paid work in addition to this unpaid work is difficult for many caregivers to fit into their schedules, especially if other supports are lacking. Although a number of states have opted to exempt caregivers of a person with a disability from TANF work requirements and time limits, other states have not. Even in states that allow exemptions, it is not clear that screening for disability is consistently done or determined by standard criteria. Caregivers of children with disabilities that are not designated severe enough, and therefore not exempted, may find it particularly difficult or impossible to obtain and sustain full employment. It may simply be too much to ask of some caregivers of children with moderate or severe disabilities to enter the workforce. Expectations set out in welfare policy or held by caseworkers that they do so are unrealistic and potentially detrimental to children with special needs. In light of this, TANF work requirements and time limits for caregivers of children with disabilities should be reassessed or modified with their circumstances and needs in mind.

In this study, all of the caregivers wanted to work and had plans for employment when they could locate appropriate child care. Yet they feared they would lose Medicaid and not be able to obtain insurance through the workplace, especially for the child with disabilities. For these families, transitional Medicaid that could be extended even longer than the current one-year limit would be a major incentive and support to work. Also, most families needed flexible and understanding workplaces. Caregivers were frequently called upon to deal with their children's health needs, which challenged their ability to maintain employment. Even when a child with a disability was in school, caregivers were often called to attend to medical crises or behavioral problems. Also, they needed to arrange before- and after-school care and coverage for the multiple days during the year when they were working but schools were closed.

Obtaining appropriate and quality child care is a problem for families regardless of income or disability status, but the difficulty is particularly acute for low-income families of children with disabilities. Although child care facilities and programs that receive government funds are required to include children with special needs under both Section 504 of the Rehabilitation Act and the Americans with Disabilities Act, a review of studies on the availability of child care for families of children with special needs indicates that whereas many centers may serve children with mild to moderate delays, there are very few child care slots for children with significant disabilities (Wolery, Holcombe, and Brookfield 1993) or children who require specialized medical care (Godfrey 1991).

The care work that families do for their members with disabilities is not recognized or valued by current social policies. It is unlikely that recommendations that family members be paid for this work will be implemented in the near (or distant) future. What could help these families now is awareness on the part of policy makers and frontline workers of the difference disability makes for families. For parents or other caregivers of children with disabilities who are required to work, work participation could become more broadly defined to include caring for children with disabilities. This is warranted because a caregiver often acts as a child's service coordinator, nurse, therapist, and teacher. To promote this approach, the Wisconsin Council on Developmental Disabilities has prepared a workbook for parents who receive TANF to document the extent of the daily care requirements predicated by their children's disabilities.

The definition of work could include participation in training programs for specialized care; service coordination; and parent advocacy for children with disabilities—training programs already federally funded in each state, such as the Parent Training and Information Centers (funded under IDEA) and Centers for Independent Living (funded under the Rehabilitation Act). Referrals to these kinds of agencies for training would ensure that lower income families and those raising children with special health care needs have a voice in future policy debates around TANF and SSI. It is critically important that these families have a place—and a voice—at the "parent advocacy table." These initiatives and groups—many of which receive some government funding—typically involve only those families who have more resources available to them, such as discretionary income, flexible child care and employment arrangements, family support and higher levels of education. It is not surprising, given the fact that these families are also struggling with their own children's disabilities and chronic conditions, that needs and concerns of lower income families who have children with disabilities are rarely addressed. Good models of this type of "family inclusion" have been developed by the Maternal and Child Health Bureau of the Health Resources Services Administration. By funding and implementing these models at the state and local levels, all families could have a voice in government policies and practices that affect them and their children. For example, the Partners in Policy Making training for families, initiated by the Administration on Developmental Disabilities and available in many states, could be revised to meet the needs of families who are TANF recipients. Obviously, participation in this type of training should be counted in fulfillment of TANF work requirements. On the workplace side, employers could offer some flexibility to allow caregivers to deal with their children's special health care needs. For caregivers with disabilities, targeted and appropriate job training and placement should be offered.

Agencies that work with families in poverty are rarely aware of disability issues and the programs in place that serve persons with disabilities. Conversely, agencies that work with persons who have disabilities are often not familiar with poverty programs (Pokempner and Roberts 2001). What would help families like those in our study is for each type of agency to become aware of the other and to collaborate in referring families to appropriate programs and services for those who live in poverty and have disabilities. TANF policies need to comply with federal laws related to persons with disabilities (the Rehabilitation Act, Individuals with Disabilities Education Act [IDEA], and the Americans with Disabilities Act [ADA]). TANF caseworkers could receive training that would provide more awareness of the impact that disability can make in their clients' lives. Caseworkers should not be expected to become disability experts, but they could gain sensitivity to disability issues and maintain a list of agencies to which they could refer clients for additional resources and support. Early intervention caseworkers and other disability professionals could receive training on TANF, Medicaid, and SSI benefits to better aid their clients in accessing these and other programs for low-income families.

In terms of entitlements, there is only one service that children with disabilities in the United States are entitled to: special education services. The other entitlements, Medicaid and SSI, are predicated upon income eligibility (except for those states that have

1915[c] waivers). This situation causes families to walk a tight rope as they struggle to remain eligible for medical care (via Medicaid) while providing food, housing, and transportation for themselves. Across federal agencies, there is no special consideration for families who are raising children with special needs at home. For example, HUD does not "count" the severity of a child's disability in determining eligibility for public housing. Coordinating services across these agencies could go a long way in helping families of children with disabilities reach economic security.

Caregivers of children with disabilities share many of the same challenges as families depicted in other chapters in this volume. They need supports similar to those of other low-income families if they are to gain economic security. But disability does make a difference for these families in a number of important ways: Child care outside the family is almost impossible to find; work is often harder to maintain in light of the frequent and acute medical needs of the child; the demands of caring for children with severe disabilities can take its toll on mothers' mental and physical health; and caregivers must negotiate the complexity of the intersection of disability and poverty programs. As the debate around reforms in social policies and programs continues, caregivers of children with disabilities and caregivers with disabilities need to be on the radar screen, and policies and practices must be evaluated from realistic perspectives on what it means to parent a child with a disability.

Notes

1. Recent exceptions to this deficiency are a series of articles relating health and welfare reform published in the *Journal of the American Medical Women's Association*, vol. 57, no. 1.

2. For a thorough account of the connection of the Americans with Disabilities Act of 1990 and Section 504 of the Rehabilitation Act of 1973 ("Section 504") to TANF programs, see LaCheen 2004. Basically, these laws prohibit discrimination against people with disabilities in receiving federal assistance. However, TANF reforms present a dilemma to persons with disabilities or caregivers of those persons. As Silverstein et al. (1998, 9) point out, "Historically, many in the disability community have been concerned that states were more likely to exempt parents with disabilities than to extend program services to them. On the other hand, unless and until the system is designed to provide meaningful services to persons with disabilities, such persons will be subject to disproportionate sanctions, and failing to exempt them or provide extensions

will have its own discriminatory impact." This dilemma seems to be playing out in current welfare practices.

3. All names of study participants are pseudonyms.

4. This pattern is comparable to that found in Polit, London, and Martinez (2001).

5. Early intervention is a complex system of medical assessments and educational and therapeutic services mandated by federal law and state regulations. Services for infants and toddlers (that is, birth through two years of age) are mandated by Part C of the Individuals with Disabilities Education Act. Part B of this act requires that special education and related services for children age three through twenty-one be provided through public school systems.

6. Faye Manaster Eldar, who worked with us in Chicago as a consultant on childhood disability programs and policies, provided many of these suggestions for collaboration of agencies.

through a quantitative and qualitative lens

Looking at the Differential Effects of Domestic Violence on Women's Welfare Receipt and Work Participation

Holly Bell, Brenda J. Lohman, and Elizabeth Votruba-Drzal

As illustrated in Lein et al. (chap. 1, this volume), low-income mothers face a number of obstacles in their attempts to support their children. One additional obstacle for some of these women is domestic violence. During the welfare debates of the mid-1990s, policy makers and advocates expressed concern that women in violent relationships would not be able to comply with the new rules of PRWORA. As a result, many states adopted the Family Violence Option (FVO), which allowed them to waive federal TANF requirements in cases where clients suffer from domestic violence. Advocates were concerned that direct attempts by women's partners to sabotage work efforts or the indirect effects of abuse on women's mental and physical well-being might make it harder for them to comply with work mandates, in turn resulting in sanctions for them and termination of their welfare benefits. Some argued that the dismantling of the safety net welfare represented would make women more dependent on violent partners for economic security and prevent battered women from leaving violent relationships.

However, research on the intersection of welfare, work, and domestic violence has not consistently found direct associations between violence and women's receipt of welfare or their ability to work. It is the goal of this chapter to explore this finding, which has differed from the early predictions by advocates for survivors of domestic violence. To do so, we draw on both survey and ethnographic data from the San Antonio site of the Three-City Study. Our study suggests that violent relationships are heterogeneous, that they often change over time, and that they do not necessarily affect women's welfare receipt or their transition from welfare to work.

Domestic Violence, Welfare, and Work

Although domestic violence cuts across class lines, research has shown that low-income women are more likely to experience domestic violence and more likely to experience severe abuse than their economically advantaged peers (Bachman and Saltzman 1995; Hotaling and Sugerman 1990). Furthermore, women on public assistance (under both the old AFDC program and the new TANF program) have been shown to suffer from higher rates of domestic violence than low-income women who are not on welfare (Allard et al. 1997; Barusch, Taylor, and Derr 1999; Browne and Bassuk 1997; Brush 1999; Curcio 1997; Lloyd and Taluc 1997; Raphael 1995, 1996; Tolman and Rosen 2001). These studies have indicated that lifetime rates of domestic violence among women on welfare are alarmingly high. Between 34 and 65 percent of women on welfare have reported experiences with domestic violence, with most reports finding a range of 50 to 60 percent. More specifically, rates of recent abuse typically range from 8 to 33 percent. The majority of studies have uncovered rates between 20 and 30 percent (Tolman and Raphael 2000).

Studies have shown that these high rates of domestic violence have both direct and indirect effects on women's employment (Tolman and Raphael 2000). Many have argued that domestic violence serves as a barrier to employment and may contribute to higher rates of welfare dependence. Both qualitative work by Raphael (1995, 1996) and quantitative studies (Allard et al. 1997; Person, Thoennes, and Griswold 1999; Sable et al. 1999) have documented the variety of ways abusers directly interfere with women's efforts to work or go to school. These manipulative and abusive behaviors include interfering with a woman's child care or transportation arrangements, interfering with her work by making harassing calls or visiting her workplace, and keeping her up at night. Additionally, domestic violence may serve as an indirect barrier to employment, as women in violent relationships suffer from higher levels of mental and physical health problems, including depression, anxiety, post-traumatic stress disorder, and drug and alcohol abuse, than do women who have not experienced domestic violence (Allard et al. 1997; Browne, Salomon, and Bassuk 1999; Salomon, Bassuk, and Huntington 2002; Straus and Gelles 1990; Tolman and Rosen 2001). Often suffering from several psychological and/or physical problems, abused women are less likely to be able to work and more likely to be dependent on welfare to survive.

The direct and indirect barriers that domestic violence presents would lead us to expect lower rates of employment among women in violent relationships. However, studies that examine the link between domestic violence and women's participation in the paid labor force have shown mixed results. Lloyd and Taluc (1999) and Tolman and Rosen (2001) have failed to find a significant association between domestic violence and women's employment, whereas Browne, Salmon, and Bassuk (1999) have found that women who had experienced violence in the past year were only one-third as likely to maintain employment for at least thirty hours per week for six months or more in comparison to women who were not in violent relationships. In fact, our prior work from the Three-City Study supports the relationships found in this literature (Votruba-Drzal, Lohman, and Chase-Lansdale 2003). Specifically, we found no significant associations between movement of women into the labor force and changes in the levels of violence they experienced over time. However, we found that the movement of women out of the labor force was significantly associated with increases in their reports of total, moderate, and work-related violence. In this chapter, we expand upon these findings using survey data and then present ethnographic data that suggest unexpected results that domestic violence does not have a consistent impact on women's movement into the labor force, which may reflect the diversity of women's experiences with intimate-partner violence.

The Diversity of Violent Relationships

Johnson and Ferraro (2000), in their review of domestic violence research in the 1990s, have argued that recognizing the diverse manifestations of domestic violence is critical to our understanding of the phenomenon. Several studies have suggested that women's responses to domestic violence differ and often change over time (Lloyd 1997; Tolman and Raphael 2000). Qualitative data collected by Lloyd (1997) and Raphael (1995) have suggested that some women in abusive relationships view work as an avenue out of violence. Other women, however, are overwhelmed by their partners' control and abuse and give up trying to work in the face of danger.

Furthermore, there is some indication that violence in relationships may change over time. In some cases the violence escalates, and in some cases it lessens or ceases. In a three-year telephone study of domestic violence deterrence (Aldarondo 1996), 30.4 percent of the men assaulted their partners at some point over the three-year period. In year two, 60.7 percent of the men who were violent in year one interrupted their violence. In year three, 50.5 percent of the men who were violent in year two interrupted their violence. However, more than one-third of all violent men assaulted their partners during all three years. In their longitudinal qualitative study, Campbell, Kub, and Nedd (1998) found that the majority of the thirty-two women they interviewed had progressed from a committed violent relationship to an "in/out" state, in which they weighed their options, to either an "out" status (leaving the relationship) or a nonabused status. Six women had not been abused emotionally or physically for at least a year at the time of the third interview. Conversely, a few women continued to be in a committed but violent relationship. Similarly, in a quantitative study of 185 self-identified postabuse survivors, 158 (85.4 percent) no longer lived with their abusive partner, whereas 28 (14.6 percent) remained in their relationships, but the abuse had ended (Horton and Johnson 1993). Although leaving a violent relationship is one option that many abused women choose, research has shown that leaving does not always end the violence. For example, Davis and Kraham (1995) have cited U.S. Department of Justice statistics indicating that divorced and separated women were battered fourteen times more often than women still living with their partners. Although the romantic involvement between partners may end, the violence may not cease, which ultimately affects a woman's ability to leave welfare or obtain employment.

Taken together, these studies suggest that domestic violence is not a monolithic experience. One reason is that violence may generally be part of a relationship, but not the whole of it. Walker (1989) identified a cycle of violence whereby episodes of violence are followed by periods of contrition and romance, which are followed by periods of tension building. Many women do not think of their relationships as violent, even though violence occurs in them, because they also experience their partners as loving and helpful at times. Women must weigh the positive and negative aspects of a relationship in deciding whether to stay or leave, and love and affection for their partner is one of the reasons that some women remain. In addition, batterers and relationships differ, as do women's responses to them. Although some women remain in relationships that are violent, others leave, thereby ending the violence. Other women leave, but the violence continues. Although rare, some women remain in such relationships but the violence ends.

Given the heterogeneity of violent relationships and how they change over time, it is important to explore whether domestic violence impacts low-income women's work and welfare receipt. Data from the Three-City Study provide an excellent opportunity to build on this body of research. This longitudinal, multimethod project allows us to examine three themes in depth and across time: (1) the exposure of low-income women to domestic violence; (2) the impact of domestic violence on women's ability to work and their reliance on welfare; and (3) the diversity of women's exposure to violent relationships and how violent relationships may change over time. The study combines the strength of an ability to generalize that comes from quantitative analysis based on a randomized survey sample with rich qualitative data that allow for an in-depth exploration of the impact of domestic violence in the lives of low-income women.

The data for this study were drawn from interviews with 628 women who lived in San Antonio and were participants in the first and second waves of the survey component of the Three-City Study, as well as from in-depth interviews with women from the San Antonio ethnography. The women who participated in the survey component of the Three-City Study took part in in-home interviews that lasted approximately two hours, during which they answered questions about themselves, their romantic relationships, their families, their households, and their children. In all, seventy-five women were interviewed at least once during the San Antonio ethnography. This analysis focuses on seventeen women identified as survivors of domestic violence by a text search of the extensive interview and field note files of the San Antonio site (more than one thousand files) using QSR NUD*IST (1999). Search terms included actions related to domestic violence (such as *assault, hit, slap, protective order, restraining order*). Demographic characteristics of the women living in San Antonio who participated in the ethnography and survey components of the Three-City Study are outlined in table 7.1.

Table 7.1 Demographic Characteristics

| Demographic variable | Survey data (n=600) | | | | Ethnographic data (n=17) | |
| | Wave 1 | | Wave 2 | | Values at time of recruitment | |
	%	SD	%	SD		#
Age (weighted mean)	31.50	8.30	32.82	8.31	Mean: 27.05 years	
Race						
African American	.07	.26				4
Hispanic	.92	.28				9
European American	.01	.11				4
Income-to-needs (weighted mean)	.72	.55	.94	.62		
Family structure					Relationship to abusive partner	
Single	.48	.50	.43	.50	Never married, no children	4
Cohabitating	.05	.22	.08	.27	Never married, father of children	6
Married	.46	.50	.49	.50	Married, with children, but separated	7
Education						
No high school education	.37	.48	.43	.49		5
GED/High school education	.50	.50	.47	.50		2
Technical education/Some college credit	.11	.31	.09	.29		9
Post-secondary education	.02	.14	.01	.08		
Missing						1
Number of children under 18 (weighted mean)	3.03	1.43	3.04	1.52	Mean: 3.23	

Note: Values for survey data are weighted percentage and standard deviations, unless otherwise indicated.

Exposure to Violent Relationships

Roughly 23 percent (seventeen out of seventy-five) of the women who participated in the San Antonio ethnography were identified as survivors of domestic violence. There was no specific focus in the ethnography on domestic violence, so we may not have identified all the women in the study who experienced it or obtained the full story of each experience. The strength of these stories is that they illustrate how women weigh their concerns about violence with those about supporting their families, either through work or welfare reliance. Reported rates of domestic violence were remarkably similar for the women who participated in the survey portion of the Three-City Study. Table 7.2 includes descriptive statistics on the rates of exposure to domestic violence. To obtain these data, the survey asked women to answer a series of questions specifically about domestic violence using a modified version of the Conflict Tactics Scale (Straus 1979) adapted for the Women's Employment Study (Tolman and Rosen 2001). To provide complete privacy for each respondent, these questions were asked using an Audio Computer Assisted Survey Interview (ACASI), in which respondents were given a field investigator's laptop computer with a set of headphones and asked to enter their responses directly into the computer.

For each item related to domestic violence, two types of questions were asked—lifetime endorsement and current exposure to domestic violence. Lifetime endorsement reflects whether or not the respondent had experienced a particular form of domestic violence in her lifetime, whereas current exposure indicates the frequency of a particular act of domestic violence during the past twelve months (using a 1–4 scale, in which 1 equals *never* and 4 equals *often*). Lifetime endorsement composites were dichotomous variables that indicate whether or not respondents reported having had at least one incident of violence of a particular type at some time in their life at either wave of the survey. Current exposure composites were created for each wave of the survey by calculating a mean across all items in a subscale. Four different types of domestic violence were created for both the lifetime endorsement and current exposure composites. The four types of violence were: total, moderate, extreme, and work related.[1]

As in prior work that assessed rates of domestic violence in poor or welfare-reliant samples, an alarmingly high number of women in

Table 7.2 Rates of Domestic Violence by Type for Women Living in San Antonio, Texas. Quantitative Survey Data, Welfare, Children, and Families: A Three-City Study

Level of violence	Wave 1	Wave 2	Lifetime endorsement
Total domestic violence	.27	.25	.76
Moderate violence	.24	.23	.73
Threatened to hit you	.14	.12	.56
Threw something at you	.14	.13	.55
Pushed, grabbed, or shoved you	.19	.19	.64
Slapped, kicked, bit, or punched you	.11	.11	.50
Extreme violence	.07	.07	.42
Beat you	.06	.04	.37
Choked or burned you	.02	.03	.25
Used a weapon against you or threatened you with a weapon	.02	.02	.26
Forced you into unwanted sexual activity	.02	.03	.26
Threatened to take away your child	.04	.04	.26
Work-related violence	.06	.07	.38
Interfered with you going to work	.04	.04	.29
Harassed you at work	.02	.03	.21
Made you miss work	.04	.06	.23
Made you lose your job due to violence	.01	.02	.13

Note: Figure contains the percentage of women endorsing each item across both waves of the survey.

the Three-City Study experienced at least one type of violence during their lifetimes. Specifically, three out of every four women reported experiencing some form of abuse during their lifetimes. These rates are roughly 10 to 15 percent higher than in other studies of low-income or welfare reliant populations (Tolman and Raphael 2000). In comparison, consistent with other studies of low-income samples, approximately one out of every four women was exposed to a moderate form of domestic violence in the twelve months prior to each wave of the survey (Lloyd 1997; Raphael and Tolman 1997; Tolman and Rosen 2001). Slightly fewer than 10 percent of the women were exposed to extreme violence during the year prior to both waves one and two of the survey. These rates are very similar to other studies of low-income-female population samples (Lloyd and Taluc 1999; Tolman and Rosen 2001). Slightly more than 40 percent of the sample reported having experienced at least one form of extreme physical violence sometime during their lifetimes. Finally, fewer than 10 percent of women in the sample reported at least one form of work-related violence during the year prior to the first and second waves of data collection. In addition, slightly more than one-third of the women in the sample reported that they had experienced at least one form of work-related violence at some point during their lifetimes, which is also consistent with other studies of low-income or welfare-reliant samples (Tolman and Rosen 2001).

Transitioning from Welfare-to-Work

In order to explore associations among employment, welfare receipt, and violence in intimate relationships over time, we estimated a series of ordinary least square regression equations using the longitudinal survey data.[2] In these models, domestic violence in women's relationships at wave two of the survey is modeled as a function of patterns of employment and welfare receipt between waves one and two, as well as of changes in individual and household characteristics.[3] From women's retrospective reports of welfare and work, we created four categories of welfare receipt: stayers (ww), nonentrants (nn), leavers (wn), and entrants (nw); and four categories of employment patterns: stably employed (ee), not employed (uu), moved into the labor force (ue), moved out of the labor force (eu). The level of domestic violence women were experiencing at wave one is included as a covariate. Kessler and Greenberg (1981) have shown that the coefficients on the explanatory variables in these models are interpreted as the effects of each variable on changes in rates of domestic violence over time. The individual and household characteristics included as covariates in these regression equations are: women's race, age, educational attainment, marital status, self-esteem, drug and alcohol use, and mental and physical health, as well as the number of children living in the household and the families' income-to-needs ratios. Three other retrospective variables were also included in the analyses: (1) whether the respondent experienced physical or sexual abuse during childhood; (2) whether the respondent had experienced domestic violence at any time during her life; and (3) whether the respondent's family of origin received welfare when the respondent was a child. For the purposes of this chapter, however, these variables are used as covariates and will not be discussed in detail. Following the regression analyses, a series of post hoc analyses were performed to make statistical comparisons between women who fell into all four welfare groups and those who fell into all four employment groups. Specifically, Adjusted Wald Tests were conducted to compare domestic violence among the welfare and employment groups.

Table 7.3 shows the results of the regression and the post hoc analyses. Here it can be seen that there were few statistically significant associations between women's patterns of welfare receipt and their exposure to domestic violence. There were two exceptions. First, as shown by the post hoc analyses at the bottom of the table, women who remained on welfare (ww) during waves one and two of the survey experienced greater increases in both total and moderate domestic violence than did women who went onto welfare (nw) during this time. Second, women who went onto welfare (nw) between waves one and two of the survey reported less of an increase in moderate violence than did those who were never on welfare during this time (the omitted group). There were not significant relations between patterns of welfare receipt and extreme violence or work interference.

Similar to the lack of significant associations between women's welfare patterns and domestic violence, the regression and post hoc analyses also revealed few significant links between women's employment patterns and changes in their reports of domestic violence over time. Specifically, women who transitioned out of a forty-hour-a-week job (eu) between waves one and two of the survey experienced greater increases in total and moderate domestic violence when compared to counterparts who fell into each of the other three employment categories (that is, women who were stably not involved in paid labor [the omitted group], women who were stably employed [ee], and women who became employed [ue]). Interestingly, there were no significant associations between women's employment patterns and changes in their reports of extreme violence or work interference over time. In summary, the quantitative data depict very few significant associations between changes in women's exposure to domestic violence over time and their patterns of welfare and employment. Domestic violence does not seem to be a barrier to women's ability to find jobs. These analyses suggest, however, that increases in domestic violence may be related to women's ability to hold jobs.

The Complexity of Women's Experiences with Violence

To better understand the few associations among work, welfare, and domestic violence, we turned to the ethnographic data and examined the interviews of the seventeen women identified as having experienced domestic violence. We were concerned that the broad definitions used in our quantitative analyses might be obscuring important heterogeneity that previous studies have shown exists in violent relationships. We reviewed each interview to develop a relationship history and to understand how women described and dealt with the violence and how these relationships affected their tenure on public assistance and their ability to gain and sustain employment (for additional analysis of this data, please see H. Bell 2003).

What emerged was a picture of great diversity in the nature of the domestic violence women experienced, in its context within the relationship, in the evolution of their relationships over time, and in women's reactions to the violence. Some violent relationships involved a single incident of violence; some involved long-term abuse. Women often experienced positive qualities of the men and the relationships, even when they sometimes experienced abuse from their partners. The nature of many of the relationships women described changed over time. A general theme that we noted was that it was much more difficult for women to work or leave violent relationships when they had children with their violent partners. Although involvement in violent relationships profoundly affected some women's tenure on welfare or ability to work, for others it did not. Specifically, six women described violent relationships that actively hindered their ability to work or comply with the requirements of TANF. Two described relationships that changed over time and, once the violence had ceased, actually helped them achieve and maintain stable work. Three others described situations in which their violent partners, at various times in their relationships, both helped and

Table 7.3 Longitudinal Multivariate Regression Models Predicting Frequency of Total, Moderate, and Extreme Domestic Violence and Work Interference at Wave 2. Quantitative Survey Data, Welfare, Children, and Families: A Three-City Study

Variable	Total	Moderate	Extreme	Work interference
Domestic violence at Wave 1	.43***	.42***	.31***	.25***
Welfare transitions				
Non-entrants (omitted)				
Stayers (ww)	.16	.14	.08	.07
Leavers (wn)	−.08	−.06	−.08	−.04
Entrants (nw)	−.07	−.09*	−.01	.01
Employment transitions				
Stably not employed (omitted)				
Stably employed forty hours a week (ee)	−.07	−.04	−.11	−.08
Move into the labor force (ue)	−.08	−.09	−.09	−.04
Move out of the labor force (eu)	.17*	.18*	.03	.03
Demographic characteristics				
Race				
Latin Americans (omitted)				
European Americans	.01	.00	.01	.01
African Americans	−.01	−.03	.01	.06
Age, Wave 1	−.02	−.02	−.02	−.04
Change in income-to-needs	.05	.06	−.01	.00
Family structure				
Cohabiting (omitted)				
Married	−.30	−.37	−.19	.04
Single	−.22	−.30	−.06	.06
Becomes single	−.10	−.13	−.13	−.01
Into marriage	−.16	−.18	−.14	.00
Into cohabitation	−.19	−.25	−.13	.05
Education				
No high school education (omitted)				
High school education	.04	.05	.00	−.02
Vocational education	.00	−.01	.00	−.02
Postsecondary education	−.01	−.01	.01	−.01
Into high school education	−.04	−.03	−.03	−.06
Into vocational education	−.03	−.03	−.04	−.03

Table 7.3 *Continued*

Variable	Total	Moderate	Extreme	Work interference
Change in the number of children in the household	−.04	−.04	.01	−.07
Mental and physical health				
Change in psychological distress	.12*	.09	−.02	.14
Change in positive self-concept	.09	.09	.07	−.01
Change in negative self-concept	.17***	.22***	.07	.05
Change in drug and alcohol use	.03	.04	−.05	−.02
Change in financial strain	−.06	−.10	.03	.00
Always disabled (omitted)				
No longer disabled	.04	.02	.05	.04
Never disabled	.01	.00	−.02	.05
Became disabled	−.08	−.07	−.03	−.04
Physical or sexual abuse during childhood[a]	.11	.12	.15*	.07
Experienced domestic violence ever in lifetime[a]	.08	.04	.11	.04
Family welfare receipt during childhood[a]	.00	.01	−.02	.00
F	6.78***	5.77***	1.38	1.48*
R^2	.36	.39	.20	.12
Employment group post-hoc tests[b]	ee < eu* ue < eu**	ee < eu* ue < eu**		
Welfare group post-hoc tests[c]	ww > nw*	ww > nw**		

Note: Standardized regression coefficients are presented.

[a]These variables are lifetime experiences and are therefore held constant over time.

[b]Post-hoc tests examine statistically significant differences among the employment groups using Adjusted Wald Tests. The omitted group is stably not employed.

[c]Post-hoc tests examine statistically significant differences among the welfare groups using Adjusted Wald Tests. The omitted group is nonentrants.

Abbreviations: ee = stably employed, eu = move out of labor force, nw = entrants, ue = move into labor force, wn = leavers, ww = stayers.

*p < .05 **p < .01 ***p < .001

hindered their efforts to gain and sustain work. Three women described relationships with partners who had at times been violent that seemed to have no impact on their ability to work. Finally, we did not have enough information from three of the respondents to establish a clear pattern of impact on their ability to work. These remaining three stories will not be described in detail.

In the following sections, we focus specifically on the impact of abuse on women's ability to work. We address associations between domestic violence and welfare receipt indirectly, since in many cases, though not all, women who were unable to work as a result of abuse were forced to rely on welfare. In a few cases, violence directly prevented a woman's ability to comply with the requirements of TANF, including work requirements, and thus jeopardized her benefits.

Violent Relationships that Hindered Women's Ability to Work

Six women described relationship violence that actively hindered their ability to work or comply with the requirements of TANF. Mandy combined TANF and a work-study job while she tried to complete her education. She told the interviewer that she lost her work-study job because of harassment by her husband and his new girlfriend. Two other women lost jobs as a result of abuse. Veronica missed a lot of work during the probationary period of a new job because of her husband's abuse, and she was fired. Though it is not clear whether this particular incident led Veronica to reapply for TANF, she described a history of cycling among work, welfare, and child support from her child's father. After years of abuse and escaping to Texas, Karen decided to return to her husband in another state to give their marriage a second chance. However, once in the car on the way back to his home, he beat her savagely and repeatedly. He kept her and their children prisoner after they arrived. Karen was finally able to contact a shelter that rescued her and helped her and her children return to Texas. Karen feared that her husband would find her. She talked about her fear that he would return, and she experienced post-traumatic stress disorder, depression, and anxiety as a result. Even though Karen had a GED, some college, and an extensive work history, she found it difficult to maintain steady and high-level employment and cycled between welfare and low-wage work.

Frankie reported that pressure from her abusive and unstable husband, who also had a gambling problem, kept her from working. During the course of our interviews with her, Frankie received TANF, held garage sales, and pawned household items to make ends meet. Ronette was sanctioned by welfare officials for not cooperating with the child support enforcement requirements of TANF. She did not want to report her abusive boyfriend, who was at that time paying informal support. However, when he later stopped paying, she reported him. Iris described a relationship that lasted for three years with a man who was not the father of any of her children. She described their relationship as stormy and admitted that she was obsessed with him. Early in their relationship, he became abusive. One night, Iris followed him to a club because she suspected him of cheating on her. They got into a fight. Iris had a gun, and when her boyfriend tried to take it from her, it went off and shot him in the hand. Iris was charged with assault with a deadly weapon and sentenced to two years' probation. She lost her job as a detention officer because of her arrest. After the trial, she never saw the man again. Iris was able to get another job as a bus driver, and she did not apply for TANF as a result of this incident. For these six women, their involvement with abusive men actively impeded their ability to work and/or meet the requirements of welfare and sometimes led them to apply or reapply for TANF.

Violent Relationships that Helped Women's Ability to Work

As stated earlier, relationships that involve violence rarely consist solely of violent episodes, but are rather a complex mixture of abuse and support, fear and love. Two women interviewed achieved a relative measure of success in terms of stable employment, which led to greater family stability overall. In both instances, these women described relationships with partners who had been abusive but who also provided needed support that helped them achieve self-sufficiency. Both women had had children with men who had been violent and had separated from the fathers of their children. Both continued to relate to these men for the sake of their children. In each case, the violence had ceased by the time of their interviews with us.

Lori described one incident of violence with her oldest child's father, Dan, while she lived with him. She called the police and went to a shelter for a month, but eventually returned to him. After several years, she separated from him permanently. Dan assisted Lori in improving her financial situation by caring for the children on the weekends so that she could work on the weekends and go to school during the week. Lori was eventually able to secure an office job with benefits and to move into a lease-to-own home as a result of Dan's help. Ysenia survived after her divorce on intermittent child support, work, and TANF. Like Lori's former husband, at one point after their separation, Ysenia's former husband kept their son on Saturdays, when regular child care was not available, so Ysenia could work as a security guard. In both of these cases, the women were no longer romantically involved with their abusive partners but maintained contact because of the children. Fathers' participation in caring for the children allowed the mothers to work and, in Lori's case, to avoid dependence on welfare.

Violent Relationships that Both Helped and Hindered Women's Ability to Work

Three women described relationships that both helped and hindered their ability to work and transition off TANF. The father of La Shonda's youngest child was on parole at the time he assaulted La Shonda. When she called the police, his parole was revoked and he was sent back to prison. La Shonda expressed concerns about her safety upon his release and questioned her decision to file charges: "Actually, I think I put myself in more danger by filing a report on him. How's he going to react? Did he have a change of heart? Did he change his mind? Does he still want to kill me?" Although she had no contact with this man, La Shonda had extensive contact with his mother, who cared for their child every weekend—an enormous help, since La Shonda had three other children to care for. La Shonda cycled between TANF and low-wage work.

During the time she lived with Rasheed, the father of her four children, Winette also cycled between TANF and low-wage work. She lost a scholarship opportunity when she had to leave her home after a particularly brutal beating. After years of abuse, Winette finally established a household away from Rasheed. She worked two jobs and stopped receiving TANF. She described an unsuccessful attempt to leave as a motivator for her later success. As she put it: "I couldn't get it together, so I eventually came back home, and ever since then, I had it in my head, 'Hey, I can do it.' Ever since then, I had it in my head, but then I had a hunger to want to up and leave and do it. . . . And from then on, that's how I started empowering myself."

Similarly, Sonya reported that Jerome, the father of her five children, had rarely worked and that Sonya had supported the family by working, mostly in fast-food restaurants, when she could find child care, and had received public assistance intermittently. Sonya reported: "[Jerome] gets mad [when I get a job] because then he figures that I don't need him." Much of the time Jerome interfered with Sonya's attempts to work, passively, by refusing to provide child care, and actively, by harassing her at work and causing her to get fired. However, at one point during our interviews with Sonya, Jerome helped her keep a job by providing child care in the summer when formal child care for five children would have been impossible to obtain.

Winette's story illustrates the diversity in women's responses to domestic violence. For some women, domestic violence serves as a barrier to employment, whereas for others what they learn from their experiences in dealing with violent relationships actually serves as a catalyst for employment and economic self-sufficiency. Sonya's and Winette's stories illustrate how violent relationships may change over time and differentially affect women's patterns of work and receipt of welfare. Violent men who once hindered their partners' ability to work may later provide necessary support that enhances women's labor-force participation.

Violent Relationships that Neither Helped nor Hindered Women's Ability to Work

Three women told of violent relationships that seemed to have no direct impact on their ability to work. Lina described such a situation. She said that her boyfriend, Raul, who was not the father of any of her children, assaulted her because she wanted to leave him. Lina spent three or four days in the hospital and, with the help of people from a local agency, filed charges and obtained a restraining order against Raul. There was no mention of him in subsequent interviews, and Lina apparently had a new boyfriend. Although we do not know the ultimate impact of Raul's violence on Lina, in her conversations with us Lina did not describe this incident as having any direct influence on her ability to care for herself or her three children. She cycled between TANF and low-wage work and cited problems with child care and transportation, not domestic violence, as her main barriers to employment.

Similarly, Helen's abusive boyfriend was not the father of any of her children. Like Lina, she reported a single incident of violence. She called the police, and since her boyfriend was on parole, he went back to prison. In the interviews that followed this event, she talked about getting back with him, but in the meantime she had another boyfriend. She received child support from the father of her children and worked off and on. While talking about her efforts to support herself and her children, Helen did not describe this incident of violence as having any effect on her ability to work.

Malinda's situation was different in that her abuser was her husband and the father of her two children. She separated from him after four and one-half years, during which time he was repeatedly violent. At the time of our first interview with Malinda, she had been separated from her husband for seven months. During the following year, he visited the children irregularly and was sometimes violent with Malinda. In January 2001, he assaulted her. They went to court, and he was jailed for repeatedly violating a protective order. He served four months for this violation. During this time, Malinda and her family survived on intermittent child support from her former husband and her income from a number of jobs. She did not attribute her job changes to her relationship with her former husband.

It appears from these stories that some relationships were easier to leave than others and were thus less likely to create ongoing barriers to employment. Long-term relationships appeared to be harder to leave than short-term ones. Women who had children with their abusive partners and were linked together by shared responsibilities for children appeared to find it harder to separate themselves from the abusers. Malinda's story, like Winette's, illustrates that even in cases of persistent violence, some women are able to work.

These stories illustrate some of the complexities of women's violent relationships. In doing so, they demonstrate the usefulness of examining qualitative data in order to understand better inconsistent results of quantitative analyses of the associations among work, welfare, and domestic violence. For the seventeen women interviewed for the ethnography, categorical answers to questions about violence in relationships are not always clear-cut and often change over time. Qualitative research can add to quantitative findings and suggest some of the reasons that domestic violence may not have a consistent effect on women's employment or welfare receipt. Since most of the women interviewed in the ethnography had children with the violent partners, they were forced to maintain some kind of contact with their abusers. In some cases, like Mandy's, ongoing abuse and harassment by the children's fathers hindered the women's ability to work. In others, the relationships cooled, the violence diminished or ended, and formerly violent partners did not hinder the women's ability to work. Some relationships involved a single incident of violence and others ongoing violence. In some cases, other factors in the women's lives, such as caring for an ill or disabled child, had more influence on the women's ability to work than did violence. Finally, women's responses to violence sometimes differed. For some, violence served as major barrier to employment; for others, violence served as a catalyst to work and obtain economic self-sufficiency.

This chapter combines qualitative and quantitative data to consider whether changes in the level and types of violence across the lifespan of a relationship may differentially impact the link between domestic violence and low-income women's welfare receipt, on one hand, and their ability to gain and sustain employment, on the other. Our findings may help explain why earlier studies of associations between work and domestic violence have generally not found significant strong links between domestic violence and women's employment (Lloyd and Taluc 1999; Tolman and Rosen 2001). The results of the survey data suggest that, although domestic violence is a challenge for many low-income women, it does not necessarily interfere with their ability to work. The vast majority of the women in our survey sample had experienced domestic violence at some point in their lives, and almost one-third had experienced at least one form of domestic violence during the past twelve months. In general, we found that the rates of current domestic violence in these analyses were comparable to other studies of low-income and welfare-reliant samples. However, as previously mentioned, lifetime reports of domestic violence in the Three-City Study were somewhat higher than those in other studies of poor or welfare-reliant populations.[4] Furthermore, our survey data suggest that women who are abused may be able to obtain jobs but may not be able to maintain them over long periods due to violence from their intimates that directly or indirectly sabotages their work. Consistent with the quantitative findings, the stories of the women interviewed for the ethnography illustrate that women may have different experiences of violence both within the course of their individual relationships and as compared to those of other battered women.

This research confirms and helps to explain unanticipated findings from quantitative research on domestic violence and welfare that fail to find a direct relationship among violence, work participation, and welfare receipt. It suggests that, although some battered women face added obstacles in transitioning off TANF and becoming self-sufficient, not all such women are hindered from working. Although these stories add to our understanding of women's experience of domestic violence, these data are limited. Future research should focus on teasing out some of the differences in violent relationships and how they may impact low-income women's transition from welfare to work.

The more complex relationship between domestic violence and work that our data present has some important implications for policy. As Johnson and Ferraro (2000) have argued, our ability to make effective policy is handicapped by a failure to take into account the distinctions within domestic violence. Our data indicate that the Family Violence Option (FVO) is a good starting point, but it is not enough. Despite the heterogeneity of women's experience with violence and the diversity of impacts it may have on their ability to work, the FVO currently offers only one solution: a temporary waiver of work requirements. Many survivors of domestic violence want to work. Survival is their concern, and domestic violence takes its place alongside many other issues that threaten them and their children (Lein et al. 2001).

In their effort to survive, low-income mothers draw on multiple resources, which include public assistance programs, family and friends, barter, and odd jobs (Lein et al. chap. 1, this vol.). For battered women, a search for resources from battering partners can lead to "dangerous dependencies" (Scott et al. 2002). As a first response to women who are being abused, welfare offices and caseworkers need to make women feel comfortable disclosing the violence they are experiencing at home, since caseworkers' responsiveness may be key to disclosure (Busch and Wolfer 2002). In particular, efforts to screen women for domestic violence who are being threatened with sanction for noncompliance with TANF work requirements may identify women for whom violence is creating a barrier to self-sufficiency. There is evidence, however, that caseworkers, in their single-minded focus on putting low-income mothers to work, may ignore or fail to inquire about domestic violence (Bell, chap. 8, this vol.). As a second response, a focus on providing work supports, in the form of substantially increased child care subsidies and extended benefits for women attempting to enter the labor force, would decrease the danger some of them face. In the absence of adequate quality subsidized child care, low-income women must rely on informal care by family and friends, which is frequently unavailable or unstable (Bruinsma, chap. 2, this vol.), or be forced into reliance on violent partners. If the woman also has a child or children with disabilities, the problem may be particularly acute (Skinner, Lachicotte, and Burton, chap. 6, this vol.). Creating safer workplaces and developing and providing training for jobs that keep survivors out of the public eye would, unlike most of the service jobs many TANF recipients find, provide more safety for survivors transitioning from welfare to work.

In sum, advocates for victims of domestic violence need to continue to work with public assistance agencies to make the special and complex needs of battered women clear and to develop programs to address those needs. Advocates can help raise public assistance caseworkers' awareness of the complicated ongoing relationships many women have with the abusive fathers of their children, and help them form strategies to deal with them in ways that enhance women's safety and economic self-sufficiency.

Notes

1. Total violence composites are based on thirteen items in the domestic violence scale and reflect all types of domestic violence women may have experienced ($\alpha_{T1} = .86$: $\alpha_{T2} = .87$). Moderate violence composites are comprised of four items, including questions related to whether women had been pushed, slapped, or threatened ($\alpha_{T1} = .87$: $\alpha_{T2} = .86$). Extreme violence composites are based on

four items, entailing more violent episodes of domestic violence such as being beaten, being burned, being threatened with a weapon, or having a weapon used against oneself ($\alpha_{T1}=.67$: $\alpha_{T2}=.70$). Finally, work-related violence composites are based on four items that reflect partners' attempts to sabotage women's work efforts, such as direct interference with women's efforts to go to work or harassment of her at work ($\alpha_{T1}=.71$: $\alpha_{T2}=.74$). To address skewness, frequency composites were subject to a square root transformation.

2. All analyses are weighted with probability weights that are inversely proportional to the likelihood of being included in the sample. Probability weights allow us to generalize to our population of inference, which includes all low-income women living in neighborhoods of San Antonio with income less than 200 percent of the poverty line.

3. For a full description of these covariates, please see Votruba-Drzal, Lohman, and Chase-Lansdale (2003).

4. This may be the result of the use of ACASI, which provides complete privacy to women as they answer questions related to partner abuse, and women may be more likely to disclose information than they would have disclosed on a questionnaire or in an in-person interview. It may also be the result of our relatively liberal definitions of lifetime domestic violence. A final factor relates to how we determined whether or not a woman had experienced domestic violence during her lifetime. Lifetime experiences of domestic violence were reported at waves one and two of the survey. Women who reported having experienced a particular form of domestic violence during their lifetime at either wave of the survey were coded as having experienced domestic violence during their lifetime. This method of assessing women's lifetime history of domestic violence differs from other studies, even those longitudinal in nature, which tend to rely on a single report of lifetime abuse.

Part Three **Working to Help**

putting mothers to work

Caseworkers' Perceptions of Low-Income Women's Roles in
the Context of Welfare Reform

Holly Bell

At the core of the debate that surrounded PRWORA was a discussion
of the rights and responsibilities of the poor single mothers who
make up the bulk of the recipients of the newly instituted TANF
program. Rather than conceiving of them primarily as mothers, entitled to be at home with their children, as they had been under the
old AFDC program, under PRWORA they were conceived of primarily as workers. Henrici and Miller (chap. 3) provide a detailed
discussion of the complex network of laws that initiated the new
welfare system. Four major changes were introduced by the new
legislation, including the conditional availability of cash assistance
(as opposed to entitlement), promotion of rapid entry into the labor
market ("work first," instead of a focus on education), increased
emphasis on services that support work, and limited expansion of
services for nonworking TANF recipients (Pavetti 2000). These
changes focused on moving low-income single mothers out of the
home and into the workplace. Whereas Henrici and Miller, as well as
Bruinsma (chap. 2), focus on the impact of this legislation on recipients, this chapter explores the ways in which caseworkers articulated and addressed the tension between low-income women's roles
as mothers and as workers.

The impact of welfare reform on both poor mothers and welfare
caseworkers occurs within a shifting understanding of women in the
welfare state as well as a changing organizational culture of welfare
provision. How these two simultaneous changes intersect will be the
focus of the following section.

Gender and Welfare

The current incarnation of welfare reform contains a number of gendered assumptions about work, citizenship, and caregiving. Historically, social welfare in the United States has been tied to the idea of a "family wage" within a nuclear family headed by a male breadwinner with a full-time female homemaker (Esping-Andersen 1999; Mink 1998). Families in the United States increasingly fail to conform to that norm; nevertheless, those stereotypes continue to influence the public welfare system. This leads to a two-tiered system of benefits. One set of programs, including unemployment and Social Security, is tied to participation in the labor force. A second set of programs, including TANF, food stamps, and Medicaid, addresses what are considered to be family failures—in particular, absence of a male breadwinner (Fraser 1989, 149). Not only are these systems separate, but they are also unequal, as they create two classes of recipients: the "deserving" and the "undeserving." Displaced workers and widows of working men (those who might receive either unemployment or Social Security) are considered deserving because of their participation, either directly or indirectly, in the labor market. The recipients of TANF are considered undeserving. They are stereotyped as women who have never worked and/or who were never legally married to wage earners. As a result, they receive lower benefits, and concerns about their moral failings saturate conversations about them (Albelda 2001b; Fraser 1989; Orloff 1996; Rice 2001).

The perceived moral failings of welfare mothers—their unwillingness to work, their failure to marry or stay married, and their irresponsible childbearing—is a central focus of the current welfare reform debate. Mink (1998) and Naples (1997) have pointed to the moral imperatives embedded in PRWORA: discouragement of unmarried parenting and childbearing (through family caps, for example), establishment of paternity and child support enforcement, prohibition of assistance to teen parents not living with parents or going to school, and mandatory work requirements. However, Mink (1998) has argued that PRWORA's attack on the rights of poor single mothers to stay at home and care for their own children is just the latest and most substantive erosion in a trend that has been ongoing since the 1960s. The intention of mothers' pensions, the grandmother of our welfare system, was economic support for mothers' caregiving work inside the home when a male breadwinner died. However, as welfare rolls expanded and more women of color and mothers who had never married entered the system, racism and fears about the erosion of the nuclear family made this politically untenable (Mink 1998). Race, in particular, has been a powerful subtext within the gendered discussion of welfare reform, and much of the concern about welfare mothers' moral fitness is rooted in racist images of black "welfare queens" who refuse to work or marry and procreate in order to receive welfare (Mink 1995, 1998; Naples 1997). Mink has argued that PRWORA has not been a reform of welfare but rather its repeal, since the law's goal is not to improve economic assistance for poor mothers but rather to end single motherhood, or, failing that, to deny poor single mothers the right to care for their own children.

As has been discussed in earlier chapters of this volume, the ideological underpinnings for welfare reform are based on a neoliberal understanding of personhood and citizenship (Kingfisher and Goldsmith 2001). Neoliberalism espouses a minimalist state in which almost all functions are market driven and focus on the responsibility of the individual in relation to the state. It degenders women's relationship to state provisions in that women who previously appealed to the state for benefits in their role as mothers are now counted as separate, autonomous individuals with the means to achieve self-sufficiency. When they do not, their failure is not seen as the failure of a social and economic system that places additional barriers, such as racial or gender bias, in the way of their success. In the neoliberal view, their failure is personal. As a result of this focus on personal responsibility, the language of empowerment, motivation, and "tough love" has become part of the current rhetoric of welfare reform.

Mink (2002) has pointed out that women's poverty in the labor market and their poverty as family caregivers are deeply intertwined, largely because women's work is not valued, either inside or outside the home. Even with substantial gains in income relative to men, women are about 50 percent more likely overall than men to live in poverty (McLanahan and Kelly n.d.). Many middle-class women balance work and parenting as a symbol of their liberation from exclusive caretaking functions. This balancing act is now mandatory for low-income women, and much more difficult (Albelda 2001b; Mink 1998). In a review of studies on welfare leavers funded by the Office of the Assistant Secretary of Planning and Evaluation (ASPE) of the federal Department of Health and Human Services, Isaacs and Lyon (2000) found that three-fifths of former welfare recipients were working; however, earning levels were low, with estimated poverty rates of close to 60 percent. Furthermore, 20 to 30 percent of former recipients returned to welfare within one year. Similar to the findings of Angel and Lein (chap. 5, this vol.), the ASPE study found that a significant percentage of leavers were uninsured and in some cases had to forgo needed medical care. Data from three states indicated that approximately one-fourth of former recipients experienced food shortages.

As several of the authors of this volume (Bruinsma; Lein et al.; Skinner, Lachicotte, and Burton) and other studies illustrate, in addition to material hardships, working single mothers face substantial and underrecognized conflicts between their roles as worker and mother. For example, Scott et al. (2001) found that most of the eighty welfare-reliant mothers in Cleveland and Pennsylvania from the project on Devolution and Urban Change stated, "My kids are my first concern." Many mothers cited financial improvement, respect as wage earners, and desire to provide better role models for their children as positive aspects of working, and most were optimistic about their future in the world of paid labor. However, they were also concerned about the costs of work to their children. Like the mothers interviewed by Bruinsma (chap. 2), the mothers in Scott and colleagues' study cited problems with child care and supervision, as many didn't trust child care centers, couldn't afford child care, or couldn't match work hours to child care hours. They also cited a lack of "quality time" with their children. Most believed that the benefits of going to work outweighed the costs, though the authors questioned this in light of wage restraints and lack of work supports for low-wage women workers.

In short, welfare reform presents a shift in low-income women's relationship to the state. Though historically eligible for benefits based on their roles as mothers, in the new era of welfare reform they are considered primarily workers. This shift from mother to worker in the eyes of the state presents tensions and conflicts for poor women. How this shift is interpreted by caseworkers, who are welfare recipients' most direct contact with the reformed welfare system, is the focus of this chapter.

The Role of Caseworkers in Welfare Reform

Welfare administrators have recognized the critical interdependence between policy reform and organizational reform (Hercik 1998). Caseworkers mediate the needs of welfare organizations and clients (Kingfisher 1996; Morgen 2001). Citing early research by Lipsky (1980) and Pressman and Wildavsky (1984), Hercik (1998) has suggested that the ways caseworkers mediate these needs are critical if policies are to be successfully implemented. Bane and Ellwood (1994) have suggested that for the "work first" philosophy of welfare reform to succeed, caseworker-client interactions must change from those that are routinized, impersonal, and focused on clients' eligibility for benefits to those that focus on preparing for work and providing assistance for clients toward that end. The philosophy of "work first" assumes that finding a job and developing work skills through personal experience will go farther in getting people off the rolls than job training; "work first" is a response to the low participation rates in the old JOBS program that preceded welfare reform, and to a concern that education was becoming an end in itself rather than a means to employment (Danziger and Seefeldt 2000; Miller and Henrici chap. 3, this vol.).

This shift in organizational culture required for the successful implementation of PRWORA presupposes that caseworkers understand and implement the new rules in a way consistent with the intent of welfare reform. The studies to date present a mixed picture of caseworkers' understanding of, agreement with, and capacity to carry out the new requirements (Danziger and Seefeldt 2000; Gerdes and Brown-Standridge 1997; Gooden 1998; Marks 1999; Meyers, Glaser, and MacDonald 1998; Morgen 2001; Nathan and Gais 2000; Poverty Law Center n.d.). Overall, they echo earlier findings based on the interviews analyzed for this chapter: most caseworkers supported the goals of welfare reform but cited structural obstacles to implementation, including high caseloads, inadequate support services for clients, lack of coordination among the organizations responsible for its implementation, and the realities of low-wage work as a barrier to client self-sufficiency (H. Bell 2005).

None of these studies emphasize the fact that in focusing on poor mothers' status as workers, caseworkers must of necessity ignore or minimize their status as mothers. In this study, I focus on this issue at the heart of welfare reform by examining how caseworkers interpret and act on the changes that have resulted from PRWORA, particularly how they view the tension between clients' roles as mother and worker.

This study relied on in-depth interviews with caseworkers in three agencies to explore how they addressed clients' parenting role, based on data from the neighborhood study of the San Antonio site of the Three-City Study.

Seventeen employees from a nonprofit organization, a state-level government agency, and a public housing authority that served low-income families in three neighborhoods were interviewed. Respondents included nine employees of the state public assistance agency that determines eligibility for TANF, Medicaid, and food stamps; seven employees of a private nonprofit organization charged with providing employment and training services; and one caseworker with the public housing authority, which collaborates with the other two organizations in public housing projects to assist residents of public housing in becoming self-sufficient.

Researchers interviewed workers from various levels of the agencies, including eleven frontline caseworkers and six supervisors and administrative personnel. Although the focus of the study was frontline caseworkers, supervisors and administrative personnel were interviewed to gain access to frontline caseworkers and to gain a sense of their organizations' histories, contexts, and changes as a result of welfare reform. Respondents included twelve women and five men, including ten Latin Americans, four European Americans, and three African Americans, ranging in age from their early twenties to mid-fifties. Although some mentioned having at least some college, none were trained as professional social workers or had either a bachelor's or a master's degree in social work.

Respondents were interviewed in the fall of 1999 and the fall of 2000 with a semistructured protocol that asked them to describe their jobs, their clients, and their opinions of the changes that resulted from welfare reform. The first few interviews were transcribed verbatim. Transcription of all interviews was later deemed unnecessary for the level of analysis intended, and the rest were selectively transcribed.

The transcript data were analyzed using QSR NUD*IST (1999), a software program for qualitative data analysis. The analysis for this chapter builds on earlier analyses of the ways in which the particular structural manifestation of welfare reform in Texas influenced case-workers' daily interactions with clients, how caseworkers assessed the reforms, and how caseworkers perceived clients' motivation and ability to become self-sufficient (H. Bell 2005). In order to analyze specifically caseworkers' perceptions of the tension between clients' roles as mothers and workers, all references caseworkers made to "mother," "family," "child," "daughter," and "son" were searched to look for patterns and themes that might indicate caseworkers' un-derstanding of the tension between these roles for TANF clients. Their views on these roles will be presented in the following section.

As found in earlier studies of welfare reform, the San Antonio caseworkers interviewed generally agreed with the goals of welfare reform and supported its focus on "work first." Their concerns about the impact that this emphasis had on clients' ability to parent were limited. In general, caseworkers focused on clients' motivation as the primary determinant of their success at transitioning from wel-fare to work. However, some caseworkers were more attuned than others to the broader context of poor mothers' lives and how this context might influence their success. Both caseworkers' views on clients' roles as mothers and workers and differences between case-workers' views will be discussed in the sections that follow.

Clients as Mothers and Workers

Caseworkers from the housing authority (HA), public assistance agency (PA), and employment and training organization (E and T) identified a common client profile. When asked how he would char-acterize clients in terms of the barriers they have to becoming self-sufficient, one male, Latin American housing caseworker said, "I think in general all of them have the same barriers. I'd say a mini-mum of two or three children. They have not worked very long in the workforce [nor do they] have too many marketable skills. They are single parents. These are the primary obstacles." Although case-workers from all three agencies used the gender-neutral term *client*, or in the case of E and T caseworkers *customer*, all of their TANF clients were mothers. Even so, rarely did any of these caseworkers talk about the parenting responsibilities of clients. Most had fully embraced the idea that clients should be primarily viewed within these agencies as workers. Many talked about the impact of the "work first" philosophy on how they accomplished their jobs, as in the following quotes from three different caseworkers:

> Well, I think the focus has gone a little bit more from, "We're here just to process your application and give you the benefits" to, "We're here, but we'd like some responsibility from you about finding work." (male European American PA caseworker)

> Prior to welfare reform, because a lot of the responsibility wasn't placed on them, it was more like a handout. When the Personal Responsibility Agreement [a contract that all clients sign in order to receive benefits] came into place, a lot of the responsibility was placed on them. (female Latin American PA caseworker)

> They [clients] have definitely seen the change, because we're bombarding them literally with, "Have you found a job?" (female Latin American PA caseworker)

Although many caseworkers had questions about the implementation of welfare reform, most did not question its basic philosophical thrust. With the primary focus being on work, caseworkers considered clients' needs and responsibilities as parents in very limited ways. They were more concerned with how parenting impacted mothers' participation in the system than with the impact of work on parenting. Caseworkers talked repeatedly about the pressures brought to bear on them to put clients to work. Even though their primary job was eligibility determination for TANF, there was a resource room in every PA office with job postings where PA caseworkers were expected to help clients focus on job searching. In addition, basic eligibility for TANF involved establishing clients' work history and sanctioning them if they did not participate in work readiness programs. The E and T workers were more directly responsible for getting TANF clients into the workforce. Under the federal "work first" policy, they had few options for clients who had little education, training, or work experience other than to refer them to GED programs, for those without a high school diploma, or a limited number of work-readiness programs. There was no funding for advanced training.

As a result, most clients were being pushed into low-wage work. Tourism is a major part of the economy of San Antonio, and the work associated with it involves low-wage, low-skill jobs (Cruz 1999). San Antonio workers earned the second-lowest average salary among the fifty largest metropolitan counties in the United States (Pesquera 2001). Similar to the experiences recounted throughout this volume by the mothers who participated in the Three-City Study, caseworkers reported that the jobs for which clients were most often eligible were part-time, involved shift work, and had no benefits—employment particularly unsuited to the needs of parents.

These realities notwithstanding, PA caseworkers, who determined eligibility for TANF, talked about parenting in terms of a limited set of behaviors that if not performed would result in a sanction. Those program requirements that related specifically to parenting involved seeing that children attended school regularly and had their immunizations and annual medical checkups. E and T caseworkers, who were responsible for seeing that clients found jobs, generally confined their concerns about mothers' parenting to encouraging them to find appropriate child care while they worked.

Again consistent with the mothers' stories examined elsewhere in this volume, almost all of the E and T caseworkers mentioned child care as a major obstacle to client self-sufficiency. A female Latin American E and T caseworker talked about the particular problems of finding child care centers that provided pickup and delivery of infants, since many TANF clients didn't have cars. (A number of day care centers refused to pick up infants because of liability issues.) Child care for shift workers was particularly challenging. Many clients had hotel and restaurant jobs that operated seven days a week at all hours. Child care was a problem when parents had to work weekends and their child care was provided only Monday through Friday. A number of clients lost their jobs because they didn't show up for work on the weekends due to lack of child care.

An African American E and T caseworker elaborated on these problems with child care. She said, "Once we get them in the system, it's not always easy to keep them on the jobs, because children are so often ill. And day care centers . . . they have their rules, and they don't hesitate to call a person on their job and say, 'You need to come pick your child up.'" According to this caseworker, issues with parenting, either a child's illness or a child's suspension from school, were challenges for mothers trying to work. However, she felt that mothers needed to find other ways to deal with these problems, because, as she said, "I, too, have a child." This caseworker admitted that when a day care called and asked a parent to pick up a child, there was no alternative to leaving the workplace unless a relative was available. She also reported that some mothers had had negative experiences with child care or feared putting their children in one.

Public assistance caseworkers complained about problems with transitional child care and were concerned that some clients "fell through the cracks" when referred to the E and T agency, which was responsible for linking clients with child care services. This problem was not merely one of perception. This E and T agency had been sanctioned several times by its parent organization for poor performance (Russell 2000a; 2000b) and was responsible for the loss of $4.4 million in child care funds for low-income parents in 2000 (Russell 1999; 2000b).

Caseworkers also cited transportation as a problem, since most clients did not own a car. Lack of transportation limited their job searches because jobs were not always located adjacent to bus lines. As a result, clients sometimes had to take two buses to get to work, and then two buses to get to the day care to pick up their child by closing time.

When asked about differences between people who transitioned off TANF and those who did not, one female European American PA caseworker responded, "Child care is a very big factor. But it's also the client and their willingness, their attitude, their determination, to work. Some of them don't have any intention of finding a job." A large number of caseworkers' conversations about clients revolved around this issue of "motivation." Consistent with the neoliberal view of individual responsibility, with rare exceptions caseworkers did not consider other reasons why clients might appear unmotivated, even when prompted. Motivation was defined in terms of clients' individual actions, as this European American male caseworker said:

> It's basically, from my perspective—it's a mind-set. You know, there are some people out there that no matter how low they get, it's "Poor me." There are other people out there that are temporary, that may have lost a job, and it's just a temporary thing. There are other people that say, "Hey, it's about time I did something about this. I don't want to be like this for the rest of my life," and they'll work to get off the benefits. So you've got a

combination of all those. But as I said before, I think now with the welfare reform, the good economy [this interview took place in 1999], we're starting to see more of the people that either don't want to, don't know how to, no matter how much you push them and try to get them to, they just don't want to.

To reinforce his point, the caseworker talked about long-term clients who were not working but had missed recertification appointments. They missed appointment after appointment until their benefits were denied. Only then did they take action to comply with agency regulations. Behaving proactively and not waiting until outside forces took over was considered evidence of motivation. Family responsibilities and the tensions inherent in parenting and working rarely entered into the conversations about clients' motivation to work.

A few caseworkers did discuss clients' family responsibilities. One female African American E and T caseworker replied as follows when asked about program successes:

I do believe that there are people who are making progress. I must admit that there are a couple whom I have always thought of as success stories; there's things that are now happening in their lives, and we're trying to look for some ways around some barriers that have come up. Because the feeling is, "If I don't do this, nobody else can," like, "My daughter's in the hospital, and I have to be there for her," or "My child is keeping me from going to work, because he's not going to school. I'm being called into court on a regular basis. I'm having problems." We do our best to give referrals to the appropriate agencies that can actually go into the home to help with some counseling. But when you're raising teenagers nowadays, and you're raising teenagers in an atmosphere like this, it's a big problem, and how to get around it, other than giving referrals for counseling in the home, I can find no other way around it, or resources. And they have to work it out in some way, shape, or form. They just have to work it out. If not, people are coming back to TANF.

In fact, there is no other person who can take the role of a parent, and this caseworker was cognizant of both that fact and of the impact this important role had on mothers' ability to work outside the home.

Another female African American PA caseworker talked about the parenting skills of some of the mothers with whom she worked. She said that many of them were so depressed, withdrawn, and wrapped up with their financial problems or their relationships with boyfriends or former partners that they couldn't give their children the attention they needed. As a result, many of the children were perceived as hyperactive and labeled with ADHD. However, such recognition of the pressures of parenting on work was rare in caseworkers' discussions of clients.

Differences Among Caseworkers' Attitudes

As in the mothers' stories presented elsewhere in this volume (Bruinsma, chap. 2; Lein et al. chap. 1; Skinner Lachicotte, and Burton chap. 6), caseworkers weighed clients' roles as mothers and workers. Unlike these mothers, however, they consistently focused on their clients' role as workers and sanctioned those mothers who did not meet work and training requirements. Caseworkers expressed the pressure they felt within the organization to put clients to work. However, there were distinctions between caseworkers. Some were much more likely to take a "tough love" stance with clients, tending to view those clients' situations largely in terms of personal motivation and responsibility. They did not focus much on circumstances, environmental problems, or social barriers that might influence clients' actions. Four of the caseworkers interviewed seemed to represent this stance. Two of them were European American men, both retired military personnel. As one of them stated:

> I think the Medicaid and food stamps [recipients], the majority of them, are working hard to try to get ahead. I think now in the TANF, especially with the economy being so good [this interview was also conducted in 1999], the TANF rolls are dropping. And I think the people that we're seeing now are what you would call the "chronic" people that probably don't want to work. When they do get a job—one of the things we always ask them for is copies of their last four pay stubs—and it's very rare that if they're working twenty hours a week that they put in twenty hours a week. Or if they're supposed to be working forty hours, it's very rare that you'll see them working forty hours. Now, understandably, a lot of them are in lower-paying jobs, domestic

jobs, hotel jobs, that sometimes depend on how busy the business is, too. But I think a lot of times it's because they just don't feel like going to work that day.

When asked if he thought this was a problem of motivation or perhaps a problem of mental health or substance abuse, he stressed, "I think there is a lot of motivation problems with a lot of the clients that we do see."

One young female Latin American E and T caseworker said that one of the most frustrating things about her job was that different generations "all use the same excuses for not participating or for quitting their job. That is frustrating, you know. Because it's, you know, the same thing over and over and over." She said clients used the excuse of having no child care, but she could go outside her office, which was located in a public housing development, and see the same women hanging out, their children nowhere in sight. Apparently someone was taking care of the children, so she believed that the excuses clients offered for not getting a job were not legitimate. Another female European American PA caseworker complained that welfare reforms in Texas, which in 2000 involved sanctioning only the parent, didn't go far enough in providing motivation for clients to work:

> I think that the time limits, I mean, it's good, but the thing is, OK, they—the mother's gonna be taken off, but not the children. So it's really not, it's not like a threat to them. You know, they can still receive TANF and cash for the children. Their needs are just removed. And that's one thing that I don't like. 'Cause if they're gonna cut them off, then—if we're telling them, "You're not gonna be eligible any longer," then I think it should be for everyone, for the whole household.

In her mind, clients needed full family sanctions to motivate them. Sanctioning only the mother was not a sufficient encouragement to work. (It should be noted that in 2004, the Texas legislature initiated full-family sanctions.)

In comparison, seven of the caseworkers interviewed were much more attuned to factors other than individual motivation that might influence clients' abilities. Three of them talked about their own experiences as mothers and seemed to empathize with women's struggles to be both parent and worker. As one Latin American E and T caseworker, a single mom and former recipient, said,

I always use myself as an example, because a lot of them say, "You don't know what I've been through."

But I can say, "Yes, I have." So I say, "I'll tell you what I've been through, and you can tell me if it's like what you've been through." Sometimes they'll tell me No, and sometimes they'll tell me Yes. I tell them, "I'm a single parent. I have two children."

So they'll say, "Well, how do you do it? It must be hard to balance all of this."

But I say, "No, it's only as hard as you make it." And then they'll tell me that they're in debt up to here and stuff like that. And I say, "I understand that." But I say, "You know what? Your kids are going to grow up, and you only have that time with your children, and you only have that time to better yourself. Why not do it now? You have all this stuff backing you up. They've got supportive services, transportation services. . . . If I can do it, then you can do it.

Other caseworkers drew on their experiences as mothers to empathize with clients. As one female African American PA caseworker said, "I'm not afraid to share myself and my successes and my failures. . . . A lot of the experiences that these residents have, I've had them in some way, shape, or form in my life. I'm not afraid to say, 'That's where I've been.'"

However, not all caseworkers who empathized with clients drew from their experience as mothers. The housing caseworker, a Latin American male, believed that residents of public housing were no different from other people. He said that most people were only two paychecks away from public housing. A female Latin American E and T supervisor looked at the bigger picture that surrounded welfare reform and asked,

What we have seen is, when they wrote this law, is it real that these people are going to make the wage at six dollars, seven dollars, and pay for child care? Everything else is a piece of cake: transportation—we're talking child care if they have four small children. Is it real? I mean, can they afford it? I think we have to go back and look at that area, the aftereffect—what happens when people are really getting off the rolls?

Caseworkers' personal histories and points of view influenced the extent to which they saw and addressed the many stresses that face poor women subject to the new constraints of welfare reform. For most caseworkers, bound as they were to the philosophy of "work first," clients' concerns as mothers were addressed only so far as they impinged on their ability to work. Even within these constraints, however, some individual caseworkers were able to articulate the tensions inherent in the effort to turn poor mothers into low-wage workers.

Implications for Welfare Policy

In carrying out the dictates of the new welfare reform regime, caseworkers in all three agencies interviewed conformed to the "work first" mandate in dealing with clients. The targets of this policy are low-income women, many of whom have responsibilities caring for children in addition to their responsibilities as wage earners. Caseworkers, who come into closest contact with these low-income mothers, were aware of the ways in which this approach conflicted with clients' roles as mothers. The problems implicit and explicit in the welfare reform law itself find expression in the contradictions faced not just by clients but also by caseworkers. By examining caseworker attitudes we can learn a lot about the underlying meaning of welfare reform and examine the assumptions on which it is based.

In general, caseworkers did not address the inherent dilemmas of this policy for clients *as parents*, but rather for them *as workers*. Parenting became a problem that interfered with work, rather than work outside the home constituting a problem that interfered with parenting. In the process of working with clients, some caseworkers were more attuned than others to the external obstacles clients faced. However, as previous studies of caseworkers have found, this exposure did not necessarily lead them to a broader critique of welfare policy (Henrici, chap. 9; Kingfisher 1996; Morgen 2001). Rather, as in these other studies, many blamed clients for their failings, labeling some "good" and some "bad," generally on the basis of their assessment of the clients' personal motivation. By blaming "bad" clients for their lack of success and using their limited discretionary power to provide extra service to "good" clients, caseworkers were able to maintain the sense that they were doing a good job. In the face of organizational pressures to turn TANF clients into workers, and with few resources to do otherwise, some caseworkers may use the concept of client motivation to help them feel OK about working in a system that asks a lot of and offers little to TANF clients. The problem with this strategy is that it reinforces the social distinction between the deserving and the undeserving poor and ignores barriers and social structures that keep poor women poor.

As we have seen elsewhere in this volume, clients may also blame "the system," or caseworkers as its representatives, for their failures (Henrici and Miller, chap. 3). It should be noted that in some cases clients' problems, like human problems generally, really are a matter of noncompliance, lack of motivation, or other personal failing. Recognizing this does not mean that caseworkers do not also bear some responsibility. However, without considering the context in which people—both caseworkers and clients—must be responsible, the idea of personal responsibility becomes almost meaningless.

Although here and elsewhere in this volume we argue that attention to low-income mothers' roles as caregivers is eroding as a result of welfare reform, it is possible that this lack of concern for poor women's ability to parent does *not* represent a shift in policy. Whereas the early history of welfare involved extensive intervention in the family lives of poor families, legislation in the 1960s seriously curtailed this type of intervention in clients' parenting except in cases of the most egregious abuse and neglect (Mink 1995, 1998). It is also possible that there are nuances in caseworkers' attitudes and possible acts of resistance to the ideology of "work first" that are lost due to the small sample, method of data collection, and secondary analysis used. It is possible that a study focused on this specific topic might produce a different picture of caseworkers' attitudes toward TANF clients' dual roles as workers and mothers.

The most fundamental questions that this study raises join those raised by others in this volume: If poor women are expected to focus on being workers rather than parents, who will care for their children? What is our responsibility as a society for our members' success, including those members who experience personal, situational, or societal barriers? The latest versions of TANF reauthorization call for increased work requirements for mothers, without proportional increases in supportive services such as child care funding. Within the framework of "work first," low-income single mothers will continue to be pushed out of their parenting role and into the workplace, without adequate supports for caring for their own children. As noted repeatedly throughout this volume, and as Bruinsma's chapter on child care (chap. 2) makes clear, child care subsidies are critical to women's ability to participate in a low-wage labor force that requires availability and flexibility.

It appears that the problems that ensue from the philosophy of welfare reform cannot be resolved within its framework. Naples (1997) suggests that we step out of that framework by examining the racial, gender, and economic assumptions embedded in PRWORA— for example, the idea of the "family wage" upon which social welfare in this country is based. Esping-Andersen (1999) argues that the male-breadwinner family is almost extinct and that social welfare policies that derive from it should be reexamined. Policies based on this model reinforce women's inequality and dependence on men. Furthermore, they stigmatize as "undeserving" racial and ethnic groups whose family structures depart most radically from this norm and drive a wedge between low-income women and middle-class women. By labeling some mothers as deserving (those attached to a male breadwinner) and others as undeserving, they mask the ways in which a focus on the family wage handicaps all women.

Mink (1998) proposes that we reconceive welfare as a payment owed to women and men who provide caregiving for dependent children or elders. Skinner, Lachicotte, and Burton (chap. 6, this vol.) make a similar suggestion with particular regard to parents who care for children with special needs. In addition to generating greater child care funding and investment in workplace equity for women, who provide most of this care work, such a rethinking of welfare would also allow for a range of choices about work and parenting, particularly for low-income women. It would ensure that those women who want to focus on child rearing are allowed to do so, whereas those who want to combine work with child rearing would have the economic support to make work a viable way to support their families. Such a paradigm shift might alleviate the potential damage to the children of poor working mothers inherent in the current pressure under PRWORA to force poor mothers to work.

Acknowledgments

The author wishes to thank Ron Angel, Julie Beausoleil, Miguel Gomez, Laura Lein, Liz Lilliott, Kathleen Murphy, Melissa Radey, Stephanie Rivaux, and Mandy Rutherford for their assistance in the preparation of this chapter, as well as the public welfare caseworkers who gave their time and attention as respondents.

agents of change

Nonprofit Organization Workers Following Welfare Reform

Jane Henrici

"People say to me, 'How can you work there?' about [the neighbor-hood]. I tell them it's changed." The social service provider sits in her tidy office in the one-year-old, brightly painted building located on the west side of San Antonio. She tells me that she is in her thirties, married, English speaking, and Hispanic. She works in the neighbor-hood, but does not live there. She characterizes those who live in the surrounding publicly subsidized houses and apartments as young, Hispanic, and English-speaking mothers. She states that those women need her and her organization "to become better parents," but mentions no mutual or reciprocal need for them. She does not indicate anything she might have in common with those to whom she provides GED and computer classes, child care, and other ser-vices, yet notes her own, as well as their, desire to "strive to become better." I am speaking with her because she is paid as one of the staff members of a private nonprofit organization, established to help low-income Mexican American women with young children, that now receives contracts to assist women regardless of race, national origin, or ethnicity as part of the neoliberal privatization of social services that Welfare-to-Work supports.

Private organizations supply social services within the current economy and benefits system of the United States, and nonprofit organization workers have to deal with that responsibility. Talking extensively with service providers in a range of San Antonio agencies as part of the neighborhood study of Welfare, Children, and Fam-ilies: A Three-City Study, other researchers and I find that, as H. Bell discusses in chapter 8, social service workers are positioned between the organizations in which they are employed, families in need of support, and larger economic and political contexts of a racialized and gendered neighborhood and nation (Gent 2002). This chapter focuses on nonprofit organization employees within San Antonio urban neighborhoods following the implementation of welfare reform in the United States, and it emphasizes issues of identity among the workers and between them and those they try to assist.

Community nonprofit workers interviewed in San Antonio, Texas, express themselves with rhetoric that cuts across differences in worker backgrounds. Meanwhile, shared responses by these providers to ongoing, as well as changing, demands following welfare reform can have differentiated, gendered, and racialized effects between them and those they work to help (M. Brown 2003).

Throughout the United States, service providers and their clients need to assist each other if organizations are to stay in business, jobs for both agency workers and their clients are to be kept, and families are to become what is known in the United States as "self-sufficient." However, many nonprofit organization workers view those who seek assistance as in need of improvement, and the agency as responsible to achieve that. Few providers attempt to change the established system in order to address either what their clients most commonly request, such as expanded child care (Bruinsma, chap. 2) or privately owned housing (Salcido, chap. 4), or even what welfare reform demands that they obtain, which is a sufficient and reliable wage so that they are able to support themselves and their families without requiring public financial support.

Those organization workers who were themselves formerly recipients of cash or other benefits now emphasize that they have "made it" as an illustration of what poorer women today should be doing right but somehow aren't. In other words, nonprofit organization staff members try to develop themselves, and they insist on the same for their clients. They note distinctions between themselves and those they help, but not the possibility that their roles and circumstances are at least similar within the larger system, if not relational or possibly mutually determined.

In addition, there is silence on the subject of gender within such rhetoric, and references to identity that do appear—to race, ethnicity, national origin, generation, and individual character—sometimes seek to lay blame on a group or person, whether clients or other practitioners, rather than give some sort of structural or systemic explanation of disparity or difference. Both the silence and speech reveal potentially adversarial relationships between professionals and clients, as other researchers have observed can occur in social service contexts (Kingfisher 1996).

I conducted interviews with service providers in San Antonio nonprofit organizations while participating in Welfare, Children, and Families: A Three-City Study. The Three-City Study design called for an examination of private and public services in the families' neighborhoods. The purpose of the neighborhood study in particular was to gather contextual information about local resource distribution and responses of community agencies to the changed benefits system, and interviews with private nonprofit as well as public agencies contributed to this part of the larger project.

I initially met with local organization workers to get their help recruiting families to interview for the larger study and to establish neighborhood information contacts. I also spent time making observations within nonprofit organizations at various points over the years of the research project, and I supervised a set of graduate students and postgraduates who produced other observations and interviews. Additionally, several of the workers within these institutions who practiced in different neighborhoods generously spoke with me for many hours about their lives, work, and attitudes, and those interviews provide the basis of this chapter.

Nonprofit Organizations and Welfare Reform

Welfare reform in the United States was set in place within the larger international economic environment of devolution and privatization of the mid-1990s. Policy makers and analysts knew, prior to PRWORA's passage, that moving system funds away from governmental agencies and toward nongovernmental institutions could bring difficulties to the private organizations, if not to their clients (Alexander 1999; Fink et al. 2001). At the same time, planners and legislators did not hesitate to shift that money, and continue to do so, because of their greater concern for a liberalized global economy (Morgen 2001; O'Connor, Orloff, and Shaver 1999).

On the one hand, that framework stimulates commercial corporations such as Lockheed Martin to create their own nonprofit units, as well as the multiplication of "faith-based" programs, all eligible to receive public contracts for Welfare-to-Work. On the other hand, the new framework means that those organizations already in place in relevant neighborhoods compete for Welfare-to-Work contracts as well. Staff and administrators in existing organizations have had to respond to the fact that the system has changed in terms of requirements for their clients and for their own agencies (Reisch and Sommerfeld 2002).

Within the changed benefits system in Texas, state-level government workers often consider it their responsibility to "divert" applicants from public assistance, as H. Bell discusses in chapter 8. Even in those circumstances in which a government agency worker approves aid to a low-income family in San Antonio, adults who seek aid must typically look for either employment, support elsewhere, or both regardless of poor health or other obstacles. Caseworkers soften the assignment with a promise of cash assistance and child care subsidies, allowable for a limited time and only with proof of employment or educational activity, regardless of the availability or quality of either the child care or adult education, issues that Lein et al. (chap. 1), Bruinsma (chap. 2), and Henrici and Miller (chap. 3) consider.

Nonprofit agency workers in San Antonio then provide, often through government subcontracting, noncash support such as child care, transportation help, and employment referrals that the low-income families have been allotted. As in other states, private agency workers structure and make available activities such as classes on parenting and job training required of many adults within Welfare-to-Work (Rom 1999).

Previous researchers were concerned that private organizations, particularly neighborhood-level nonprofits, would be too small and specialized to successfully take on the new levels of work that devolution sent their way. Primarily, investigators worried about how the inability to follow through might affect the clients that neighborhood agencies serve (Edin and Lein 1998).

Some researchers also focus on privatization with specific concern for its increasing support of for-profit businesses within the benefits system, out of concern for evaluating its effectiveness in providing help to low-income families (Rom 1999). Another interest has been in the change to the neighborhood as a context (Coulton 2000–1). Finally, a number of scholars have investigated responses of government agency workers to their continuing, though changing, relations with clients (Morgen 2001).

Few studies of nonprofit workers' responses to welfare reform exist, and those that do tend to be framed as part of analyses of the nonprofit agencies themselves (Fink et al. 2001; Reisch and Sommerfeld 2002). Although more research needs to address issues of race and ethnic identity among communities, providers, and clients, such studies that do exist report that nonprofit organizations developed three patterns in the 1990s, which affect the workers hired and their interactions with clients. These three are of interest here.

First, efforts to "professionalize" nongovernment organizations (NGOs) and nonprofits in the mold of for-profit businesses seem to attract funding but discourages less conventional programming and activities, including those that target local concerns and customs (Alexander 1999; Markowitz and Tice 2001; Morgen 1990). Recent documentation indicates that accompanying emphasis on standardization and "accountability" limits the ability of agencies to assist clients who need long-term case management and those who have low incomes, particularly racial and ethnic minorities. Furthermore, not all nonprofits receive additional support and funding in return for investment in the expenses and limitations of for-profit operating standards (Alexander 1999; Reisch and Sommerfeld 2002, 169).

A second development is that a nonprofit may focus in practice on helping a specific category of client along lines of gender, race, class, or ethnicity, but in mission statements it could leave that focus unacknowledged. Meanwhile, the primary categories of clients served might be suggested indirectly and imprecisely, for example, within San Antonio by use of a non-English word or a community leader's surname in the agency's name, or vaguely through broader categories of affiliation, as in "faith-based." One reason that neighborhood founders might imply such an affiliation rather than openly state it is to afford flexibility in negotiating with participants in the wider political system who may not share the basic values of those founders (Quane et al. 2002). Although stating a direct link to a specific ethnicity or race for an organization, its workers, or an event might seem unnecessary, implying them nevertheless affects how community residents and other institutions view and use an activity or service (Goode 2001). At the same time, keeping such an affiliation vague suggests ecumenical and multicultural tolerance and capacity.

These two major issues combine within governmental devolution and privatization to form a third: the possibility of inequitable resource distribution. From a local response to a neighborhood need, a participating organization's program within Welfare-to-Work comes to replace the earlier and maligned central government's one-size-fits-all package. Nonprofit organizations might originate with one client base and possibly locally sensitive or politically activist objectives, but then must take on a wider constituency and still make their programs work. At the same time as they work within a new climate of increased "accountability," these agencies have contracts to help across neighborhoods and regions, races and ethnicities.

Agency activities should in theory be easier to track and their programs easier to evaluate, even as all of those activities might lose some of their special character. Instead, devolution of national responsibilities to state and local entities can obscure revealing practices both of difference and of discrimination. To learn whether an organization in fact principally serves one group or another at any one time, intake and treatment records must be used (Alexander 1999; Reisch and Sommerfeld 2002). Meanwhile, as a woman with decades of experience in San Antonio private and public welfare agencies put it, the new directors of new agencies charged with choosing and evaluating the new Texas Welfare-to-Work contractors were in fact the "Old Boys" who ran things long before the benefits system changed, but the special interests of those directors remained unchanged.

Money moved, but perhaps not the distance that supporters of restructuring and privatization claimed. Certain programs in some neighborhoods no longer operate, whereas other organizations continue to swell; meanwhile, tracing the actual flow of the money in Welfare-to-Work is difficult.

At junctures, San Antonio service providers seem not to question whether their community-based programs can expand to cover all contingencies and populations. They seem to consider the new model capable of being simultaneously community-based and able to respond to situations in a range of contexts. However, do the organization workers provide broader awareness of and commitment to a diversifying clientele and to the wider neighborhood? Observations and interviews indicate that the reactions of workers vary: some implement long-term adaptations whereas others resist.

This chapter considers individual workers rather than the organizations. In part, this research approach was intended to explore the choices made by such service providers. For example, like the private agencies in which they are employed, specific workers must "professionalize"; as they reach goals such as acquisition of titles and degrees, these staff members may leave to take positions with better salaries or benefits, which, in turn, can affect agencies and relationships with clients.

Furthermore, this approach encompasses the backgrounds of these workers and considers whether they had experience as welfare or other public assistance recipients. Examining overlapping categories of identity can highlight patterns of shared expectation and opportunities for communication between service providers and clients (compare Kingfisher 1996). Most of the workers we interviewed are women who are, or have been, changing their situations and organizations following welfare reform. Their views and activities add to the larger configuration of low-income families, neighborhoods, and public and private service agencies and their articulation with gender, race, ethnicity, national origin, and generation.

In the following section, I will describe briefly the methods used to gather information from individual workers in service organizations. I will follow with a short depiction of San Antonio and its low-income, mixed resource neighborhoods and their organizations at the time of research. Then I will concentrate on narratives from interviews with service providers who worked in two agencies that operate in historically and culturally distinct neighborhoods within San Antonio. One of these neighborhoods is almost entirely Mexican American, whereas the other is historically African American, though as one service provider puts it, "Right now I guess it's about equal with the blacks and the Hispanics." I have reviewed the 255 documents of the Neighborhood Study in San Antonio for a longer paper, but in the following I will select and address four issues that seem to concentrate both on nonprofit organization service providers and on the general context of neighborhood agencies after welfare reform.

Interviews and Nonprofits

Both governmental and nongovernmental organizations in San Antonio are critical to the qualitative and quantitative components of the Three-City Study at many levels. Researchers of the San Antonio site team talked with neighborhood and state agency directors and their staff to gain permission and access to groups of appropriate families, as well as to gather neighborhood resource information.

The project required families with preschool-aged children, so researchers initially approached community agencies that house child and day care centers. These included the only Head Start contractor in San Antonio at that time, an organization that owned most of the city's child care centers. Only a few of the organizations expressed reluctance directly, and that was due to skepticism that the results would be used to help the communities being studied. Only one child care agency checked researcher credentials and backgrounds before allowing access to families with small children. Most of the organizations simply looked over the documentation on the project and welcomed researchers as volunteer workers, so any subsequent difficulties obtaining interviews with family members or service providers had to do less with institutional obstructions than with respondents' time constraints.

The San Antonio team contacted approximately fifteen private nonprofit community centers that contained child care centers, two of which were faith-based. It also sought families through other institutions, such as government and nongovernmental health and housing facilities. The former could not provide contact information for ethnographers to reach families, nor would most of their staff ask families to make contact with the ethnographers. Small agencies that work with low-cost housing turned out to have the same time and resource constraints as the smaller child care centers and thus rarely could help provide interviews or contacts for interviews. However, they were resources for observations that fieldworkers collected about the range of responses organization workers made after welfare reform. Meanwhile, the San Antonio Housing Authority gave enormous assistance to low-income families and access to service providers.

In their efforts to obtain recruiting help and as gestures of gratitude the San Antonio ethnographers offered the organizations policy information, public presentations of study findings, computer training, and grant proposal assistance. A range of incentives was provided to nongovernmental agencies or their staff members when appropriate, from supplies for day cares to public lectures for agency conferences. Furthermore, student field ethnographers spent time volunteering in after-school and weekend projects in order to meet children and their parents directly, to lessen unease about talking to researchers, and to help out with organization activities.

After establishing and keeping in contact with roughly forty agencies and program workers, researchers met low-income families through direct contact, staff introductions, or occasionally lists provided by service providers. The same pool of public and private agencies provided the core of interviews for the Neighborhood Study, and a variety of other individuals who worked with municipal, federal, and private concerns in the communities spoke with project researchers.

San Antonio is a Southwestern city with a growing population. This growth has come primarily through an increase in the percentage of recent immigrants and Latinos/as, of which Mexican Americans continue to form the preponderance. The ties with Mexico are not limited to historic background and geographic proximity, but also include strengthened economic connections due to the existence of a major highway corridor that extends through the southern Texas city of San Antonio directly to the northern Mexican city of Monterrey. Meanwhile, the percentage of African Americans within San Antonio is diminishing slightly, while that of families of mixed race and ethnicity is growing. As already noted, service agencies that participate in Welfare-to-Work programs declare themselves citywide in reach, but the women workers interviewed individually reveal that resources vary according to different local communities and neighborhoods.

Race and ethnicity, as well as generation, gender, and class, were factors in the relationships that agencies had established within zip codes, census tracts, voting districts, and the related geopolitical units of neighborhoods. Research methods for the Three-City Study responded to differences among these community-agency relationships. For example, the most consistent strategy in recruiting African American families was to go to child care and Head Start centers and assist the instructors with the children in the afternoon until the parents came. For Mexican American families, a parenting program with a child care facility proved extremely helpful after the director permitted researchers to work there in fall of 1999. Service providers introduced ethnographers to women who were participating in GED preparation and parenting classes as part of their Welfare-to-Work requirements. The strategy in this center, and in all of those that primarily involved Mexican American workers and families, tended to be slightly more structured and hierarchical than for other organizations: the GED and Welfare-to-Work training instructors would introduce the project manager and field researchers to a class of women during a prearranged class time and then allow a set number of minutes for exchanges and sign-ups to take place.

Concurrent with the implementation of welfare reform during the mid to late 1990s, federal housing changes (Salcido, chap. 4, this vol.), military base cuts, and other factors of migration and immigration changed the neighborhoods in San Antonio. Altered composition affected overall counts of racial and ethnic categories so that more Spanish speakers appeared in neighborhoods that had historically been primarily African American, and more families of mixed African descent listed themselves in neighborhoods that had been almost exclusively Mexican American for more than a century. In addition, movement of families away from the central parts of the city pulled large numbers of children away from the elementary schools and child care centers in these neighborhoods, which in turn caused cuts in federal funds and city subsidies formerly used to pay for resources such as child counselors and after-school programs.

In response to new or growing demands, such as needs for counseling after school staff cuts and for aid from food pantries following welfare reform, neighborhood organizations reported a necessity to make adjustments and find new funding. This was a preoccupation that intensified time and resource constraints in the late 1990s, and it affected how service providers viewed families in the neighborhoods. That is, an increasing number of families were relatively unknown to agency staff at that time; no longer were these neighborhoods made up of long-time associates, neighbors, or extended kin relations that had comprised many of the clientele during the preceding decades. A sense of distrust, often limited to a literal interpretation of contracts or government requirements, appeared in some of the worker-client relations, rather than a shared sense of obligation or affection between organization workers and those who had relied on assistance for years, if not generations.

Women and Their Work

Women workers in private nonprofits and those who labor in community centers across the United States currently deal with increased demands for accountability, as do their clients. Thus, women caseworkers and their clients occasionally have analogously chang-ing conditions, and occasionally they come from similar back-grounds. Although few agency workers and aid recipients in San Antonio claimed to share identities of gender, race, or ethnicity, many case workers described having uncomfortably close experi-ences with difficult jobs, low incomes, unrealized educational aspira-tions, and negotiations and calculations brought on by poverty. Women in these contexts often battle against blame as circum-stances worsen, as has been shown to have been the case even before welfare reform (Kingfisher 1996).

The changing construct of low-income woman with children as they move from "mother" to "worker," which Bruinsma and H. Bell (chaps. 2 and 8) discuss, and the current focus on the employability of women with few resources occur as part of contemporary rela-tionships that government policy and civic response have formed. Certainly, women are crucial to change in benefits policy and allo-cation. Within U.S. public practice and globalizing development, women are subjects of study and objects of improvement, as well as activists and volunteers who make policy possible (Henrici 2002; Susser 1997).

The descriptions I provide here are based on conversations with women in diverse neighborhoods. These women service providers tell stories filled with self-diagnosis, explanations that use varied terms derived from different training and backgrounds, to help lis-teners understand long-term commitment to a community. In rich anecdotes and life narratives, practitioners describe how they came to work in day care and youth activity centers, food pantries, hous-ing developments, and adult education programs. They offer their own personal views about their work and neighborhoods. In addi-tion, these women make suggestions about what they believe would be improvements.

To begin, I would like to present more background concerning the words of Elena, quoted earlier, who works with classes on parent-ing and other subjects in a primarily Mexican American neighbor-hood of San Antonio. Elena is from San Antonio, but from a different part of town than the one in which she now works on a daily basis. She recognizes that difference in background rather than any com-monality with her clients, and she notices other differences, as well.

Of those women in the neighborhood who participate in GED,

computer literacy, and parenting classes, and come directly from Mexico or other nations, she says, "They're more into wanting to learn, wanting to get ahead," than those born in the United States. This statement, representative of stereotypes about the first-generation migrant and immigrant, is shared by others in her agency, but it is often expressed by other workers with less admiration for the Mexican national and more frustration for U.S.-born women.

The families in the surrounding neighborhood are primarily Mexican American. Relatively few of them come from Central America or the Caribbean, whereas another minority is comprised of African Americans whose families have lived for generations on this tract of land, which was once part of Mexico. One section of the neighborhood is a sprawling, newly rebuilt housing development that surrounds the agency building, and two other housing developments can be found within a few miles. Residents of these developments and the streets of one- and two-bedroom wooden homes that form them are almost exclusively U.S.-born Mexican Americans with a minority of biracial families, who have recently been increasing in number. Another section of the neighborhood also has a housing development at its center. African Americans and the growing number of recent Spanish-speaking Mexican American and Caribbean immigrants of various races tend to live here, although the majority of this section also remains Mexican American. Elena says there is a difference between the women in these two sections: her clients in the first are more alert, and "you kind of have to convince them" of their need for the programs. With the others, "you just have to tell them," and they will go along with your program as it is set up.

Elena says that she has noticed this contrast growing between the populations of the two parts of the neighborhood over the years she has worked there. She argues that another change has also taken place among younger generations of Latinas in both sections in that they are not quite as cooperative as those who are older. In this sense, Elena observes a difference within families in San Antonio beyond what she detects in the distinct racial, ethnic, and national origin backgrounds of these women and their families.

However, despite Elena's description of relative passivity among residents in the second section of the neighborhood, which centers on a historically black community, her organization had not succeeded at the time of my interviews in setting up classes for parenting in other San Antonio neighborhoods where African Americans have historically formed historic majorities. Elena says that, among other things, African American women seem to object to the forms of address she and her coworkers use to refer to clients and their small children, for example, *m'jita* (my daughter) and *bebito* (baby boy). She is uncertain about the reason for being unsuccessful in the past, but is optimistic about success in the future because of her organization's expanded state contracts. In other words, she seems to attribute differences and difficulties to young Latinas within one neighborhood—and to African Americans within others—rather than to any possible need of her own or her program to changes.

Next, I would like to turn to the words of two service providers who worked together at the time of my interviews in a San Antonio neighborhood occupied primarily by African Americans for at least one hundred years. The stories of these two agency workers converge and diverge in ways that seem connected to their own personal histories and that of the neighborhood. Both women are in their forties, have raised several children, and live in this historically African American part of the city. One of them, Rosa, is a U.S. citizen who immigrated to the United States from Mexico, whereas the other, Kathy, is an African American originally from this area.

After living in a small Texas town, Rosa moved to San Antonio in order to be closer to the national border and other Hispanics. She chose San Antonio rather than a border town because she "had the idea that more interior cities had better education for kids." In addition, she had learned through an Internet search at her former shelter about a Catholic college in San Antonio where she could get a degree in a pilot program in social work.

At the time she sought social welfare assistance in the early 1990s, Rosa was living in a San Antonio shelter hiding from an abusive husband. The caseworker assigned to Rosa wanted her to seek employment immediately. However, Rosa insisted on going to college for her degree in social work and asked for help getting subsidized housing so that she could afford school. The government caseworker provided this aid, but placed her in a housing development located across the city from the college. Rosa has grown to prefer that neighborhood, where she now works, and eventually bought a home for herself nearby. Nevertheless, Rosa says that initially she was frightened to be surrounded by African American neighbors, which was a new experience for her. When asked why she thought the caseworker had assigned her to this neighborhood, Rosa said she believed that the caseworker had done it "to punish" her for not complying with advice given during counseling and to push her to "go to work" and to get her out of an uncomfortable environment.

When asked about this idea of punishment, Rosa responded as if both to judge and pardon the behavior of the counselor that the caseworker had provided Rosa with advice about getting food stamps and housing. Rosa noted that initially there was "blame and resentment" between herself and her service provider. However, the intervention turned out to help Rosa, since it let her know that she "really had to make it" to prove herself to that practitioner. It also introduced Rosa to the community with which she has formed links and in which she has invested her money and career.

"In 1990, there were no Hispanics on [this side of town]," says Rosa. "After I moved, I realized that I was the second white family [in that public apartment building], the first family, Anglo." Rosa formed a safety net of friendships at the housing development with women of African descent and completed college using elaborate bus routes. Now, she says, "All of my friends are black. All of the people I associate with are black." Later, local housing authorities moved families of Mexican descent or nationality to the privately owned but publicly subsidized apartments where she lived because, Rosa speculates, the manager "wanted to upgrade families." These families and her own "would not talk among ourselves," says Rosa. "They were not as helpful [as the blacks]." Rosa blames the Hispanic families themselves for their isolation, and winces as she attributes racialized housing decisions to administrators.

When discussing her clients, whether Latina or African American, Rosa avoids blaming individual women but questions their actions. "I don't see them getting ready" for time limits, observes Rosa, and for what she tells them will be a "phasing out" of other provisions. In this context, Rosa reserves her stronger criticisms for government policies that do not provide affordable child care despite expectations that mothers secure employment.

The other respondent within the same neighborhood of San Antonio, Kathy, is an African American who grew up nearby. "Low income people mostly live in this neighborhood, mostly blacks and

Hispanics, . . ." she observes. "Right now, I guess it's about equal with the blacks and the Hispanics. . . . You have a lot of them that's on welfare, you have some that *do* work, then you have some that decide to make ends meet the best way they can by doing some things that's not ethically correct, like selling drugs." There are jobs, Kathy says, but "Mostly young families, they want fast money and you can't get fast money working in restaurants." Although Kathy admits that recent reports of crime in the neighborhood are few in number, and decreasing compared to figures from past years, she places emphasis on these facts as part of her personal story and of the circumstances through which her family and others are still working.

Kathy talks freely about her own history and those of the children she raised in this neighborhood of two-story, century-old wooden homes interspersed with newer brick and cement apartment complexes. Stating that one son is "a follower," she analyzes choices in terms of personal character in order to explain where her other children have ended up. In her view, character traits such as being a "leader" can be taught. "I guess I was lucky," she states. In Kathy's assessment, two of the three children she raised "took it in," whereas the third is in prison for dealing drugs. Kathy herself is completing work toward professional titles and certificates in child development through a small, historically black private college. She is not doing this because of specific encouragement or challenges from others, she says, but rather because she is a "school-a-holic."

Kathy's description of the changing racial and ethnic mixture in the neighborhood is similar to that of Rosa. However, Kathy's view of the relationships developing in that mixture contrasts with Rosa's. The neighborhood includes a few Puerto Ricans and others of Caribbean origin or ancestry. Kathy classifies these persons as "black" regardless of whether or not English is their first language. Rosa asserts that Hispanic families in the neighborhood, by which she means Mexicans or Mexican Americans, work exclusively neither with one another nor with African American families. However, Kathy argues that Hispanic women help one another's families to the potential detriment of the community's families of non-Latino African descent. When Hispanics preferentially assist one another, as Kathy states they do, it is hard to know the extent to which a demand exists for service. As an example, she points to "certain families" who take more than their share of food from a pantry. Kathy herself admits that they might do this because their families are larger, but this comment is expressed more as a fault than a fact. Regardless of her intention, Kathy's suggestion of blame is not attributed to individual personality.

In general, however, Kathy does not focus her criticisms exclusively on one population or another. She does not place credit or blame on any single set of mothers who seek child care through her agency. Aside from her comment that "they" have moved more Hispanics into her neighborhood and blacks out, she finds nothing particularly problematic about the benefits system. Individuals receive most of Kathy's praise or skepticism, and although "personal responsibility" is not a phrase that she uses, the concept seems close to the way she understands matters.

Interviews and observations with agency workers in nonprofit organizations in San Antonio neighborhoods indicate that these service providers often blame their clients, and sometimes each other, when trying to describe current conditions of poverty. Additional research indicates that women who receive assistance sometimes blame their difficulties on service providers. Further study should also incorporate the experiences and rhetoric of men who work in nonprofits. However, in the context of this chapter, which focuses on the histories women workers share with each other and on calls for caseworkers and clients to "professionalize" and "show responsibility," it seems both divisive and ironic for women to blame someone else.

Simple consideration of the effects that sanctions and reports of such matters as child neglect can have on a woman and her family should be enough to prompt searching for ways either to smooth out or eliminate frictional contacts (Sullivan 1999). Laying blame is certainly one part of these narratives, but ideally it should not be the main focus with respect to nonprofit organization workers, their clients, and the neighborhoods in which they are all struggling. The two main categories of women discussed here, service providers and clients, are related to each other in such a manner that the power held by one helps limit that of the other. As long as they remain divided, they are relatively helpless in comparison to the larger neoliberal system with which both of them must contend.

These matters are of particular concern not because of an imagined construct of some multicultural ideal with the potential to smooth over racial, ethnic, and national differences and erase distinctions among generations and genders. Rather, this chapter is an effort to examine critically the potential consequences of such tensions within neighborhoods and households already divided among themselves and hurt by larger socioeconomic circumstances. Other parts of the discussion left unexplored in this brief chapter are a fuller exploration of the political and historical context of San Antonio (Rosales 2000) and enormous issues of race and ethnicity faced by peoples throughout the Americas (Arreola, 2004; Harrison 1995). The findings of this chapter seem particularly crucial within the context of the social service, workforce, and educational systems of the United States, which are currently racialized and will probably remain that way into the future (Dill et al. 1998; Edin and Harris 1999; England, Christopher, and Reid 1999; Gilens 1996; Kushnick and Jennings 1999; Mink 1990, 2002; Neubeck and Cazenave 2001; Neubeck 2004; K. Newman 2001; Reisch and Sommerfeld 2002; Schneider 2000b; Thomas 1998).

Privatization and devolution in Welfare-to-Work require increasing amounts of effort from women service providers in private nonprofit and public agencies, and from recipients. In many contexts, privatization relates to the apparent lessening of power by nation-states and the growth of power elsewhere in civil society. There is quite a bit of current academic interest in civil society since developments within it involve what some consider movement toward domination by privately owned nongovernmental operations. The shift of power and money away from central control would mean that entrepreneurs, activists, and radicals might all seek opportunities to take part in a matter that crosses boundaries (Mohanty 2004; Reisch and Bischoff 2002). Ideally, these agents of change would collaborate with one another, particularly since "exclusionary practices" can exacerbate racialized and gendered conditions (Ochoa 2004, 227).

Meanwhile, at the local level and on a small scale, perhaps the origin and maintenance of identity within the context of nonprofits needs greater scrutiny, which this chapter attempts to initiate. Privatization can give nonprofit organizations and their workers increased opportunity to direct resources toward local needs and concerns. At the same time, nonprofit organizations and workers can avoid committing themselves and those resources elsewhere.

It is increasingly important to be creatively involved with the system that is currently taking shape, whether nation-states and civil societies actually will share space and regardless of any influence that positioning might have over the changing benefits system. In their ongoing responses to welfare reform, individuals like Elena, Kathy, and Rosa must focus both very narrowly and very broadly. Those of us who study women service providers and benefits recipients simultaneously must avoid "blaming" one set of participants or another if a civil society that includes women's active involvement, one for which we hope, has not yet emerged.

Before interviewing community workers in San Antonio, I was concerned primarily with transformations in policy that affected contemporary nonprofits and grassroots organizations within a neoliberal society. This research project led me to invert my initial focus on large-scale developments even as it extended my concern with issues of local identity. That is, although devolution, privatization, and other global contemporary conditions affect neighborhood nonprofit organizations, workers in those organizations continue to influence impressively the changed benefits system and those who seek aid, just as they often have for decades. Yet they also continue to be, perhaps increasingly, divided among themselves and with those they work so hard to help.

conclusion: welfare reform and low-wage work

A Troubled and Troubling Environment for
Mothers and Children

Linda Burton and Laura Lein

The chapters in this volume all draw on data from the Three-City Study, with substantial emphasis on the experiences of families in San Antonio after welfare reform. There are several reasons for this emphasis. First, Texas, like many southern states, is a "low-payment" state, with relatively small cash transfer payments for welfare recipients and strenuous limits on other support services. Chicago and Boston were both guided by policies that included more generous cash transfers. However, in this current time of budgetary retrenchment, states are increasingly taking an austere approach to social spending. An emphasis on Texas experiences may illuminate the future low-income families will face in a time of constrained social welfare expenditure.

San Antonio, the study site in Texas, is also a "majority minority" city, with a population more than half Hispanic and a sizable (7 percent) African American segment. The growing presence of minority households—and among minority groups, those that are Latino and Latin American—is a national phenomenon. As several of the chapters in this volume indicate, Latino families' experiences with health care (Angel and Lein, chap. 5) and housing (Salcido, chap. 4), among other issues, are distinctive.

A compelling literature explores the relationship between race and public attitudes toward those on welfare, including the relationship after welfare reform. Both the welfare population itself and images of women on welfare have changed over the past century. As the image of a woman on welfare became identified more as an unmarried minority mother, public attitudes toward welfare programs hardened. Welfare reform is based on assumptions that welfare mothers need to be coerced to work and strongly encouraged to get and stay married. However, many of the women we spoke with experienced their own problems with both welfare and family stability around issues of poverty and lack of education, at least as much as race. This is reflected in the central role played by poverty in much of the analysis presented here, in the context of larger-scale analysis that indicates the driving significance of race in the production and conception of poverty.

The Texas economy and the employment options offered to low-income mothers reflect trends that are occurring nationally. San Antonio has lost manufacturing jobs as its economy has turned more to service, health, and tourism. Compared to manufacturing jobs, employment in these sectors is much more likely to be seasonal, irregular, and without benefits.

For these reasons, Texas is an important setting within which to study family life under welfare reform. An analysis of the interplay between low-income, mother-headed families and the institutions that serve them allows us to critically examine the ways in which both welfare and work, as they are organized in the United States, affect the lives of mothers and children. The chapters in this volume, taken together, highlight the comparisons and contrasts between the lived experiences of families in poverty and the assumptions underlying the regulatory environment of the welfare system.

Indeed, welfare reform, as encoded in PRWORA, is based on several myths or assumptions that the chapters in this book, as well as other research, challenge. These myths include the following, as we discussed in the Introduction:

- That the U.S. economy provides workers, including single mothers, with an appropriate arena within which hard work and motivation can achieve success, even where extensive skills, background, and education are lacking.
- That paid employment is the means by which single mothers should assume responsibility; that the jobs they acquire will stabilize families by imposing order on family life as well as providing an earned income sufficient to provide basic necessities.
- That welfare reforms such as time limits can change the behavior and the overall well-being of families in poverty; that they will establish important goals and milestones for mothers, providing limited assistance but also clarifying the expectation that

even low-income mothers are expected to achieve self-sufficiency; that women can seek other necessary support from their
own familial and community resources.
· That the primary danger of the welfare system is that mothers
will settle into a comfortable dependence on welfare, without
taking responsibility for themselves; that new policy must provide an impetus for mothers to move off welfare and take
greater personal responsibility.

From their different perspectives, the chapters in this volume
confront each of these assumptions and raise additional issues. A
brief critique of each assumption follows, in which we briefly review
how the research reported in these chapters illuminates life realities
in contradistinction to these myths. We then finish with suggested
policy arenas in which more significant change is needed if we are to
confront these assumptions in ways that will allow low-income
mothers and their children to truly benefit.

The Labor Market Is Not a Level Playing Field

There are several reasons, as illustrated in this work, that impoverished single mothers are handicapped in a competitive labor market.
First, the jobs that low-income mothers typically hold are somewhat
removed from the steady manufacturing jobs that have been more
likely to provide regular hours and pay and some access to benefits.
As Lein et al. (chap. 1) point out, these jobs are likely to leave women
experiencing periods of unemployment without welfare. Furthermore, as Henrici and Miller (chap. 3) illuminate, mothers on welfare
have little access to the kind of extensive job training and transitional support that might actually provide entrée into stable employment. Several experiments in San Antonio (Morales 1996) and
elsewhere (Gueron and Hamilton 2002) indicate the usefulness of
more intensive approaches to preparation for employment. Mothers
with sufficient training and education may be able to locate the
kinds of jobs that stabilize their families. Mothers without much
previous experience and with limited education and skills are likely
to be employed in the service industries, with variable hours and pay
and a lack of benefits. Bell, Lohman, and Votruba-Drzal (chap. 7) and
Skinner, Lachicotte, and Burton (chap. 6) point out that mothers
whose economic issues are compounded by other serious problems,

such as domestic violence or disability, may face multiple jeopardies simultaneously.

Low-Wage Jobs Do Not Provide Family Stability

Of the single mothers who leave welfare, large-scale studies both nationally (Isaacs and Lyon 2000) and in Texas (Schexnayder, Lein, and Douglas 2002) tell us that approximately half are employed. Lein et al. (chap. 1) tell us about life after welfare without a job, an experience shared in their first year off welfare by the majority of those who leave welfare. Only a minority of mothers who leave welfare are employed during every quarter of their first year off welfare (Schexnayder, Lein, and Douglas 2002). There are a number of barriers that keep low-income single mothers from regular employment. One factor not fully described in this volume but alluded to above is the nature of the labor market mothers face. As illuminated by other scholars (Lambert, Waxman, and Haley-Lock 2002), their jobs do not supply regular hours, regular wages, job security, or regular benefits for the employee or the employee's family. Women who work in health facilities, restaurants, hotels, retail, and a range of other service-oriented businesses often face schedules that change on a weekly basis and provide an uncertain number of work hours.

Furthermore, neither jobs nor the now-curtailed welfare system provide them two key services, either of which could well cost most of their income: child care and family health insurance. As Angel and Lein point out in chapter 5, these families are likely to be uninsured, and the more attached to the labor force the mother is, the less likely the family is to have complete health insurance. Furthermore, in chapter 2 Bruinsma discusses low-income mothers' struggle, often in isolation, to obtain the kind of care and supervision they need for their children so they can engage in either employment or education.

Low-income single mothers, like most parents, have dreams beyond the provision of the most basic essentials for their families. Salcido writes of mothers' desires for a home (chap. 4). The Latina mothers she interviewed discussed in detail their desire for a home of their own, a place where their children could play, a place they could expect to keep. The jobs these mothers acquire barely provide rent money. Mothers must often depend on subsidies even when employed, and they are unlikely to be able to put aside funds to buy a home.

Thus, the jobs that low-income mothers tend to hold destabilize their families in several ways. First, with low wages and few benefits, they leave families, as we pointed out above, with little access to health insurance and child care, two supports essential to family well-being. Second, rather than allowing families to settle into a recognized routine, jobs in the service industry tend to change schedules arbitrarily. Third, the wages these jobs pay don't offer access to the dream of most American families: a stable home of their own.

Welfare Reform Has Not Changed Life for Low Income Families

Although it is undeniable that the welfare rolls have dropped (S. Bell 2001), critics and proponents alike realize that both welfare reform and the study reported here were initiated during an economic boom. We are now beginning to see the impact on low-wage families of the combined impact of welfare reform and economic doldrums, but that is a story for another volume.

The materials presented here, however, collected as they were during that period of economic growth at the turn of this century, still raise considerable doubt about the efficacy of the current version of welfare reform in promoting real-life benefits for impoverished families. Families continue to face a series of destabilizing problems whether they are on welfare or in the low-wage jobs welfare recipients are likely to move into. The ethnographic data on which this volume is based allow us to see how welfare reform interacts with the realities of life in low-income American families.

Texas is highlighted in this analysis, and there are some differences in the life stories of mothers across the three cities. They were less likely to have health insurance in San Antonio than in the other three cities. Jobs and wages were distinctive among the three cities. The quality of available housing differed. However, families also clearly experienced core similarities among the three research sites. Mothers in all three cities faced irregular and low-paid work, had difficulties dealing with the welfare bureaucracy, and found it difficult to obtain stable health insurance and child care, as well as stable employment. The chapters included in this volume explore many facets in the lives of low-income mothers, including their work, their

relationships with other families and with institutions, their housing, and their health. All of these areas are affected by the persistent
poverty that marks these women's family lives, whether their families are drawing on welfare, wages, or a combination of both.

Bell and Henrici (chaps. 8 and 9) illustrate the degree to which
families are removed from the welfare rolls without many of the
supports necessary to succeed at employment. Bruinsma, in her
examination of child care (chap. 2), shows how difficult it is for
mothers to negotiate child care, and both she and Angel and Lein
(chap. 5), in writing about health insurance, show that community
and family networks cannot meet the needs of impoverished families in these and other pivotal areas.

Low-Income Family Needs Are Not
Comprehensively Met by the Welfare System

Calls for welfare reform came from many points on the political
spectrum, many of them motivated by the belief that welfare created
dependence. Even before reforms were enacted, many liberals saw
the old welfare system as poorly structured and insufficient in promoting life-changing benefits for low-income families. More conser-
vative critics saw it as a "giveaway" program, with few incentives for
welfare users to become less dependent on federal support. Welfare
reform was clearly designed to move families off TANF, the program
that replaced AFDC. Many of those calling for reform also hoped
that the ensuing wage-earning activities would promote family well-
being.

Recent ethnographic research (such as Edin and Lein 1997; K.
Newman 1999, 2001) as well as classic studies of poverty (Howell
1973; Liebow 1967; Stack 1974) have documented the difficulties
experienced by mothers who try to support their families on welfare.
In fact, under both recent welfare reforms and the pre-1996 welfare
system, many families tended to cycle off and on welfare, rather
than settling into long-term welfare receipt (Harris 1996, 1997;
Loprest 2002). With its new time limits, welfare reform ensures that
families will not, in general, collect benefits for a lifetime. However,
the restrictions on welfare interact in decisive ways even on families
who would ordinarily have cycled off welfare in any case.

In Texas, where welfare cash grants for a family of three never went much over two hundred dollars per month, it has always been clear that families required additional sources of income to survive even while they were receiving welfare (Edin and Lein 1996, 1997). In Illinois and Massachusetts, which had somewhat more generous cash grants, families still struggled. Even before welfare reform, families could not survive in any of these states on welfare alone. The combined use with welfare of such associated programs as food stamps and subsidized child care and public housing (never available even to the majority of those eligible) still left families on welfare struggling.

In fact, families on welfare are almost always, of necessity, dependent on other programs in addition to TANF. They need the benefits of food stamps, Medicaid, subsidized child care, and often other local and state services to meet their households' needs. Food stamps and welfare cash grants rarely cover all of a family's ordinary needs, and, as several of the chapters in this book point out, low-income families in the era of welfare reform are often scrambling to make ends meet. In their analysis of women's economic lives, Lein et al. (chap. 1) illustrate a number of the strategies on which low-income mothers depend during the frequent occasions when they have neither work nor welfare. As they detail it, mothers fight for access to other programs, such as SSI, when they are eligible for such support. They turn to other people, either in their household or in their families outside the household, for cash assistance or help in areas such as child care and transportation. They experience brief episodes of homelessness, periods without adequate health care, and other material hardships.

As Bell (chap. 8) explains, interactions with service providers that occur during the process of seeking out additional services are not always efficient or transparent. Caseworkers at different agencies, themselves often undertrained and under considerable pressure, make their own decisions about who to help and who not to help. At both state offices and local agencies, women who appear less worthy of public investment may well receive less information about programs and less access to them. They may not understand all of the requirements they face or have the time, energy, and organizational resources to meet them. In the area where they perhaps need the greatest long-term help—preparing for and gathering the resources to enter the labor market—some states, Texas among them, as illustrated by Henrici and Miller (chap. 3), provide only minimal, short-term assistance, except for small experimental programs that offer more holistic services. These programs and other local efforts tend to be sponsored by smaller not-for-profit organizations that, as Henrici points out, make decisions about who to invest in. These decisions may well create further barriers for the most disadvantaged and contribute to ethnic and racial discrimination.

The welfare system, in its new streamlined form, can interact with other family needs to increase the pressure on low-wage families—whether the families are on welfare or at work—without offering the necessary resources for a constructive response. As Bell, Lohman, and Votruba-Drzal (chap. 7) point out, victims of domestic violence, although eligible for welfare and waivers from requirements, often need more help, including extended services for child care, health care, and job training and placement, which are only sporadically available. Furthermore, according to Skinner, Lachicotte, and Burton (chap. 6), families that include someone with a disability may have needs beyond what a welfare budget can support, both in terms of the cash grant provided and the time the caretaker must spend providing services to that family member, in addition to the effort required to retain welfare eligibility.

In fact, given the limited time and money available through cash grants (a situation most austere in the Texas research site), virtually all of the mothers on welfare are scrambling to gather additional resources. Many of them are already employed—although often in the informal labor market—before they leave welfare. It is only in unlikely circumstances that mothers can settle into a life of welfare dependence, without frequent forays into some level of employment, dependence on other individuals, or access to additional institutional supports. This is not a new message. What is new, under welfare reform, is the degree to which all mothers on welfare must undertake these activities while preparing for employment.

If we accept the challenges to the myths that were incorporated into welfare reform, we see the need for policy changes in at least four areas, as outlined below.

Health Care

Low-income families, including the working poor, need access to a seamless health insurance system that supplies health care coverage to all members of the household, including coverage for nonprescription necessities for caring for household members with disabilities. Workers without health insurance may leave their jobs in order to acquire health insurance coverage through welfare if the financial costs of family illness become unbearable and are not covered through employer-assisted plans. We need a more universal health insurance system that provides family coverage to low-income households.

Child Care

Low-income families need access to affordable child care that provides services during the hours they are required to work. The market rates for care for a single child can cost a substantial percentage of a low-wage salary, and the child care subsidy system meets only a fraction of the need. Furthermore, the child care market, as it is now structured, provides very little care for infants, very little care outside of the 8 a.m. to 6 p.m. working hours, and very little care for mildly ill children or children with disabilities. We need a more centrally organized child care system with sufficient subsidies to support the needs of low-income families.

Education/Training

Low-income mothers need access, while they have welfare and afterward, to the kind of extensive education and training that will make them eligible for the kinds of jobs that will sustain them and their families over the long run. Small-scale experiments, as mentioned above, have demonstrated the efficacy of some programs in increasing mothers' earnings. Furthermore, the higher-wage jobs they acquire are more likely to include some types of benefits and job security that are equally important in securing family stability.

Labor Force Policies

The nature of the jobs open to low-wage mothers often works to the detriment of their family life. Job conditions that preclude regularities in family life include the lack of set schedules or regular numbers of hours, wages based on a commission, and the lack of benefits. Mothers subject to unpredictable schedule changes cannot easily arrange adequate child care. Mothers without even the minimal benefit of sick days or personal days cannot retain their status as responsible employees while also meeting the needs of family dependents. Mothers working at jobs that provide earnings below the poverty line cannot take adequate care of their households. We need to maintain such programs as the Earned Income Tax Credit, but also increase the minimum wage. We need to work at the national and state levels to ensure that jobs provide the basics in terms of benefits and that there are public programs to step in where employer-based benefits do not provide a safety net. If work is to be the road to stabilization, we need to make sure that the mothers with family responsibilities have access to jobs that allow them to support their households.

Welfare, as it has been envisioned and implemented, has not been well informed by an understanding of the realities faced by low-income women and their families. The analysis here moves us toward an increased understanding of the difficult and complex work and regulatory environment within which low-income families try to sustain themselves. It suggests a number of directions for policy development that could increase family well-being and improve the odds that a family might leave poverty. This research is a first step in the road ahead.

Glossary

ADHD (Attention Deficit Hyperactivity Disorder) is a condition commonly diagnosed in children characterized by problems in concentration, ability to follow directions, and patience.

AFDC (Aid to Families with Dependent Children) prior to 1996, was the federally funded and regulated cash assistance program to income-eligible households.

Block grant is a sum of federal money allocated to a state that it may administer and regulate.

CareLink is a health coverage program unique to Bexar County, Texas. It provides access to a network of health care for residents not qualified for medical assistance programs in return for a monthly payment based on income and family size.

CHIP (State Children's Health Insurance Program, or SCHIP), also known as Title XXI, was part of the Balanced Budget Act of 1997. It offers coverage for minors through federal matching funds that are administered and regulated at the state level.

Food stamps (Food Stamp Act of 1977) is a 1964 program that went nationwide in 1974 to provide coupons for food to income-eligible individuals.

FSS (Family Self-Sufficiency Program) is an escrow and case management program created by the San Antonio Housing Authority in 1998 to help families assisted by the public housing and Section 8 program achieve financial independence.

GED (General Education Development) is an exam administered toward high school diploma equivalency. It was set up in 1942 to help World War II veterans finish their studies.

Head Start Program was a preschool program first implemented in 1965 as an experimental eight-week summer program by the Office of Economic Opportunity. It was transferred in 1969 to the Office of Child Development in the U.S. Department of Health, Education, and Welfare, and is now a program within the Administration on Children, Youth and Families in the Department of Health and Human Services.

PRWORA (Personal Responsibility and Work Opportunity Reconciliation Act) of 1996 is legislation that ended AFDC and began TANF (Temporary Assistance to Needy Families). Under PRWORA, the emphasis shifted to workforce preparation and a lifetime limit of benefits set at five years/sixty months, although states can specify shorter time limits.

SSDI (Social Security Disability Insurance) was expanded to include disability benefits in the Social Security Amendments of 1954. Payments under SSDI are based on prior work under Social Security. The program is financed with Social Security taxes.

SSI (Supplemental Security Income) pays monthly income to those who are more than sixty-five years old, blind, or disabled, as well as those who are income eligible. Unlike SSDI (see above), SSI is not related to employment.

TANF (Temporary Aid for Needy Families) was created in August 1996. It offers federally funded and state-regulated cash assistance to eligible families, broadly defined, that include a pregnant woman or one or more minor children cared for by an adult (not necessarily a relative). Eligibility is set by state requirements within federal guidelines. Criteria for eligibility include income level, as well as Welfare-to-Work expectations and time limits.

TWC (Texas Workforce Commission) is a state government agency that provides workforce development to employers and potential employees in Texas. It is the state's primary public agency for coordinating Welfare-to-Work activities and subcontracting them to private agencies.

Welfare-to-Work programs are aimed at moving welfare applicants into the workforce by providing a variety of supports that range from incentives for employers to direct training for low-income and low-skill adults.

WIC (Women, Infants, and Children) was enacted in the Child Nutrition Act of 1966. The program provides supplemental food assistance, referrals for health care, and information on nutrition for families with children up to the age of five.

Workers' Compensation is a program put into effect by the Occupational Safety and Health Act of 1970.

References

Abramovitz, Mimi. 1996. *Regulating the Lives of Women: Social Welfare Policy from Colonial Times to the Present.* Boston: South End Press.

——. 2001. Everyone is still on welfare: The role of redistribution in social policy. *Social Work* 46 (4):297–308.

Acs, Gregory, and Pamela Loprest with Tracy Roberts. 2001. *Final synthesis report of findings from ASPE "leavers" grants.* Report submitted to Office of the Assistant Secretary for Planning and Evaluation, U.S. Department of Health and Human Services. Washington, D.C.: Urban Institute. Available at http://aspe.hhs.gov/hsp/leavers99/synthesis02/index.htm. Date last accessed April 20, 2005.

Acuña, Rodolfo. 1988. *Occupied America: A history of Chicanos.* New York: Harper and Row.

Albelda, Randy. 2001a. Fallacies of Welfare-to-Work policies. *Annals of the American Academy* 577:66–78.

——. 2001b. Welfare-to-Work, farewell to families? U.S. welfare reform and work/family debates. *Feminist Economics* 71: 119–35.

Aldarondo, Etiony. 1996. Cessation and persistence of wife assault: A longitudinal analysis. *American Journal of Orthopsychiatry* 661: 141–51.

Alexander, Jennifer. 1999. The impact of devolution on nonprofits: A multiphase study of social service organizations. *Nonprofit Management and Leadership* 10: 57–70.

Allard, M. A., R. Albelda, M. E. Colton, and C. Cosenza. 1997. *In harm's way? Domestic violence, AFDC receipt, and welfare reform in Massachusetts.* Boston: University of Massachusetts, McCormack Institute.

Angel, Ronald J., and Jacqueline L. Angel. 1997. *Who will care for us: Aging and long-term care in multicultural America.* New York: New York University Press.

Angel, Ronald, Laura Lein, Jane Henrici, and Emily Leventhal. 2001. The health safety net for poor families. *Welfare, children, and families: A three-city study policy brief 01-2.* Baltimore: Johns Hopkins University. Available at http://www.jhu.edu/~welfare. Date last accessed April 20, 2005.

Arreola, Daniel D., ed. 2004. Hispanic American legacy, Latino American diaspora. In *Hispanic places, Latino places.* Austin: University of Texas Press.

Bachman, Ronet, and Linda Saltzman. 1995. *Bureau of Justice statistics special report: Violence against women: Estimates from the redesigned survey.* Washington, D.C.: U.S. Department of Justice, Office of Justice Programs.

Bane, Mary Jo, and David Ellwood. 1994. *Welfare realities: From rhetoric to reform.* Cambridge, Mass.: Harvard University Press.

Bartik, Timothy J. 2001. *Jobs for the poor: Can labor demand policies help?* New York: Russell Sage Foundation.

Barusch, Amanda, Mary Jane Taylor, and Michelle Derr. 1999. *Understanding families with multiple barriers to self sufficiency.* Salt Lake City: University of Utah, Social Research Institute.

Bass, Greg. 2000. Adult and dislocated worker job training provisions of Title I of the *Workforce Investment Act of 1998*: Part I—Federal, state, and local workforce investment system. *Clearinghouse Review* 33 (9–10):524–57.

Bell, Holly. 2000. Neighborhood ethnography: Preliminary housing report. *Welfare, children, and families: A three-city study.* Unpublished manuscript.

——. 2003. Cycles within cycles: Domestic violence, welfare, and low-wage work. *Violence Against Women* 9 (10):1245–62.

——. 2005. Caseworkers' assessment of welfare reform: Report from the frontlines. *Journal of Human Behavior in the Social Environment.* 12 (2/3):241–57.

Bell, Stephen H. 2000. The prevalence of education and training activities among welfare and food stamp recipients. *The New Federalism: National survey of America's families, no. B-24.* Washington, D.C.: Urban Institute. Available at http://www.urban.org/publications/309711.html. Date last accessed December 20, 2005.

——. 2001. Why are welfare caseloads falling? Discussion paper at Assessing the New Federalism, no. 01-02. Washington, D.C.: Urban Institute. Available at http://www.urban.org/publications/310302.html. Date last accessed December 20, 2005.

Blau, Francine D. 1998. Trends in the well-being of American women, 1970–1995. *Journal of Economic Literature* 36: 112–65.

Bogdon, Amy. 2001. What can we learn from previous housing-based self-sufficiency programs? In *The home front: Implications of welfare reform for housing policy,* edited by Sandra J. Newman. Washington D.C.: Urban Institute Press.

Bourdieu, Pierre. 2002. Essence of neoliberalism. *Analetica.* Available at http://www.analitica.com/bitblioteca/bourdieu/neoliberalism.asp. Date last accessed April 20, 2005.

Brookings Institution. 2003. *San Antonio in focus: A profile from Census 2000.* Center on Urban and Metropolitan Policy, Living Cities Series. Available at http://www.brookings.edu/es/urban/livingcities/sanantonio.htm. Date last accessed December 8, 2005.

Brown, Amy. 2001. *Beyond work first: How to help hard-to-employ individuals get jobs and succeed in the workforce.* New York: Manpower Demonstration Research.

Brown, Michael K. 2003. Ghettos, fiscal federalism, and welfare reform. In *Race and the politics of welfare reform*, edited by Sanford F. Schram, Joe Soss, and Richard C. Fording. Ann Arbor: University of Michigan Press.

Browne, Angela, Amy Salomon, and Shari Bassuk. 1999. The impact of recent partner violence on poor women's capacity to maintain work. *Violence Against Women* 5: 393–426.

Browne, Angela, and Shari Bassuk. 1997. Intimate violence in the lives of homeless and poor housed women: Prevalence and patterns in an ethnically diverse sample. *American Journal of Orthopsychiatry* 67: 261–78.

Browne, Irene. 2000. Opportunities lost? Race, industrial restructuring, and employment among young women heading households. *Social Forces* 73 (3):907–29.

Brush, Lisa. 1999. Women battering and welfare reform: The view from a welfare-to-work program. *Journal of Sociology and Social Welfare* 26: 46–90.

Buck, Pem Davidson. 1996. Sacrificing human rights on the altar of "morality": White desperation, far right explanation, and punitive social welfare reform. *Urban Anthropology* 25 (2):195–219.

Busch, Noël, and Terry Wolfer. 2002. Battered women speak out. *Violence Against Women* 8: 566–84.

Campbell, J., L. Rose, J. Kub, and D. Nedd. 1998. Voices of strength and resistance: A contextual and longitudinal analysis of women's responses to battering. *Journal of Interpersonal Violence* 13 (6):743–62.

Capps, Randolph, Nancy M. Pindus, Kathleen Snyder, and Jacob Leos-Urbelet. 2001. Recent changes in Texas welfare and work, child care, and child welfare systems. *Assessing the New Federalism*, State Update No. 1. Washington, D.C.: Urban Institute.

Catanzarite, Lisa, and Vilma Ortiz. 1996. Family matters, work matters? Poverty among women of color and white women. In *For crying out loud: Women's poverty in the United States*, edited by Diane Dujon and Ann Withorn. Boston: South End Press.

Center on Budget and Policy Priorities. 2000. State policy documentation project. Washington, D.C.: Center for Law and Social Policy and Center on Budget and Policy Priorities. Available at http://www.spdp.org. Date last accessed April 20, 2005.

Cherlin, Andrew, Paula Fomby, Ronald Angel, and Jane Henrici. 2001a. Public assistance receipt among U.S.–born children of immigrants. *Welfare, children, and families: A three-city study policy brief 01-3*. Baltimore: Johns Hopkins University. Available at http://www.jhu.edu/~welfare. Date last accessed April 20, 2005.

———. 2001b. Sanctions and case closings for rules violations: Who is affected and why. *Welfare, children, and families: A three-city study policy brief 01-1*. Baltimore: Johns Hopkins University. Available at http://www.jhu.edu/~welfare. Date last accessed April 20, 2005.

Cleaver, Harry. 1997. Nature, neoliberalism, and sustainable development: Between Charybdis and Scylla? Paper prepared for the fourth Ecology Meeting, Viseu, Portugal. Available at http://www.eco.utexas.edu/Homepages/ Faculty/Cleaver/port.html. Date last accessed April 20, 2005.

Committee on Children with Disabilities (2001). The Continued Importance of Supplemental Security Income (SSI) for Children and Adolescents with Disabilities. *Pediatrics* 107:790–93.

Coulton, Claudia. 2000–1. Neighborhoods and welfare reform. *Journal of Applied Social Sciences* 25 (1):41–56.

Crump, Jeff R. 2003. The end of public housing as we know it: Public housing policy, labor regulation and the U.S. city. *International Journal of Urban and Regional Research* 27 (1):179–87.

Cruz, Monica D. 1999. An analysis of welfare-to-work coordination in San Antonio. Master's thesis, University of Texas at Austin, LBJ School of Public Affairs, Center for the Study of Human Resources.

Curcio, William. 1997. *The Passaic County study of AFDC recipients in a welfare-to-work program.* Passaic County, N.J.: Passaic County Board of Social Services.

Danziger, Sheldon K., and Kristin S. Seefeldt. 2000. Ending welfare through work first: Manager and client views. *Families in Society: The Journal of Contemporary Human Services* 81 (6):593–601.

Danziger, Sandra K., Mary E. Corcoran, Sheldon Danziger, Colleen M. Heflin, Ariel Kalil, J. Levine, Daniel Rosen, Kristin Seefeldt, Kristine A. Siefert, and Richard Tolmanet. 2000. *Barriers to the employment of welfare recipients*, rev. version. Ann Arbor, Mich.: University of Michigan, Poverty Research and Training Center.

Davis, Martha, and Susan Kraham. 1995. Protecting women's welfare in the face of violence. *Fordham Urban Law Journal* 22:1141–57.

Dill, Bonnie, Maxine Thornton, Baca Zinn, and Sandra Patton. 1998. Valuing families differently: Race, poverty, and welfare reform. *Sage Race Relations Abstracts* 23 (3):5–30.

Earle, Alison, and S. Jody Heymann. 2002. What causes job loss among former welfare recipients: The role of family health problems. *Journal of the American Medical Women's Association* 57: 5–10.

Edin, Kathryn, and Kathleen Mullan Harris. 1999. Getting off and staying off: Racial differences in the work route off welfare. In *Latinas and African American women at work*, edited by Irene Browne. New York: Russell Sage Foundation.

Edin, Kathryn, and Laura Lein. 1996. Work, welfare, and single mothers' economic survivals strategies. *American Sociological Review* 61: 253–66.

———. 1997. *Making ends meet: How single mothers survive welfare and low-wage work.* New York: Russell Sage Foundation.

———. 1998. The private safety net: The role of charitable organizations in the lives of the poor. *Housing Policy Debate* 9 (3):541–73.

Ehrenreich, Barbara. 2001. *Nickel and dimed: On (not) getting by in America.* New York: Metropolitan Books.

England, Paula, Karen Christopher, and Lori L. Reid. 1999. Gender, race, ethnicity, and wages. In *Latinas and African American women at work*, edited by Irene Browne. New York: Russell Sage Foundation.

Esping-Andersen, Gøsta. 1990. *The three worlds of welfare capitalism*. Princeton, N.J.: Princeton University Press.

———. 1999. *Social foundations of postindustrial economies*. New York: Oxford University Press.

Fink, Barbara, Rebecca Widom, with Richard Beaulaurier, Gilbert Contreras, Lorna Dilley, and Rebecca Joyce Kissane. 2001. *Social service organizations and welfare reform*. New York: Manpower Demonstration Research, Project on Devolution and Urban Change.

Fisher, James C. 1999. Research on adult literacy education in the Welfare-to-Work transition. *New Directions for Adult and Continuing Education* 83: 29–41.

Foner, Nancy, and George M. Fredrickson, eds. 2004. *Not just black and white: Historical and contemporary perspectives on immigration, race, and ethnicity in the United States*. New York: Russell Sage Foundation.

Fraser, Nancy. 1989. Women, welfare, and the politics of need interpretation. In *Unruly practices: Power, discourse, and gender in contemporary social theory*, edited by Nancy Fraser. Minneapolis: University of Minnesota Press.

Fraser, Nancy, and Linda Gordon. 1994. A genealogy of dependence: Tracing a key word in the U.S. welfare state. *Signs: Journal of Women in Culture and Society* 19 (2):309–36.

Friedlander, Daniel, and David H. Greenberg. 1997. Evaluating government training programs for the economically disadvantaged. *Journal of Economic Literature* 35: 1809–55.

Friedlander, Daniel, and Gary Burtless. 1995. *Five years after: The long-term effects of welfare-to-work programs*. New York: Russell Sage Foundation.

Fujiura, Glenn T., and Kiyoshi Yamaki. 2000. Trends in demography of childhood poverty and disability. *Exceptional Children* 66: 187–99.

Garbarino, James, and Barbara Ganzel. 2000. The human ecology of early risk. In *Handbook of early intervention*, 2d ed., edited by Jack P. Shonkoff and Samuel J. Meisels. New York: Cambridge University Press.

Gent, Chariti. 2002. Talking across the welfare divide. In *Work, welfare, and politics: Confronting poverty in the wake of welfare reform*, edited by Frances Fox Piven, Joan Acker, Margaret Hallock, and Sandra Morgen. Eugene: University of Oregon Press.

Gerdes, Karen, and M. C. Brown-Standridge. 1997. Discovering rules that govern AFDC recipient-worker interactions: A qualitative study. *Journal of Applied Social Sciences* 21 (2):123–30.

Gilens, Martin. 1996. "Race coding" and white opposition to welfare. *American Political Science Review* 90 (3):593–604.

Godfrey, A. Blanton. 1991. Providing health services to facilitate benefit from early intervention. *Infants and Young Children* 4: 47–55.

Goode, Judith. 2001. Let's get our act together: How racial discources disrupt neighborhood activism. In *The new poverty studies: The ethnography of power, politics, and impoverished people in the United States*, edited by Judith Goode and Jeff Maskovsky. New York: New York University Press.

Goode, Judith, and Jeff Maskovsky, eds. 2001. *The new poverty studies: The ethnography of power, politics, and impoverished people in the United States*. New York: New York University.

Gooden, Susan. 1998. All things not being equal: Differences in caseworker support toward black and white welfare clients. *Harvard Journal of African American Public Policy* 4: 23–33.

Greenbaum, Susan D., and Cheryl Rodriguez. 2001. Ethnography and public housing: HOPE VI in Tampa. *Anthropology News* 42 (1):31.

Greenberg, Mark. 1998. Participation in welfare and Medicaid enrollment. Washington, D.C.: Issue paper for the Henry J. Kaiser Family Foundation Commission on Medicaid and the Uninsured. Available at http://www.kff .org/. Date last accessed February 23, 2006.

Grubb, W. Norton. 2001. Second chances in changing times: The roles of community colleges in advancing low-skilled workers. In *Low-wage workers in the new economy*, edited by Richard Kazis and Marc S. Miller. Washington, D.C.: Urban Institute Press.

Gueron, Judith, and Gayle Hamilton. 2002. The role of education and training in welfare reform. Welfare reform and barriers to employment brief #20 and #151. New York: Manpower Development Research.

Guyer, Jocelyn. 2000. *Health care after welfare: an update of findings from state-level leaver studies*. Washington, D.C.: Center on Budget and Policy Priorities. Available at http://www.cbpp.org/8-16-00wel.pdf. Date last accessed April 20, 2005.

Hacker, Jacob S. 2002. *The divided welfare state*. New York: Cambridge University Press.

Hao, Lingxin. 1994. *Kin support, welfare, and out-of-wedlock mothers*. New York: Garland.

Harlen, Sharon L., and Ronnie J. Steinberg, eds. 1989. *Job training for women: The promise and limits of public policies*. Philadelphia: Temple University Press.

Harris, Kathleen Mullan. 1993. Work and welfare among single mothers in poverty. *American Journal of Sociology* 99 (2):317–52.

——. 1996. Life after welfare: Women, work, and repeat dependency. *American Sociological Review* 61: 407–26.

——. 1997. *Teenage mothers and the revolving welfare door*. Philadelphia: Temple University Press.

Harrison, Faye V. 1995. The persistent power of "race" in the cultural and political economy of racism. *Annual Review of Anthropology* 24 (1995):47–74.

Hays, Sharon. 2003. *Flat broke with children: Women in the age of welfare reform*. New York: Oxford University Press.

Henrici, Jane. 2002. U.S. women and poverty. *Voices*. December: 27–31.

Hercik, Jeanette. 1998. At the frontline: Changing the business of welfare reform. *Welfare Information Network Issue Notes* 2 (7). Available at http://www.financeproject.org/Publications/frontline.htm. Date last accessed December 20, 2005.

Hicks, Alexander. 1999. *Social democracy and welfare capitalism*. Ithaca, N.Y.: Cornell University Press.

Hill, Ian, and Amy Westpfahl Lutzky. 2003. Getting in, not getting in, and why: Understanding SCHIP enrollment. *Assessing the New Federalism occasional paper no. 66*. Washington, D.C.: Urban Institute.

Hochschild, Jennifer. 1995. *Facing up to the American dream*. Princeton, N.J.: Princeton University Press.

Holcomb, Pamela A., LaDonna Pavetti, Caroline Ratcliffe, and Susan A. Riedinger. 1998, June. *Building an employment focused welfare system: Work first and other work-oriented strategies in five states*. Executive Summary. Washington, D.C.: Urban Institute.

Holtzworth-Munroe, Amy. 2000. A typology of men who are violent toward their female partners: Making sense of the heterogeneity in husband violence. *Current Directions in Psychological Science* 9 (4):140–43.

Holzer, Harry J. 2001. Career advancement prospects and strategies for low-wage minority workers. In *Low-wage workers in the new economy*, edited by Richard Kazis and Marc S. Miller. Washington, D.C.: Urban Institute Press.

Horton, Anne, and Barry Johnson. 1993. Profiles and strategies of women who have ended abuse. *Families in Society: The Journal of Contemporary Human Services*. October: 481–92.

Hotaling, Gerald, and David Sugerman. 1990. A risk marker analysis of assaulted wives. *Journal of Family Violence* 5: 1–13.

Howell, Joseph T. 1973. *Hard living on Clay Street: Portraits of blue collar families*. Garden City, N.Y.: Anchor Press.

Isaacs, Julia B., and Mathew R. Lyon. 2000. *A cross-state examination of families leaving welfare: Findings from the ASPE-funded leavers studies*. Washington, D.C.: U.S. Department of Health and Human Services, Office of the Assistant Secretary for Planning and Evaluation.

Itzigsohn, José. 2004. The formation of Latino and Latina panethnic identities. In *Not just black and white: Historical and contemporary perspectives on immigration, race, and ethnicity in the United States*, edited by Nancy Foner and George M. Fredrickson. New York: Russell Sage Foundation.

Johnson, Amy, and Alicia Meckstroth. 1998. Ancillary services to support welfare to work. Report to the Office of the Assistant Secretary for Planning and Evaluation, U.S. Department of Health and Human Services. Princeton, N.J.: Mathematica Policy Research. Available at http://aspe.hhs.gov/hsp/isp/ancillary/front.htm. Date last accessed April 20, 2005.

Johnson, Jennifer. 2002. *Getting by on the minimum: The lives of working-class women*. New York: Routledge Press.

Johnson, Michael, and Kathleen Ferraro. 2000. Research on domestic violence in the 1990s: Making distinctions. *Journal of Marriage and the Family* 62 (4):948–63.

Joyce Foundation. 2002. *Welfare to work: What have we learned?* Chicago: Joyce Foundation.

Kaiser Commission on Medicaid and the Uninsured. 2003. *The health insurance status of low-income children and their parents: Recent trends in coverage and state-level data*. Washington, D.C.: Henry J. Kaiser Family Foundation Commission on Medicaid and the Uninsured.

Kapstein, Ethan B., and Brank Milanovic. 2003. Income and influence: Social policy in emerging market economies. *Employment Research* 10 (3):1–2.

Katz, Michael B. 2001. *The price of citizenship: Redefining the American welfare state*. New York: Henry Holt.

Kazis, Richard, and Marc S. Miller, eds. 2001. *Low-wage workers in the new economy*. Washington, D.C.: Urban Institute.

Kenney, Genevieve M., Jennifer M. Haley, and Alexandra Tebay. 2003. *Children's insurance coverage and service use improve*. Washington, D.C.: Urban Institute.

Kessler, Ronald, and David Greenberg. 1981. *Linear panel analysis: Models of quantitative change*. New York: Academic Press.

King, Christopher T. 2004. The effectiveness of publicly financed training in the United States: Implications for WIA and related programs. In *Job training policy in the United States*, edited by Christopher J. O'Leary, Robert A. Straits, and Stephen A. Wandner. Kalamazoo, Mich.: W. E. Upjohn Institute for Employment Research.

Kingfisher, Catherine. 1996. *Women in the American welfare trap*. Philadelphia: University of Pennsylvania Press.

——. 2002a. Introduction. In *Western welfare in decline: Globalization and women's poverty*, edited by Catherine Kingfisher. Philadelphia: University of Pennsylvania Press.

——. 2002b. Neoliberalism I: Discourses of personhood and welfare reform. In *Western welfare in decline: Globalization and women's poverty*, edited by Catherine Kingfisher. Philadelphia: University of Pennsylvania Press.

——. 2002c. Neoliberalism II: The global free market. In *Western welfare in decline: Globalization and women's poverty*, edited by Catherine Kingfisher. Philadelphia: University of Pennsylvania Press.

Kingfisher, Catherine, and Michael Goldsmith. 2001. Reforming women in the United States and Aotearoa/New Zealand. *American Anthropologist* 103 (3):714–32.

Korneman, Sanders. 2002. Commentary: The low-wage market and welfare reform. In *Laboring below the line: The new ethnography of poverty, low-wage work, and survival in the global economy*, edited by Frank Munger. New York: Russell Sage Foundation.

Kushnick, Louis, and James Jennings, eds. 1999. *A new introduction to poverty: The role of race, power, and politics*. New York: New York University Press.

LaCheen, Cary. 2004. *Using the Americans with Disabilities Act to protect the rights* of individuals with disabilities in TANF programs: A manual for non-litigation. New York: Welfare Law Center. Available at www.welfarelaw.org/contents/ADA2004_manual.html. Date last accessed December 28, 2005.

Lafer, Gordon. 1994. The politics of job training: Urban poverty and the false promise of JTPA. *Politics and Society* 22 (3):349–88.

———. 1999. Sleight of hand: The political success and economic failure of job training policy in the United States. *International Journal of Manpower* 20 (3/4):139–51.

———. 2002. *The job training charade.* Ithaca, N.Y.: Cornell University Press.

———. 2003. Job training for welfare recipients: A hand up or a slap down? In *Work, welfare and politics: Confronting poverty in the wake of welfare reform,* edited by Frances Fox Piven, Joan Acker, Margaret Hallock, and Sandra Morgan. Eugene: University of Oregon Press.

Lambert, Susan, Elaine Waxman, and Anna Haley-Lock. 2002. *Against the odds: A study of instability in lower-skilled jobs.* Working paper, Project on the Public Economy of Work. Chicago: University of Chicago.

Lamphere, Louise, Patricia Zavella, Filipe Gonzales, and Peter B. Evans, eds. 1993. *Sunbelt working mothers: Reconciling family and factory.* Ithaca, N.Y.: Cornell University Press.

Lane, Julia, Kelly S. Mikelson, Patrick T. Sharkey, and Douglas Wissoker. 2001. *Low-income and low-skilled workers' involvement in nonstandard employment: Final report.* Washington, D.C.: U.S. Department of Health and Human Resources/ASPE.

Lein, Laura, Alan F. Benjamin, Monica McManus, and Kevin Roy. 2002. Economic roulette: When is a job not a job? Paper presented at the American Sociological Association Annual Meeting, Chicago. August.

Lein, Laura, Susan Jacquet, Carol Lewis, Patricia Cole, and Bernice Williams. 2001. With the best of intentions: Family violence option and abused women's needs. *Violence Against Women* 2: 193–209.

Lennon, Mary Clare, Juliana Blome, and Kevin English. 2002. Depression among women on welfare: A review of the literature. *Journal of the American Medical Women's Association* 57: 27–32.

Levit, K., C. Cowan, H. Lazenby, A. Sensenig, P. McDonnell, J. Stiller, and A. Martin. 2000. Health spending in 1998: Signals of change. *Health Affairs* 19: 124–32.

Lewis, Dan A., Amy Bush Stevens, Laura B. Amsden. 2003. Preserving the gains, rethinking the losses: Welfare in Illinois five years after reform. *Summary of Third Annual Report, Illinois Families Study.* University Consortium on Welfare Reform. Available at http://www.northwestern.edu/ipr/research/IFS.html. Date last accessed December 27, 2005.

Liebow, Elliott. 1967. *Tally's Corner: A study of Negro street corner men.* Boston: Little, Brown.

Limoncelli, Stephanie. 2002. "Some of us are excellent at babies": Paid work, mothering, and the construction of need in a welfare-to-work program. In

Work, welfare and politics: Confronting poverty in the wake of welfare reform, edited by Frances Fox Piven, Joan Acker, Margaret Hallock, and Sandra Morgan. Eugene: University of Oregon Press.

Link, Bruce, and Jo Phelan. 1995. Social conditions as functional causes of disease. *Journal of Health and Social Behavior* 35 (extra issue): 80–94.

Lipsky, Michael. 1980. *Street level bureaucracy: Dilemmas of the individual in public services.* New York: Russell Sage Foundation.

Lloyd, Susan. 1997. The effects of domestic violence on women's employment. *Law and Policy* 19: 139–67.

Lloyd, Susan, and Nina Taluc. 1997. Effects of violence on work and family project. Paper presented at the conference Trapped by Poverty/Trapped by Abuse: Developing a New Research Agenda, Chicago. September.

——. 1999. The effects of domestic violence on women's employment. *Violence Against Women* 5: 370–92.

Long, Sharon K. 2003. Hardship among the uninsured: Choosing among food, housing, and health insurance. *The new federalism: National survey of America's families*, no. B-54. Washington, D.C.: Urban Institute.

Loprest, Pamela. 2002. *Who returns to welfare?* no. B-49. Washington, D.C.: Urban Institute.

Loprest, Pamela, and Gregory Acs. 1996. *Profile of disability among families on AFDC.* Washington, D.C.: Urban Institute.

Lukemeyer, Anna, Marcia K. Meyers, and Timothy M. Smeeding. 2000. Expensive children in poor families: Out-of-pocket expenditures for the care of disabled and chronically ill children in welfare families. *Journal of Marriage and the Family* 62: 399–415.

Mann, C., J. Hudman, A. Salganicoff, and A. Folsom. 2002. Five years later: Poor women's health care coverage after welfare reform. *Journal of the American Medical Women's Association* 57: 16–22.

Manski, Charles F., and Irwin Garfinkel, eds. 1992. *Evaluating welfare and training programs.* Cambridge, Mass.: Harvard University Press.

Mark, Melvin M., Gary T. Henry, and George Julnes. 2000. *Evaluation: An integrated framework for understanding, guiding, and improving public and nonprofit policies and programs.* San Francisco: Jossey-Bass.

Markowitz, Lisa, and Karen W. Tice. 2001. *Precarious balance of "scaling up": Women's organizations in the Americas.* Working Paper #271, Women and International Development. East Lansing: Michigan State University.

Marks, Ellen. 1999. Changing the culture of the welfare office: Report from frontline workers. Paper presented at the 39th Annual Workshop of the National Association for Welfare Research and Statistics, Cleveland, Ohio. Available at http://www.nawrs.org/ClevelandPDF/marks.pdf. Date last accessed April 20, 2005.

Martin, Emily. 1994. *Flexible bodies: Tracking immunity in American culture, from the days of Polio to the age of AIDS.* Boston: Beacon Press.

McDowell, Linda. 1999. *Gender, identity, and place: Understanding feminist geographies.* Minneapolis: University of Minnesota Press.

McFate, Katherine. 1995. Trampolines, safety nets, or free fall? Labor market policies and social assistance in the 1980s. In *Poverty, inequality, and the future of social policy: Western states and the new world order*, edited by Katherine McFate, Roger Lawson, and William Julius Wilson. New York: Russell Sage Foundation.

McKeever, Patricia, and Karen-Lee Miller. 2004. Mothering children who have disabilities: A Bourdieusian interpretation of maternal practices. *Social Science and Medicine* 59: 1177–91.

Meyers, Marcia K., Bonnie Glaser, and Karin MacDonald. 1998. On the frontlines of welfare delivery: Are workers implementing reforms? *Journal of Policy Analysis and Management* 17 (1):1–22.

Meyers, Marcia K., Henry E. Brady, and Eva Y. Seto. 2000. *Expensive children in poor families: The intersection of childhood disabilities and welfare*. San Francisco: Public Policy Institute of California.

Meyers, Marcia K., Wen-Jui Han, Jane Waldfogel, and Irwin Garfinkel. 2001. Child care in the wake of welfare reform: The impact of government subsidies on the economic well-being of single-mother families. *Social Service Review* 75 (1):29–59.

Miles, Matthew B., and A. Michael Huberman. 1994. *Qualitative data analysis*, 2d ed. Thousand Oaks, Calif.: Sage Publications.

Mink, Gwendolyn. 1990. The lady and the tramp: Gender, race, and the origins of the American welfare state. In *Women, the state, and welfare*, edited by Linda Gordon. Madison: University of Wisconsin Press.

——. 1995. *The wages of motherhood*. Ithaca, N.Y.: Cornell University Press.

——. 1998. *Welfare's end*. Ithaca, N.Y.: Cornell University Press.

——. 2002. Valuing women's work. In *From poverty to punishment: How welfare reform punishes the poor*, edited by Guillermo Delgado. Oakland, Calif.: Applied Research Center.

Moffitt, Robert, and Andrew Cherlin. 2002. Disadvantage among families remaining on welfare. Paper prepared for the Joint Center for Poverty Research Conference, the Hard to Employ and Welfare Reform. February–March.

Mohanty, Chandra Talpade. 2004. *Feminism without borders: Decolonizing theory, practicing solidarity*. Chapel Hill, N.C.: Duke University Press.

Morales, Rebecca. 1996. *Project QUEST: An embedded network employment and training organization*. Center for Urban Economic Development. University of Illinois at Chicago. Project no. 421.

Morgen, Sandra. 1990. Two faces of the state: Women, social control, and empowerment. In *Uncertain terms: negotiating gender in American society*, edited by Faye Ginsburg and Anna Lownhaupt Tsing. Boston: Beacon Press.

——. 2001. The agency of welfare workers: Negotiating devolution, privatization, and the meaning of self-sufficiency. *American Anthropologist* 103 (3): 747–61.

Morgen, Sandra, and Jeff Maskovsky. 2003. The anthropology of welfare "reform": New perspectives on U.S. urban poverty in the post-welfare era. *Annual Review of Anthropology.* 32 (2003):315–38.

Morgen, Sandra, and Jill Weigt. 2001. Poor women, fair work, and welfare-to-work that works. In *The new poverty studies: The ethnography of power, politics, and impoverished people in the United States*, edited by Judith Goode and Jeff Maskovsky. New York: New York University Press.

Mullahy, John, and Barbara Wolfe. 2001. Health policies for the non-elderly poor. In *Understanding poverty*, edited by Sheldon H. Danziger and Robert H. Haveman. New York: Russell Sage Foundation and Harvard University Press.

Mulroy, Elizabeth A. 1995 *The new uprooted: Single mothers in urban life.* Westport, Conn.: Auburn House.

———. 2002. Low-income women and housing: Where will they live? In *Women at the margins: Neglect, punishment, and resistance*, edited by Josefina Figueira-McDonough and Rosemary C. Sarri. New York: Haworth.

Munger, Frank, ed. 2003. *Laboring below the line: The new ethnography of poverty, low-wage work, and survival in the global economy.* New York: Russell Sage Foundation.

Myles, John. 1989. *Old age in the welfare state: The political economy of public pensions.* Lawrence: University of Kansas Press.

Naples, Nancy. 1997. The "new consensus" on the gendered "social contract": The 1987–1988 U.S. congressional hearings on welfare reform. *Signs: Journal of Women in Culture and Society* 224: 907–45.

Nathan, Richard, and Thomas L. Gais. 2000. *Implementing the personal responsibility act of 1996: A first look.* State University of New York, Nelson A. Rockefeller Institute of Government, Federalism Research Group. Available at http://www.rockinst.org/publications/federalsim/first_look. Date last accessed December 27, 2005.

Navarro, Vicente. 1998. Neoliberalism, "globalization," unemployment, inequalities, and the welfare state. *International Journal of Health Services* 28 (4):607–82.

Negrey, Cynthia, Stacie Golin, Sunhwa Lee, Holly Mead, and Barbara Gault. 2002. *Working first but working poor: The need for education and training following welfare reform.* Washington, D.C.: Institute for Women's Policy.

Nelson, Hal, and Anthony Paredes. 1984. Welfare for the unemployed: The rise and fall of a social experiment. *Human Organization* 43: 168–77.

Neubeck, Kenneth J. and Noel A. Cazenave. 2001. *Welfare racism: Playing the race card against America's poor.* New York: Routledge.

———. 2004. Welfare racism and its consequences: The demise of AFDC and the return of the states' rights era. In *Work, welfare and politics: Confronting poverty in the wake of welfare reform*, edited by Frances Fox Piven, Joan Acker, Margaret Hallock, and Sandra Morgan. Eugene: University of Oregon Press.

Neustrom, Alison, Forrest A. Deseran, and Don Moore. 2001. Sources and types of formal and informal assistance patterns among Louisiana's welfare populations. Paper presented at the Forty-first Annual Workshop of the National Association for Welfare Research and Statistics, Baltimore. August.

Newman, Katherine S. 1998. *Tyesha's dilemmas: Anthropological ruminations on the consequences of welfare reform.* JCPR Working Paper 34. Evanston, Ill.: Joint Center for Poverty Research.

———. 1999. *No shame in my game: The working poor in the inner city.* New York: Russell Sage Foundation and Knopf.

———. 2001. Hard times on 125th Street: Harlem's poor confront welfare reform. *American Anthropologist* 103 (3):762–78.

Newman, Sandra J. 1999. Introduction and overview. In *The home front: The implications of welfare reform for housing policy.* Washington D.C.: Urban Institute Press.

Ochoa, Gilda L. 2004. *Becoming neighbors in a Mexican American community: power, conflict, and solidarity.* Austin: University of Texas Press.

O'Connor, Alice. 2001. *Poverty knowledge: Social science, social policy, and the poor in twentieth-century U.S. history.* Princeton, N.J.: Princeton University Press.

O'Connor, Julia S. 1996. From women in the welfare state to gendering welfare state regimes: Trend report. *Current Sociology* 44 (2):1–124.

O'Connor, Julia, Ann Orloff, and Sheila Shaver. 1999. *States, markets, families: Gender, liberalism and social policy in Australia, Canada, Great Britain, and the United States.* Cambridge: Cambridge University Press.

Ohlson, Cheryl. 1998. Welfare reform: Implications for young children with disabilities, their families, and service providers. *Journal of Early Intervention* 21: 191–206.

Oliker, Stacey J. 2000. Examining care at welfare's end. In *Care work: Gender, labor, and the welfare state*, edited by Madonna Harringon Meyer. New York: Routledge.

Olson, Krista K., and LaDonna Pavetti. 1996. *Personal and family challenges to the successful transition from welfare to work.* Washington, D.C.: Urban Institute.

Orloff, Ann. 1996. Gender in the welfare state. *Annual Review of Sociology* 22: 51–78.

Patel, Nisha, and Julie Strawn. 2003. *WIA reauthorization recommendations.* Washington, D.C.: Center for Law and Social Policy. Available at http://www.clasp.org/publications/WIA_Recomm.pdf. Date last accessed April 20, 2005.

Pavetti, LaDonna. 2000. Creating a new welfare reality: Early implementation of the Temporary Assistance for Needy Families Program. *Journal of Social Issues* 56 (4):601–16.

Pearce, Diana. 1979. Women, work, and welfare: The feminization of poverty. In *Working women and families*, edited by Karen Wolk Feinstein. Beverly Hills, Calif.: Sage.

Peña, Devon. 1997. *Terror of the machine: Technology, work, gender and ecology on the U.S.–Mexico border.* Austin, Tex.: Center for Mexican American Studies Books.

Pérez, Sonia M., amd Cecilia Muñoz. 2001. Latino low-wage workers: A look at immigrant workers. In *Low-wage workers in the new economy*, edited by Richard Kazis and Marc S. Miller. Washington, D.C.: Urban Institute Press.

Perez-Johnson, Irma Hershey, and Alan M. Hershey. 1999. *Early implementation of the Welfare-to-Work grants program: Report to Congress*. Princeton, N.J.: Mathematica Policy Research, Inc.

Person, Jessica, Nancy Thoennes, and Esther Griswold. 1999. Child support and domestic violence: The victims speak out. *Violence Against Women* 4: 427–48.

Pesquera, Adolfo. 2001. Affordable rental market crawls. *San Antonio Express-News*. Business section, 8E. March 16.

Peterson, Janice, Xue Song, and Avis Jones-DeWeever. 2002. *Life after welfare reform: Low-income single parent families, pre- and post-PRWORA*. Washington, D.C.: Institute for Women's Policy Research.

Pindus, Nancy M., Robin Koralek, Karin Martinson, and John Trutko. 2000. *Coordination and integration of welfare and workforce development systems*. Washington, D.C.: Urban Institute.

Piven, Frances Fox. 1998. Welfare reform and the economic and cultural reconstruction of low wage labor markets. *City and Society Annual Review*, 21–36.

———. 2001. Welfare reform and the economic and cultural reconstruction of low wage labor markets. In *The new poverty studies: The ethnography of power, politics, and impoverished people in the United States*, edited by Judith Goode and Jeff Maskovsky. New York: New York University Press.

Plimpton, Lisa, and Demetra Smith Nightingale. 2000. Welfare employment programs: Impacts and cost-effectiveness of employment and training activities. In *Improving the odds: Increasing the effectiveness of publicly funded training*, edited by Burt S. Barnow and Christopher T. King. Washington, D.C.: Urban Institute Press.

Pokempner, Jennifer, and Dorothy Roberts. 2001. Poverty, welfare reform, and the meaning of disability. *Ohio State Law Journal* 62:1–23.

Polit, Denise F., Andrew S. London, and John M. Martinez. 2001. *The health of poor urban women: Findings from the project on devolution and urban change*. New York: Manpower Demonstration Research.

Polk, Caroline. 2000. Representative Mink introduces fixes to 1996 welfare law. Available at http://www.womensenews.org/article.cfm/dyn/aid/695/context/archive. Date last accessed April 20, 2005.

Portes, Alejandro, and Patricia Landolt. 2000. Social capital: Promise and pitfalls of its role in development. *Journal Of Latin American Studies* 32: 529–47.

Poverty Law Center. n.d. *Caseworkers are overworked, clients underserved, union survey finds*. Available at http://www.povertylaw.org/advocacy/iwn/index.cfm?action=show_article&id=327. Date last accessed April 20, 2005.

Presser, Harriet B., and Amy G. Cox. 1997. Work schedules of low-educated American women and welfare reform. *Monthly Labor Review* 120 (4):25–35.

Pressman, Jeffrey, and Aaron Wildavsky. 1984. *Implementation*. Berkeley: University of California Press.

QSR NUD*IST [Computer software]. 1999. Thousand Oaks, Calif.: Scolari, Sage Publications Software.

Quadagno, Jill S. 1994. *The color of welfare: How racism undermined the war on poverty*. New York: Oxford University Press.

Quane, James, Pamela Joshi, Gwendolyn Dordick, and Jane Henrici. 2002. Neighborhood organizations and the people who use them: a spatial consideration of welfare reform. Paper presented at the 2002 Annual Meeting of the American Sociological Association, Chicago. August.

Rangarajan, Anu. 1998. *Keeping welfare recipients employed: A guide for states designing job retention services*. Princeton, N.J.: Mathematica Policy Research.

Raphael, Jody. 1995. *Domestic violence: Telling the untold welfare-to-work story*. Chicago: Taylor Institute.

———. 1996. *Prisoners of abuse: Domestic violence and welfare receipt*. Chicago: Taylor Institute Women, Welfare, and Abuse Project.

Raphael, Jody, and Richard Tolman. 1997. *Trapped by poverty, trapped by abuse*. Chicago: Taylor Institute and the University of Michigan.

Reisch, Michael, and David Sommerfeld. 2002. Race, welfare reform, and nonprofit organizations. *Journal of Sociology and Social Welfare* 29 (1):155–77.

Reisch, Michael, and Ursula Bischoff. 2002. Welfare reform strategies and community-based organizations: The impact of family well-being in an urban neighborhood. In *Work, welfare and politics: Confronting poverty in the wake of welfare reform*, edited by Frances Fox Piven, Joan Acker, Margaret Hallock, and Sandra Morgan. Eugene: University of Oregon Press.

Reskin, Barbara F. 1999. Occupational segregation by race and ethnicity among women workers. In *Latinas and African American women at work*, edited by Irene Browne. New York: Russell Sage Foundation.

Rice, Joy. 2001. Poverty, welfare, and patriarchy: How macro-level changes in social policy can help low-income women. *Journal of Social Issues* 572: 355–74.

Riley, Susan A., ed. 1999. *Texas Workforce Commission: An audit report on welfare reform implementation at the Texas Workforce Commission*. Austin: Office of the State Auditor.

Rodriguez, Cheryl. 2003. Invoking Fannie Lou Hamer: Research, ethnography and activism in low-income communities. *Urban Anthropology* 32: 231–51.

Rodriguez, Clara E. 2000. *Changing race: Latinos, the census and the history of ethnicity in the United States*. New York: New York University Press.

Rolett, A., J. Parker, K. Heck, and D. Makuc. 2001. Parental employment, family structure, and child's health insurance. *Ambulatory Pediatrics* 1: 306–13.

Rom, Mark Carl. 1999. From welfare state to Opportunity, Inc.: Public-private partnerships in welfare reform. *American Behavioral Scientist*. 43 (1):155–76.

Rosales, Rodolfo. 2000. *The illusion of inclusion: The untold political story of San Antonio*. Austin: University of Texas Press, Center for Mexican American Studies, History, Culture, and Society Series.

Rose, Elizabeth. 1999. *A mother's job: The history of daycare: 1890–1960*. New York: Oxford University Press.

Rosman, Elisa A., and Jane J. Knitzer. 2001. Welfare reform: The special case of young children with disabilities and their families. *Infants and Young Children* 13: 25–35.

Rossi, Peter H., Howard E. Freeman, and Mark W. Lipsey. 1999. *Evaluation: A Systematic Approach*, 6th ed. Thousand Oaks, Calif.: Sage.

Roy, Kevin, Carolyn Tubbs, and Linda Burton. 2004. Don't have no time: Daily rhythms and the organization of time for low-income families. *Family Relations* 52: 168–78.

Russell, Andrew, and Iain R. Edgar. 1998. Research and practice in the anthropology of welfare. In *The anthropology of welfare*, edited by Iain R. Edgar and Andrew Russell. London: Routledge.

Russell, Jeanne. 1999. Leaders probe loss of childcare funds; Peak asks staff for answers. *San Antonio Express-News*. Metro/South Texas section, 1B. December 11.

———. 2000a. Inspectors scrutinize workforce centers. *San Antonio Express-News*. Metro/South Texas section, 1B. April 12.

———. 2000b. Kid Care fund loss is probed. *San Antonio Express-News*. Metro/South Texas section, 1B. April 1.

———. 2000c. Local contractor loses Kelly job-training deal. *San Antonio Express-News*. Metro/South Texas section, 8B. June 23.

Ryscavage, Paul. 1999. *Income inequality in America: An analysis of trends*. Armonk, N.Y.: M. E. Sharpe.

Sable, M. R., M. K. Libbus, D. Huneke, and K. Anger. 1999. Domestic violence among AFDC recipients: Implications for welfare-to-work programs. *AFFILIA* 14: 199–216.

Sainsbury, Diane. 1996. *Gender, equality, and welfare states*. New York: Cambridge University Press.

Salomon, Amy, Shari Bassuk, and Nicholas Huntington. 2002. The relationship between intimate partner violence and the use of addictive substances in poor and homeless single mothers. *Violence Against Women* 8: 785–815.

San Antonio Housing Trust Fund. 2000. Market analysis for affordable single family housing in San Antonio's inner city. Unpublished manuscript.

Sard, Barbara, and Amy S. Bogdon. 2003. What has changed, what have we learned, and what don't we know. In *A place to live, a means to work: How housing assistance can strengthen welfare policy*. Washington, D.C.: Fannie Mae Foundation.

Sard, Barbara, and Margy Waller. 2002. *Housing strategies to strengthen welfare policy and support working families*. Washington, D.C.: Brookings Institution and the Center for Budget and Policy Priorities, Center on Urban and Metropolitan Policy.

Sassen, Saskia. 1998. *Globalization and its discontents: Essays on the new mobility of people and money*. New York: New Press.

———. 2000. Spatialities and temporalities of the global: elements for a theorization. *Public Culture* 12 (1):215–32.

——. 2002. Commentary: Deconstructing labor demand in today's advance economies: Implications for low-wage employment. In *Laboring below the line: The new ethnography of poverty, low-wage work, and survival in the global economy*, edited by Frank Munger. New York: Russell Sage Foundation.

Schexnayder, Deanna, Laura Lein, and Karen Douglas. 2002. *Texas families in transition—Surviving without TANF: An analysis of families diverted from or leaving TANF*. Austin: Texas Department of Human Services.

Schneider, Jo Anne. 2000a. Introduction: Social welfare and welfare reform. *American Anthropologist* 103 (3):705–13.

——. 2000b. Pathways to opportunity: The role of race, social networks, institutions, and neighborhood in career and educational paths for people on welfare. *Human Organization* 59 (1):72–85.

——. 2001. Introduction: social welfare and welfare reform. *American Anthropologist* 103 (3):705–13.

Schorr, Lisbeth B. 1997. *Common purpose: Strengthening families and neighborhoods to rebuild America*. New York: Anchor Books.

Schram, Sanford F. 2001. *After welfare: The culture of postindustrial social policy*. New York: New York University Press.

Schram, Sanford F., Joe Soss, and Richard C. Fording, eds. 2003. *Race and the politics of welfare reform*. Ann Arbor: University of Michigan Press.

Scott, Ellen, Kathryn Edin, Andrew S. London, and Joan Mazelis. 2001. My children come first: Welfare-reliant women's post-TANF views of work-family trade-offs and marriage. In *For better and for worse: Welfare reform and the well-being of children and families*, edited by Greg J. Duncan and P. Lindsay Chase-Lansdale. New York: Russell Sage.

Scott, Ellen, Andrew London, and Nancy Myers. 2002. Dangerous dependencies: The intersection of welfare reform and domestic violence. *Gender and Society* 16 (6):878–97.

Scott, K. 1996. The dilemma of liberal citizenship: Women and social assistance reform in the 1990s. *Studies in Political Economy* 50: 7–36.

Seccombe, Karen. 1999. "So you think I drive a Cadillac?": Welfare recipients' perspectives on the system and its reform. Needham Heights, Mass.: Allyn and Bacon.

Seelman, Katherine, and Sean Sweeney. 1995. The changing universe of disability. *American Rehabilitation* 21 (3):2–13.

Segura, Denise A. 1994. Working at motherhood: Chicana and Mexican immigrant mothers and employment. In *Mothering: Ideology, experience, and agency*, edited Grace Chang, Evelyn Nakano Glenn, and Linda Rennie Forcey. New York: Routledge.

Shields, John, and Mitchell B. Evans. 1998. *Shrinking the state: Globalization and public administration "reform."* Halifax, N.S.: Fernwood.

Sidel, Ruth. 1990. *On her own: Growing up in the shadow of the American dream*. New York: Viking.

Silverstein, Bobby, Mark Greenberg, Malika Saada Saar, Curt Decker, Ruth Bourquin, Herbert Semmel, Cary LaCheen, Marty Ford, and Tony Young. 1998. Analysis of issues regarding the implementation of TANF for individuals with disabilities. Memorandum to National Task Force on Employment of Adults with Disabilities. August 11.

Skinner, Debra, Stephen Matthews, and Linda Burton. 2005. Combining ethnography and GIS technology to examine constructions of developmental opportunities in contexts of poverty and disability. In *Discovering successful pathways in children's development: Mixed methods in the study of childhood and family life*, edited by Thomas Weisner. Chicago: University of Chicago Press.

Skinner, Debra, Elisa Slattery, William Lachicotte, Andrew Cherlin, and Linda Burton. 2002. *Disability, health coverage, and welfare reform*. Washington, D.C.: Kaiser Commission on Medicaid and the Uninsured.

Skocpol, Theda. 2000. *The missing middle: Working families and the future of American social policy*. New York: W. W. Norton.

Smith, L. A., D. Romero, P. R. Wood, N.S. Wampler, W. Chavkin, and P. H. Wise. 2002. Employment barriers among welfare recipients and applicants with chronically ill children. *American Journal of Public Health* 92: 1453–57.

Stack, Carol. 1974. *All my kin: Strategies for survival in a black community*. New York: Harper and Row.

———. 2002. In exile on main street. In *Laboring below the line: The new ethnography of poverty, low-wage work, and survival in the global economy*, edited by Frank Munger. New York: Russell Sage Foundation.

Stern, M. P., M. Rosenthal, S. M. Haffner, H. P. Hazuda, and L. J. Franco. 1984. Sex difference in the effects of sociocultural status on diabetes and cardiovascular risk factors in Mexican Americans: The San Antonio Heat Study. *American Journal of Epidemiology* 120 (6):834–51.

———. 1992. Genetic and environmental determinants of type II diabetes in Mexico City and San Antonio. *Diabetes* 41: 494–99.

Stewart, Dianne. 1999. Bridging the income gap: For many Texans, the promise of prosperity in exchange for hard work rings hollow. Austin, Tex.: Center for Public Policy Priorities.

Straus, Murray. 1979. Measuring intrafamily conflict and violence: The conflict tactics (CT) scales. *Journal of Marriage and the Family* 14: 75–88.

Straus, Murray, and Richard Gelles, eds. 1990. *Physical violence in American families: Risk factors and adaptations to violence in 8,145 families*. New Brunswick, N.J.: Transaction Books.

Strawn, Julie. 1999. *Welfare-to-work programs: The critical role of skills*. Washington, D.C.: Center for Law and Social Policy.

Strawn, Julie, and Karin Martinson. 2000. *Steady work and better jobs: How to help low-income parents sustain employment and advance in the workforce*. New York: Manpower Demonstration Research.

Sullivan, Kathleen A. 1999. The perils of advocacy: listening, labeling, appropriating. In *Hard labor: Women and work in the post-welfare era*, edited by Joel F. Handler and Lucy White. Armonk, N.Y.: M. E. Sharpe.

Sullivan, Teresa A., Elizabeth Warren, and Jay Lawrence Westbrook. 2000. *Fragile middle class: Americans in debt*. New Haven: Yale University Press.

Susser, Ida. 1997. The flexible woman: Regendering labor in the informational society. *Critique of Anthropology* 17 (4):389–402.

Swartz, Rebecca, and Brian Miller. 2002. Welfare reform and housing. Policy Brief No. 16. Washington, D.C.: Brookings Institution, Center of Budget and Policy Priorities. Available at http://www.brookings.edu/printme.wbs?page =/es/research/projects/wrb/publications/pb/pb16.htm. Date last accessed December 27, 2005.

Texas Workforce Commission. 2000. *How Texas works: 1999 annual report*. Austin: Texas Workforce Commission. Available at http://www.twc.state.tx.us/news/ar99.pdf. Date last accessed February 15, 2004.

———. 2001. *How Texas works: 2000 annual report*. Austin: Texas Workforce Commission. Available at http://www.twc.state.tx.us/news/ar00/pdf. Date last accessed February 15, 2004.

Thomas, Susan L. 1998. Race, gender, and welfare reform: the Antinatalist response. *Journal of Black Studies* 28 (4):419–46.

Thompson, Terri S., and Kelli S. Mikelson. 2001. *Screening and assessment in TANF/Welfare-to-Work: Ten important questions TANF agencies and their partners should consider*. Washington, D.C.: Urban Institute.

Tolman, Richard, and Daniel Rosen. 2001. Domestic violence in the lives of women receiving welfare. *Violence Against Women* 7: 141–58.

Tolman, Richard, and Jody Raphael. 2000. A review of research on welfare and domestic violence. *Journal of Social Issues* 56: 655–82.

Tubbs, Carolyn, Kevin Roy, and Linda Burton. 2005. Family ties: Constructing family time in low-income families. *Family Process* 44: 77–91.

United Nations Development Programme. 2005. *Human development reports*. Available at http://hdr.undp.org/. Date last accessed September 17, 2005.

U.S. Department of Health and Human Services. 1998. *Building an employment-focused welfare system: Work first and other work-oriented strategies in five states—executive summary*. Washington, D.C.: U.S. Department of Health and Human Services.

———. 2000a. *Changes in TANF caseloads since enactment of new welfare law*. Washington, D.C.: U.S. Department of Health and Human Services. Available at http://www.acf.dhhs.gov/news/stats/aug-dec.htm. Date last accessed April 20, 2005.

———. 2000b. *Temporary Assistance for Needy Families (TANF) Program: third annual report to Congress*. Washington, D.C.: U.S. Department of Health and Human Services. Available at http://www.acf.hhs.gov/programs/ofa/index ar.htm. Date last accessed December 27, 2005.

U.S. Department of Health and Human Services, Administration for Children and Families, Office of the Assistant Secretary for Planning and Evaluation; U.S. Department of Education, Office of the Under Secretary, Office of Vocational and Adult Education; and Manpower Demonstration Research Corporation. 2002. *Moving people from welfare to work: Lessons from the national evaluation of Welfare-to-Work strategies*. Washington, D.C.: U.S. Department of Health and Human Services.

U.S. Department of Labor, Employment and Training Administration. 2001. *Training and employment guidance letter no. 15-00*. Washington, D.C.: U.S. Department of Labor, Employment and Training Administration. Available at http://wdr.doleta.gov/directives/attach/TEGL15-00.pdf. Date last accessed April 20, 2005.

U.S. General Accounting Office. 2001. *Welfare reform: More coordinated effort could help states and localities move TANF recipients with impairments toward employment* (GAO-02-37). Washington, D.C.: U.S. General Accounting Office.

Votruba-Drzal, Elizabeth, Brenda Lohman, and Lindsay Chase-Lansdale. 2003. Violence in intimate relationships as women transition from welfare to work. Unpublished manuscript.

Walker, Lenore A. 1989. Psychology and violence against women. *American Psychologist*. 44 (4):695–702.

Waller, Margy, and Alan Berube. 2002. *Timing out: Long-term welfare caseloads in large cities and counties*. Survey series. Washington, D.C.: Brookings Institution and Center for Budget and Policy Priorities, Center on Urban and Metropolitan Policy.

Warren, Mark R. 1998. Community building and political power. *American Behavioral Scientist* 42 (1):78–92.

Weir, Margaret, Ann Shola Orloff, and Theda Skocpol. 1988. *The politics of social policy in the United States*. Princeton, N.J.: Princeton University Press.

Weisbrot, Mark. 1997. *Welfare reform: The jobs aren't there*. Washington, D.C.: Preamble Center for Public Policy.

Welfare-to-Work and Child Support Amendments of the Consolidated Appropriations Act of 1999, Public Law 106–113. Available at http://wtw.doleta.gov/wtw/laws-regs/99amendsum.cfm. Date last accessed April 20, 2005.

Westbrook, Lauren E., Ellen J. Silver, and Ruth E. K. Stein. 1998. Implications for estimates of disability in children: A comparison of definitional components. *Pediatrics* 101: 1025–30.

Wilson, William J. 1996. *When work disappears: The world of the new urban poor*. New York: Knopf.

Winston, Pamela, Ronald J. Angel, Linda M. Burton, P. Lindsey Chase-Lansdale, Andrew J. Cherlin, Robert A. Moffitt, and William J. Wilson. 1999. *Welfare, children, and families: A three-city study overview and design*. Baltimore: Johns Hopkins University. Available at www.jhu.edu/~welfare/overviewanddesign.pdf. Date last accessed April 20, 2005.

Wolery, M., A. Holcombe, and J. Brookfield. 1993. The extent and nature of preschool mainstreaming: A survey of general early educators. *Journal of Special Education* 27: 222–34.

Wood, Robert G., and Diane Paulsell. 1999. *Helping TANF recipients stay employed: Early evidence from the GAPS initiative*. Princeton, N.J.: Mathematica Policy Research, Inc.

Zavella, Patricia. 1996. Living on the edge: Everyday lives of poor Chicano/ Mexicano families. In *Mapping multiculturalism*, edited by Avery F. Gordon and Christopher Newfield. Minneapolis: University of Minnesota Press.

Zedlewski, Shelia R., Sandi Nelson, Kathryn Edin, Hether Koball, Kate Pomper, and Tracy Roberts. 2003. *Families coping without earnings or government cash assistance*. Occasional Paper Number 64. Washington, D.C.: Urban Institute.

About the Contributors

Ronald J. Angel, Ph.D., is professor of sociology at the University of Texas at Austin. His work focuses on social policy, with specific reference to health care among vulnerable populations.

Holly Bell, Ph.D., LCSW, is a research associate at the Center for Social Work Research, University of Texas at Austin. Her work focuses on the intersection of poverty and violence against women, particularly domestic violence, sexual assault, and prostitution.

Alan F. Benjamin, Ph.D., is a lecturer in the Jewish Studies Program at the Pennsylvania State University. He received his Ph.D. in cultural anthropology from the University of North Carolina at Chapel Hill in 1997. His research focuses on practices of social boundary- and identity-making.

Beth H. Bruinsma, M.A., is a doctoral candidate in the Department of Anthropology at the University of Texas at Austin. As an ethnographer for the San Antonio site of the Three-City Study, she developed her research interests in gender, class, welfare policy, and the American dream.

Linda Burton, Ph.D., is currently professor of Human Development and Sociology at The Pennsylvania State University. Burton was the director of the ethnographic component of the Three-City Study. She currently directs a comparable cross-site ethnography of low-income families in rural Pennsylvania and North Carolina.

William Lachicotte, Ph.D., is adjunct assistant professor in the Department of Anthropology and research associate, FPG Child Development Institute, University of North Carolina at Chapel Hill. His research explores, through the lens of personal and social identity, the effects of institutional and professional conditions on the production of medical care and, consequently, on the health and lives of individuals, families, and communities in the United States.

Laura Lein, Ph.D., is professor in the Department of Anthropology and the School of Social Work at the University of Texas at Austin. She served at the senior ethnographer for the Three-City Study. Her research concentrates on families in poverty and the public and private policies and institutions that structure poverty programs and family supports.

Brenda J. Lohman, Ph.D., is assistant professor of Human Development and Family Studies and faculty affiliate of the Institute for Social and Behavior Research at Iowa State University. With a Ph.D. in Human Development and Family Studies from the Ohio State University and an M.S. in developmental psychology from Illinois State University, Lohman uses a multidisciplinary framework to research the successful academic and psychosocial adjustment of adolescents and their families, especially those from economically disadvantaged minority communities.

Monica McManus, Ph.D., is an independent scholar working in the U.S. Midwest. She served as a research scientist and field research coordinator, and then site director for the Three-City Study. In addition to her work on families, poverty, and welfare, she pursues research in linguistic anthropology and Latin America.

E. Carol Miller, LMSW, is government relations coordinator of member political action for the National Association of Social Workers/Texas Chapter, and a registered lobbyist working at the state capital. Formerly, Miller worked as a program manager at the Center for Social Work Research at the University of Texas at Austin. Of particular significance in her past and current work are the rights of vulnerable populations.

Kevin Roy, Ph.D., is assistant professor in the Department of Family Studies at the University of Maryland. He served as a postdoctoral fellow with the Three-City Study. His research concentrates on low-income fathers and on impoverished families' contributions to their children's social capital.

Lillian M. Salcido, M.A., a doctoral candidate in the Department of Anthropology at the University of Texas at Austin, is also a postgraduate researcher in the Department of Human and Community Development at the University of California, Davis, with the Early Growth and Development Study.

Debra Skinner, Ph.D., a sociocultural anthropologist, is senior scientist at the FPG Child Development Institute, University of North Carolina at Chapel Hill. Her research focuses on poverty and disability, and sociocultural aspects of genetic disorder.

Elizabeth Votruba-Drzal, Ph.D., is a faculty member in the Department of Psychology at the University of Pittsburgh. Her research examines the environmental origins of economic disparities in school readiness and early academic achievement.

Index

African Americans, 85–86, 100, 103, 185; children and, 111, 183–84; neighborhoods of, 90, 96, 178, 183–85, 187, 190; research project and, 8, 9, 11, 180

Aid to Families with Dependent Children (AFDC), 5, 43, 114, 132, 155, 195, 201, 202

assistance, public, 4, 19, 27, 38, 41, 70, 78–79, 150; disability and, 114, 116, 125; eligibility for, 119, 155; forms of, 29–31, 99; as temporary, 6, 36, 43

Balanced Budget Act of 1997, 65–66, 115, 201

Barb (pseudonym), 51, 57–58

Boston, 5, 8, 10, 85–86, 102, 190, 194, 196

caregivers, 197; devaluation of, 42–43, 169, 171; disability and, 109, 113–14, 128; employment and, 69, 122–24, 126–27, 129; health of, 39, 115, 117, 119–20, 166; women as, 48, 170

"cash" assistance, 38, 73, 173, 195–97; as an incentive, 68, 92, 94; qualifying for, 69, 70, 88, 123, 167, 197, 202; research project families and, 10, 69, 196; welfare

reform and, 6, 75–76, 90, 109, 155, 175

Chicago, 5, 8, 10, 85–86, 102, 190, 194, 196

child care, 13, 40, 90, 197; access to, 8, 15, 26, 31–32, 46, 69, 173, 194; cost of, 59, 62n8; disability and, 16–17, 123–24, 126, 129; early childhood development and, 25, 47, 179; emergencies and, 72, 120–21, 163–64, 199; employment and, 14, 39–40, 42, 66, 74; extended families and, 34, 35, 37, 46–47, 55–56, 146, 196; government policies and, 17, 90, 185; household stability and, 37, 56, 79, 158; informal economy and, 49, 53, 55, 57–58, 62n7; job training and, 32, 48, 73, 90; low-wage jobs and, 25–26, 44, 68, 193–94, 198; men and, 36, 59, 90, 146, 147; quality of, 26, 31–32, 53, 58, 164; schedule restrictions and, 51–53, 106, 146–47, 158, 163, 198–99; self-sufficiency and, 92, 112, 163, 167; social networks and, 19, 41; as a support service, 70, 179, 187; types of, 13, 30, 124, 179; as work, 39, 52

child care, subsidized: access to, 55, 60, 126–27, 151, 171, 196;

About the Editor

Jane M. Henrici is an anthropologist who studies gender and ethnicity in relation to poverty and development. Henrici is assistant professor in the Department of Anthropology and an affiliate of the Center for Research on Women and the Hooks Institute for Social Change at the University of Memphis. Adding to research she has conducted in Peru and elsewhere in the United States, Henrici has begun studies in Memphis, Tennessee, on job training for low-income women and on community effects of the forthcoming regional NAFTA corridor. She has published on tourism and export development and their interaction with ethnicity and gender in Peru, and on policy change and social programs and their effects on poorer women in the United States. With respect to the latter, she is a coauthor for the forthcoming *Poor Families in America's Health Care Crisis* (New York: Cambridge University Press). As a Fulbright Scholar to Peru in 2006, Henrici will conduct fieldwork on the effects of free trade agreements on Peruvian women's alternative trading organizations.